HERE'S WHERE I STAND

SENATOR JESSE HELMS

Here's Where I Stand

A MEMOIR

RANDOM HOUSE NEW YORK

Grateful acknowledgment is made to the following for permission to reprint previously published material:

The Washington Post Company: Excerpt from "Reorganized State Dept. Will Accommodate Republicans" by John F. Harris and Thomas W. Lippmann. Originally published in *The Washington Post,* April 18, 1997, page A2. Reprinted by permission of the Washington Post Company.

The Durham Herald Company: Excerpt from "Political Gladiators Promise a Slugfest." Originally published in June 1983 in the *Durham Morning Herald.* Reprinted by permission of the Durham Herald Company.

Dr. Norman L. Geisler: "10 Reasons for Voluntary Prayer" by Dr. Norman Geisler. Reprinted by permission of Dr. Norman L. Geisler.

WorldNetDaily.com: Excerpt from "A Fond Farewell to Senator 'No Sir'" by Jane Chastain. Originally published by WorldNetDaily.com on January 2, 2003. Reprinted by permission of WorldNetDaily.com.

LIBRARY OF CONGRESS CATALOGING-IN-PUBLICATION DATA

Helms, Jesse.
Here's where I stand : a memoir / Jesse Helms.
p. cm.
Includes index.
ISBN 0-375-50884-8
1. Helms, Jesse. 2. Legislators—United States—Biography. 3. United States.
Congress. Senate—Biography. 4. United States—Politics and government—
1945–1989. 5. United States—Politics and government—1989– . Conservatism—
United States—History—20th century. 7. Southern States—Politics and
government—1951– . Monroe (N.C.)—Biography. I. Title.
E840.8.H44A3 2005
328.73'092—dc22
[B]   2005042795

*All photographs, except as otherwise credited,
courtesy of the Jesse Helms Center*

I HAVE SAID MANY TIMES THAT NO ONE EVER HAD a better wife than I do, and I mean it. This book is dedicated first to her, my best friend and truest love, Dorothy, and to our family, whose love for us means more than I can ever say; and also to the voters and friends who gave their earnest support when we were most embattled; and especially to those remarkable young people who served on my federal or political staffs, whose lives and dedication make me proud that they were, and still are, a part of the "Helms family."

PREFACE

THIS BOOK IS THE RESULT of the process of bringing together a conglomeration of memories and thoughts and fragments. At times it has seemed like an old man's exercise in the futility of trying to piece together the thousand memories and dozens of matters of possible interest that this octogenarian can assemble. Many wonderful friends have helped in assembling names, dates, events, and details. Their support has been both meaningful and helpful. You see, I had never given thought to putting together a missive like this until asked. But hopefully, and if so in large part because of the help I've received, my efforts to make this book interesting, and thereby this project worthwhile, will have succeeded.

Honest confessions have often been described to me as beneficial for all humans. I trust I may be forgiven by those who suspect that I may have been planning an exhibit of holier-than-thou memorabilia. I cannot even think of pleading guilty to even having considered that notion. But I do readily confess that scarcely a day passes that I don't express to our Maker my gratitude for having been born when I was and where I was, in the best hometown this grateful soul can imagine. I am indebted to so many—no, to *most*—of the people I have known, who have helped me, in a life during which I have been witness to so many things that I never could have hoped to see.

Mine has been such a good life—for me and, I hope, for the remarkable lady who has been my best friend for more than six decades, and, I trust, for our three children and seven grandchildren.

I will digress no more but begin to try to put together a tapestry of memories and countless other things so essential to making this project justifiable, let alone possible.

Jesse Helms
MARCH 2005

FOREWORD
SENATOR WILLIAM H. FRIST, M.D.

NEARLY NINETEEN HUNDRED men and women have served in the United States Senate since its inception in 1789. Yet only a couple dozen stand out in history as Senators who truly were defining leaders of their times. I would include Senator Jesse Helms in those select ranks.

Although one might find it hard to believe, Senator Helms began his career in the media. After World War II, Jesse worked as city editor of *The Raleigh Times*. Later he became director of news and programs for the Tobacco Radio Network and radio station WRAL in Raleigh.

The media also made possible Senator Helms' transition into politics and public affairs. In 1952, he directed radio and television for the presidential campaign of Senator Richard Russell of Georgia. One year later, Jesse became Executive Director of the North Carolina Bankers Association and editor of *The Tarheel Banker*, which he grew into the largest state banking publication in America.

As a journalist, Senator Helms earned the respect of his readers and his peers. From 1960 to 1972, Jesse delivered daily editorials on WRAL-TV, wrote columns that appeared regularly in more than two hundred newspapers nationwide, and broadcast on more than seventy radio stations in North Carolina. He received the Freedoms Foundation Award for the best television editorial in America. He won the same award for the best newspaper article.

Jesse Helms' arrival in the Senate in January of 1973 made history. He was the first Republican elected to the Senate from North Carolina since Reconstruction. His star immediately began to rise. At the 1976 Republican National Convention, he was the only Senator to endorse Ronald Reagan for President. And though he asked for his name to be removed from the ballot, ninety-nine delegates voted to make him the party's nominee for Vice President of the United States.

While in the Senate, Jesse Helms became one of those unique leaders who combine fierce conservatism with fierce populism. His love for country and conservatism was matched only by his love for the people he represented. He always prided himself on standing up for the people of North Carolina—for the values they hold dear, for the beauty of their land, and for the work that is their lifeblood.

While in the Senate, Jesse also stood up for the cause of liberty and democracy in the world. He stood side by side with President Reagan in the battle to win the Cold War. He believed in peace through strength and still does.

He also believes in the value and dignity of every human life. I know this firsthand. Jesse and I worked hard as members of the Foreign Relations Committee to secure hundreds of millions of dollars to save young Africans from the plague of HIV/AIDS. Today, through the Jesse Helms Center, the Senator and his family are launching new initiatives to continue his work to protect children from this terrible scourge.

Always one to practice what he preaches, Jesse Helms has served as a deacon and Sunday-school teacher and as a director of Camp Willow Run, a Christian youth camp he helped found. He has generously given his time to combat cerebral palsy. And he spent countless hours with the more than one hundred thousand children and young adults who stopped by his office in Washington to shake his hand. Jesse has inspired them all to be better citizens; many have even gone on to serve in public office.

I know that all of us in the Senate have missed having Jesse Helms as a part of our everyday lives and deliberations. And America has missed a courageous and impassioned leader. But our loss has been the gain of the great state of North Carolina and of his family. I know how much Dot has enjoyed having more time to spend with her husband and with their children and grandchildren. Seeing Dot and Jesse together these days fills my heart with the same joy I felt when I saw my parents together in their later years.

We are so fortunate that Jesse Helms did not fade away when he retired from the Senate at the beginning of 2003. Of course, we knew he wouldn't. And with this memoir, he doesn't. This is a rich resource that helps us discover not just what Senator Helms did, but why he pursued the singular—and sometimes controversial—course he forged. We have here a guidebook for understanding what it means to hold clear convictions and champion them without regard for the mood of the moment. Even when you disagreed with him, you respected the clarity and conviction he brought to the public square.

I am so glad that Senator Helms' retirement has provided him with the time to complete this book. I have said many times that it would take ten Senators to equal the impact of one Senator Helms. I believe that this memoir will be a powerful tool for those who follow Senator Helms, one that will ensure that his voice will be heard for many years. Long after he and Dot finally have time to sit on the porch and enjoy the rest they have earned, we will still be able to profit from the Senator's wisdom.

CONTENTS

INTRODUCTION

I WAS BORN AND REARED IN A SMALL TOWN—which, come to think about it, may be why I have never been able to drive past the magnificent structure in Washington known as the U.S. Capitol without feeling a renewed sense of pride in our country. Pride, yes, but also gratitude for America's great heritage of freedom. Every day I become more firmly convinced that freedom just has to be a very special blessing from God.

I was born and raised in Monroe, the seat of Union County, North Carolina. That makes me, as an indulgent friend once put it, a "country boy." In any event, I thank the Lord for my parents—and my teachers—who left no doubt in my mind that being an American is the greatest fortune that can befall a human being.

In the years since then, my life has taken me far from my childhood and into a career during which I have been privileged to associate not only with some of the top leaders of our country, but with those of many other nations. In a very real sense, I have often been an eyewitness to history—and sometimes even a part of the history being made.

There is no sight in the world that has ever been more stirring—for me—than that majestic white dome, brilliantly illuminated against the evening sky. Many are the times—especially after some tumultuous days in the Senate—when I made a point of stopping my car, occasionally getting out of it to stand with a tingle down my spine, to admire this great edifice, hoping for another day's opportunity to do my small part to uphold the Republic for which it stands.

Though we passed through some dark days during my thirty years as a United States Senator in that great city, and darker days may yet befall us, this thrilling spectacle that crowns Capitol Hill has never disappointed me. Our Capitol, when all is done and said, remains the great shining beacon of freedom in the world. It represents our heritage, our values, our belief that anyone—

even country boys from Monroe, North Carolina, can go as far as hard work will take us, no matter how humble our beginnings. That promise, made possible because of our system of free enterprise, is truly the Miracle of America.

Growing up in Monroe between the two world wars was an experience I would not now trade for any material thing. From the perspective of years, I look back today and am reminded that my contemporaries and I clearly absorbed—from our homes and our Southern environment—great ideals (and few illusions).

Our home ties were very strong, and our little church on Monroe's Main Street was a dominant influence in our lives. Small towns in the South, moreover, have seldom been known as havens of affluence, and the Great Depression hit them with a particular virulence.

These were times when our faith in God, and in our country's institutions, was put to a severe test, but on the whole, we kept the faith and surmounted adversity. In the process, life was not without its rewards. The sense of community compassion, resourcefulness, courage, pride, and self-reliance that we knew then seems conspicuously absent from many of today's luxurious new neighborhoods and gated communities.

No one can deny that for comfort and convenience, American life today is a far cry from what it was in the thirties. And yet, in all my reading and reflection over the years, I never detected during the days of the Depression the kind of spiritual desolation and cynicism, nor the urge toward violence, that have gripped our country in the recent past, including the attempts to disrupt trade conferences or silence speakers whose ideas are not welcome on our university campuses.

Characteristically, Americans have always been a buoyant, optimistic people, and this change in outlook has become all the more ominous. There is a constant theme in the thousands of letters I have received through the years from people all over the country. They ask: What has happened to our moral fiber? Where have we lost the way? Why has corruption become so rampant in so many levels of government? Why are all of us so desperately frightened of and preoccupied with crime and terror?

Our political problems are nothing but our psychological and moral problems writ large. There is a great crisis of the spirit, a weariness of soul that has gradually paralyzed much of the Christian West. As a result, Communism succeeded in taking over almost half of the world's population in our own lifetimes—with little serious opposition—and now terrorists are allowed to flourish because of our lack of attention to their growing expressions of hatred and threats of violence.

When the Soviet Union began to self-destruct in the early 1990s, some "intellectual" in some think tank gathered headlines for himself by proclaiming that, with the extinction of Russian Communism, mankind had arrived at a watershed which he termed the "end of history." That nonsense notwithstanding, history marches on. Communism may be dead in Russia and Eastern Europe, but man's inhumanity to man has continued unabated. A spiritual famine lingers across our beloved land. Our citizens remain apprehensive about our future as a nation.

For nearly two thousand years, the Christian religion warned that among the greatest sins we can fall into are those of presumption and despair. Because I believe this, I feel a duty to reiterate, however inadequately and unworthily, the great moral and political truths that have sustained America as an independent nation for two centuries—truths that are now gravely endangered in a climate of apathy and skepticism.

A famous writer once said of Christianity that it had not been tried and found wanting; rather, it had been found difficult, and left untried. He was right, of course. And I believe a similar statement could be made about the philosophy of government which I myself have tried to espouse and which today is known as "conservatism."

For decades, there has been an unending barrage of "deals"—the New Deal, the Fair Deal, the New Frontier, and the Great Society, not to mention court decisions tending in the same direction. These have regimented our people and our economy and federalized almost every human enterprise. This onslaught has installed a gigantic scheme for redistributing the wealth that often rewards the indolent and penalizes the hardworking.

We have bought every nostrum the liberals have been so insistent on selling us, and we have abandoned the sure prescription for freedom, for prosperity, and for survival that is the very genius of the Declaration of Independence and the Constitution.

I believe we can halt the long decline, and that is what I wanted my career to be about. There is nothing inevitable about America's travail. There is a way back. I believe that the Miracle of America is just as possible in this new century as it has always been.

While we often say "times have changed," *some* things have not changed, even slightly, and those are the principles that we must follow if we are to restore and preserve our nation's moral and spiritual priorities—and the liberties which a gracious and merciful God has granted to us so that we might see more and more miracles in our midst.

Like many of you, I love America, and I know, as I'm sure you do, that we owe the Lord our gratitude for letting us live in America.

HERE'S WHERE I STAND

CHAPTER 1

My Family in Monroe

N OBODY GROWING UP EVER HAD better home folks than I did. My boyhood days were golden. Monroe was the kind of place where you knew just about everybody and just about everybody knew you.

The Monroe of my childhood was a community of about three thousand, surrounded by farmland. Today, it is a thriving small city; it is the county seat of North Carolina's fastest-growing county, and among the twenty-five fastest-growing counties in the United States. Down through the years, countless farms have given way to new homes, yet my hometown has never, to me, lost its attraction, and it never will.

Even now, after all these decades, when I see that ancient town clock facing all four ways atop the Union County Court House, or when I ride through what is now known as the historic district, I see those familiar buildings of my boyhood days. At those moments, my memories instantly become as vivid as today's headlines.

In the late 1740s, three Helms brothers—George, Jonathan, and Tilman— migrated from Pennsylvania to North Carolina and the Union County area. Both my mother, Ethel Mae Helms, and my father, Jesse Alexander Helms, who were not directly related, could trace their respective Helms roots back to those pioneers.

I am a part of the seventh generation of Tilman Helms' family to claim "Sweet Union" as my birthplace. (Nowadays the Helms listings in the local phone directory take up several pages, and scores of kin attended a family reunion organized some years ago.)

There were five of us in our immediate family: my late brother, Wriston, who was five years older than I; my sister, Mary Elizabeth (Lib), who is eight years younger; and our parents, both now deceased.

There was never a moment when I did not know that my parents loved me and my siblings. My mother might be described as a homebody. Other than being in church with us on Sunday morning, there was no place where she was happier than in her own home. She quietly took care of us and encouraged us by creating an environment where we were free of worry. She taught by example and was devoted to making sure we were well fed with vegetables from her garden and chickens from her little flock. One year during the Depression she even bought a cow to make sure that we would have enough fresh milk. Somehow, she managed to stretch every resource far enough to take care of us—and have something to share when my father found someone in need of a meal.

During the Depression, my dad served as both chief of police and chief of the fire department at the same time. By covering both jobs, the town of Monroe could provide my father a monthly salary of just $65. As little as that was, we somehow always had the essentials that we needed. Therefore, we considered ourselves exceedingly fortunate to have plenty to eat and a warm and comfortable home.

So, to me, the good old days in Monroe *were* indeed the good old days. I don't suggest that there weren't occasional difficult times, but they were more than balanced by the good fortune of being surrounded with people who cared for us and for one another.

We were poor, yes—awesomely poor by today's standards of poverty. The Great Depression was a fact of our lives, just as it was for the rest of the country. We knew that fortunes had been lost, and our own local bank had to take a bank holiday to prevent a run on its holdings, but we were no strangers to simple living, and our economy was tied to agriculture more than manufacturing. We stuck to the basics and hoped for the best.

All of us worked at whatever jobs we could find to bring in some extra money. At age nine I got my first job sweeping the floors at the offices of *The Monroe Enquirer*. I was proud of that job! My friends were doing the same thing, delivering groceries, helping out at the local stores, helping to sell eggs and vegetables—and all of us turned out to pick cotton in the fall. The schools closed so we wouldn't get behind in our classes, and out we went to pick the snowy crop and deliver it for ginning. It was not an easy time, but it was invaluable to me, and to a whole generation of people who would be asked to give so much to their country in the years ahead. But, of course, we could not have imagined any of that back then. We were living in challenging days, days of love and hope—and, as it turned out for so many young people from Monroe, we were living in days of opportunity.

I will never forget the delightful aroma of my mother's fried chicken every Sunday after church. Like many other families, we raised chickens in our backyard, and there were those painful moments when I realized that *my* pet chicken was next in line to become Sunday dinner. But, after a while, I became accustomed to the realities of life. I tried to learn to dismiss from my mind each episode involving the fate of one of my pets and concentrate on my mother's good cooking.

One instance in particular comes to mind with some frequency—a late-night experience when I was awakened by the unmistakable aroma of frying breakfast bacon and scrambled eggs—hours after everyone should have been asleep. I couldn't believe that it was already getting-up time, but the aroma from the kitchen commanded me to slip out of bed and investigate.

I saw my father busily setting the kitchen table and pouring coffee for two strangers, both poorly dressed and unshaven. Just as I entered the kitchen, my mother handed my father two plates, each filled with scrambled eggs, Mama's homemade biscuits, and generous helpings of fried fatback. The two strangers began to gobble down the food, pouring homemade molasses on two or three of Mama's biscuits and gulping down the hot coffee. I heard one of them say "Thank God" for the kindness of my father and mother.

It was later that I understood the meaning of what I had seen, an unforgettable lesson during the heart of the Great Depression. It was a painful time, when jobless men caught rides unnoticed in empty railroad boxcars, desperately seeking work in an effort to somehow survive and find jobs enabling them to provide food for their families. We caught sight of them sometimes when the train pulled into the station down the hill from the courthouse. They kept to the shadows because they were breaking the law by hopping on the train.

But that night, when I entered the kitchen and my father firmly instructed me to go back to bed—after presenting me to the two men as "my son, Jesse Junior," I had no idea that my father was supposed to have put these weary, hungry men under arrest.

These two strangers were called "hobos." Hobos violated the law when they slipped aboard empty railroad boxcars. They were penniless, their clothes were ragged, and they often were approaching starvation, so perhaps they decided the risk was the best of their limited options.

Years later, when my father and I talked about those men, he said, "Son, I guess I was supposed to throw them in jail—but what good would that have done? These people were trying to find work so that they could feed their families." In short, they needed a helping hand, not punishment for doing their best to find work. My father said he felt vindicated when he got a postcard signed by those two men reporting that they had found work in nearby Charlotte helping to keep the streets there clean.

Years later, my parents received a box of oranges from Florida with a card signed by one of the two men. "Best Wishes," it read, and "Merry Christmas to you and your wife. You saved two lives that night."

MY DAD WAS an imposing figure—six feet five inches tall and tough when he needed to be. But I remember him as kind and gentle. He taught me to respect people, no matter what their circumstances. He enforced the law even when some of his friends, even a fellow church member on occasion, violated the law.

He lived the way he wanted to teach me to live. Once, when I was about five years old, he was walking with me toward the swimming hole on my grandfather's farm when we saw a turtle sitting up on a fence post about three feet from our pathway. He stopped, pointed to the little turtle struggling to get off the post, and said to me, "Don't you think we'd better help that little fellow get down?" He reached over and put the squirming little turtle on the ground, then said, "One thing is for sure, that turtle didn't get up there by himself." He looked at me for a minute, then added, "None of us gets very far by ourselves." He paused, looked at me, then said, "Son, that's why I hope you will try to help others when they need it."

My dad never got past the fifth grade in school, but he was the smartest man I ever knew. There was the time when I was home from college and I went to visit my dad at the police station. The phone rang. Dad answered it, and I heard him say, "Mr. Bob, I'll be right there." Then he added, "I'm going to bring my son."

Mr. Bob met us at the door of his grocery store and said, "I was broken into last night and a slab of fatback and some dried beans are gone."

My dad thought a minute, then said, "I guess a lot of people are hungry these days. Let me see what I can do."

Minutes later I was in the front seat of the police car riding proudly with my father as we set off to solve the break-in. In a very few minutes we parked in front of a house. My father got out and went up on the porch, where he knocked on the door.

A man's voice from inside the house said, "Mr. Jesse, you looking for me?" My dad responded, "Robert, you know why I'm here. I want you to get that fatback and the other things that you took last night when you broke into Mr. Bob's." The voice inside responded, "No, Mr. Jesse, I ain't got no fatback. I don't know what you're talking about," to which my father said, "Yep, you do, and I believe *you* took it because you and your family were hungry."

Robert hesitated, then opened the door, shook hands with my father, and said in subdued desperation, "Yes, sir, that's how it was. My family was hungry."

My father replied, "Robert, get what remains of that fatback and dried beans and let's go see Mr. Bob and apologize."

When the stolen goods were offered to Mr. Bob, he hugged this man who had robbed him, then handed back the fatback and dry beans, saying, "When and if you and your family get hungry again, come in the front door of my store and tell me."

I remember thinking how much kindness my father showed as he handled this problem and how Mr. Bob responded with love and sympathy.

This wisdom marked his whole career. My good friend Bud Nance said his definition of "police brutality" was my father telling his mother that Bud had been caught misbehaving. That was true for most of the kids in town. Parents in those days could be counted on to administer their own discipline and have their children make restitution for any damage or loss.

Around the time of my father's funeral another man who had struggled to feed his family in those Depression years revealed an agreement my father had made with him. The man had a small still and used the money from the "white lightning" he brewed and sold to take care of his children. Mr. Jesse told the man he knew the still was his source of income and he would ignore its existence as long as the business didn't expand. That arrangement held, and while it did not follow the "letter of the law," it was true to the spirit of kindness that made my father unique.

That wise and caring man was my leader and my teacher, and I loved him dearly. He made clear the difference between right and wrong, and I was expected to do right.

When I was five years old, I was playing with a boy who lived a block over from us. We got into a little dispute, as little boys are inclined to do. He called me a "white cracker" and I retorted with that "N" word.

My dad had happened by and heard what I said. He reached down, took my hand, and led me into our home.

Gently he taught me a lesson I've never forgotten: "There's nothing *you* did that made you white, and there's not a thing *he* did that made him colored. Son, I don't want to hear you say that word again. Do you understand?"

I said, "Yes, sir." I've kept my word ever since. I don't care anything about the color of skin; I want to know what's in the head and what's in the heart.

His instruction on respecting "womenfolks," as he called them, was just as plain and direct. When I was old enough to date, he simply reminded me that the young lady I was about to go out with was somebody's sister and I ought to treat her the way I would expect someone to treat my sister.

The Fourth of July was an occasion that our Monroe neighbors always celebrated with enthusiasm. Being the son of the fire chief was a decided advantage for me on July 4, because my friends and I were among those who enjoyed the parade from the back of the fire truck as we waved our way through town. We loved every minute of it.

It was during one of those times of celebration that another lesson burned indelibly into my consciousness. One year the Monroe merchants got together for a big sales promotion and purchased an automobile that was to be given away at noon on Independence Day in a special ceremony at the courthouse.

Each merchant distributed tickets, and the stubs were deposited in a large container. During the weeks of the sales promotion, prior to the big day, everyone collected and preserved numerous ticket stubs. I recall my father giving each of us children three stubs that he had acquired when making purchases. "Keep them," he said, "but don't count on getting an automobile for nothing." (I don't know what an eight-year-old boy would have done with a car, even if I had won it.)

That was one of the few times that I doubted Papa's advice. I kept those stubs and examined them so often that they were almost tattered. I slept with them under my pillow. I knew that Papa just had to be wrong this time: Surely fortune would smile on me.

It didn't, of course. Someone else won the car. But I got something decidedly more valuable. I had a heart-to-heart talk with an understanding father who realized my deep disappointment. In that talk he taught me that the way to achieve, the way to acquire something that I really wanted, was to work for it.

"Earn it," he said in his gentle way. He told me that in America, people who work hard and save can do amazing things. "Someday," Papa said, "you'll have a car—but it will be because you *earned* the money to pay for it, not because you happened to hold a lucky ticket stub."

The one subject we never talked about much was politics. Looking back, I think one reason for that was the political climate of the times. Almost everybody we knew was a Democrat. There hadn't been a Republican in any statewide office since Reconstruction, and nobody in Union County could expect to be elected to any office by running as a Republican. Unless the circumstances were very unusual, like they were in 1928 when the Democrats nominated Al Smith to run for President, we already knew who was going to win the general election. Even in 1928, when Herbert Hoover carried all but eight states (including North Carolina, which went Republican for the first time in history), nine of Union County's precincts went for Smith, including both north and south Monroe—not a bad showing for a New York Governor who opposed Prohibition in a small Southern town full of teetotaling Baptists.

Of course, we were right back in that Democrat fold in 1932, when Franklin Roosevelt ran for President. We hoped Roosevelt's leadership would be good for America and get people back with their families and off the road.

I have worked since I was nine years old. I guess you could say my work has always been my hobby. My first jobs were with *The Monroe Journal* and *The Monroe Enquirer*. I earned a dollar a week. I swept floors and melted down type for the *Enquirer*. Mr. John Ashcraft, the *Enquirer*'s owner, trusted me with a key to the door of the *Enquirer* shop, and I've always been proud of that. How many employers today would give a nine-year-old boy a key to their business? For a while, as a high school student, I wrote a column titled "This Day of Daze" for the *Journal*, and by 1939 I had my own byline for a regular sports column. I also worked as a paperboy for both *The Monroe Journal* and the *Enquirer*, and for *The Charlotte News*. And I worked as a soda jerk at both Gamble's Drug Store and Wilson's Drug Store at the same time. At one point in high school, I was balancing four different jobs. That turned out to be good practice for my college days.

Looking back on it, I am glad I didn't win that automobile or have wealthy parents. If I had, I might never have had that important heart-to-heart talk with my father. That moment was the beginning of a little boy's understanding of the free-enterprise system. My father wanted me to learn that America never promises anybody happiness — only the freedom to *pursue* happiness. The genius of America is not in *winning* something or in being *given* it, it is in having the opportunity to strive and work and *earn* the things we really want.

We had several churches in our little town. Our family went to First Baptist on Main Street, as did most of my friends. I always stood next to my dad when we were singing hymns. He couldn't carry a tune in a basket, but I'd give a thousand dollars to hear his voice singing a hymn one more time.

But years have passed since the last Sunday I stood in that church on Main Street with my dad. I no longer live in Monroe. My father is no longer around to drive the town's American LaFrance hook-and-ladder fire engine, or to introduce me to wondrous things, like the time he showed me how to place a penny on the railroad track at the depot at the foot of Main Street, then wait, each passing minute feeling like an hour, until finally the huffing-and-puffing locomotive rounded the curve and roared down the track, flattening the penny. Once the train had disgorged its passengers and taken others aboard, then chugged out of sight, we retrieved our penny, now flattened and slick. I still have one or two of those pennies, and they remind me of my father. When I think of him, I imagine him "up there" doing whatever angels do. And I'm confident he knows how much those times meant to that little boy so long ago. I shall forever have wonderful memories of a caring, loving father who took the time to listen and to explain things to his wide-eyed son.

FAMILY AND FAITH FED my roots, and it was at school that I was challenged to grow. We never doubted that every one of our teachers cared about us. There were Miss Anna Bernard Benson, Miss Ollie Alexander, Mr. Alton Hall, Miss Lura Heath, Miss Annie Lee, and the remarkable principal of our high school, Mr. Ray W. House. All of them left their marks. They were dedicated Americans; they taught because they loved to be teachers, and it was no accident that what they taught were the principles that led to what I like to call the Miracle of America.

Miss Annie Lee taught us that grammar mattered. Her lessons stuck, and I have put them to use at every stage of my life, even in drafting legislation.

I was once serving on a Senate conference committee along with Senator Hubert Humphrey. We were ironing out that year's agriculture appropriations bill. After most of the issues had been hammered out and the members of the committee had a bill we could all agree to help enact into law, Hubert and I were the final two to stay on the job to perfect the details of the conference report. Hubert was exasperated by this point because I had made so many changes.

Finally, Hubert said, "Well, Jesse, is there *anything* else?"

I said, "Yes, as a matter of fact, there is one more thing that I must correct for Miss Annie Lee."

"What is it?" he asked.

"A split infinitive," I replied.

He said, "Fine. Is there anything else?"

I said, "No."

He said, "Let's go!" and he agreed to pull it out.

When the bill was finished, he looked at me and pointedly asked, "Who in the hell is Miss Annie Lee?"

When I told him, he said, "Well, we'll just call this the Miss Annie Lee bill."

That evening, I called Miss Annie and told her about the conference report meeting, about Senator Humphrey asking, "Who in the hell is Miss Annie Lee?," and about the conference report being named for her. She laughed and laughed.

An entire book could be written about Ray W. House, the principal of Monroe High School. He never saw limitations, only challenges.

He arrived at our school one September and within weeks declared, "We're going to get ourselves a band." He went out and he begged and borrowed (but didn't quite steal) used instruments that we could put to use as the Monroe High School Band. One of the horns was the sousaphone that I wound up playing—a battered relic; from where, I never knew, but Mr. House got it somewhere. Mr. House could not, strangely enough, read music, but he took a bunch of kids and got them together in the latter part of September, and the following May, the Monroe High School Band won the state championship in our division. One year I was a drum major, and there's an old picture of me leading the band down Monroe's Main Street. Each of us used what we had available to make a "uniform," and I improvised with the white jacket I was issued to wear at one of the drugstores while I was working as a soda jerk. Being a part of that band was a wonderful experience.

Mr. House could (and did) do anything with young people, even turn us into award-winning musicians. If it were possible to assemble all the young people who went to school under him and take a poll about what we thought about him, every one would say, "I loved him."

In our senior year, Mr. House summoned a group of us to his office. He looked around at us for a minute or so, then told us that if we were willing to work hard, we could earn more than we ever imagined.

He said to me, "Jesse. You may not believe this, but you're going to own your own home. You will have two cars, and you can do a lot for your city and county, and your state and country." At the time, I thought Mr. House's predictions were just a pep talk, albeit an effective one—after all, the country was still in the Depression—but Mr. House was serious. When I told him I wasn't going to be able to go to college because I couldn't afford it, Mr. House told me there were jobs available to help anybody who wanted to go, as long as that person was willing to do whatever was necessary (as long as it was honest). He told me, "It will all come in time, if you're willing to work hard enough for it."

When I did go to college, I studied journalism, only to discover that much of what was offered in the classroom I had already been taught by the editors of *The Monroe Journal* and *The Monroe Enquirer*. I am so grateful that in his retirement Mr. House was able to visit with me in Washington several times during the years I was a U.S. Senator. He certainly deserved a generous share of the credit for how my life turned out.

Among my boyhood companions, Bud Nance stands out. He was far more than a childhood friend. His life and mine touched time and again, drawing us closer each time. One of the many blessings that came my way during my years in the Senate was the renewal of our friendship and our daily contact. I could depend on him in every way.

Just about everybody in our hometown of Monroe knew Bud Nance during our formative years, and I think both of us were adults before it even occurred to me that Bud's name was James W. Nance. Our homes in Monroe were only a couple of blocks apart, and we played together, and gathered with our other friends to listen to our favorite radio programs, or to go to the movies when we had a quarter to spare. We studied together and shared our youthful hopes and dreams with each other. As small boys, we would climb high into the clock tower of our county courthouse, where we would peer out into the horizon at what we were sure was the whole world.

We were kids without affluence in a town without affluence, but we had no notion that anyone might regard us as poor. In terms of moral guidance from our parents, pastors, teachers, and city leaders, Bud Nance and I grew up blessed with a more valuable sort of wealth, having pursued careers that enabled both of us to serve our country—albeit in different ways. We could not have known it then, but our lives and our careers would bring us as close in our later years as we were in those wonderful days in Monroe.

CHAPTER 2

Getting "Educated"

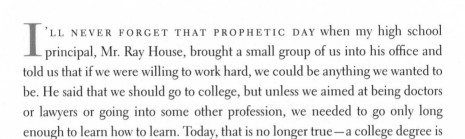

I'LL NEVER FORGET THAT PROPHETIC DAY when my high school principal, Mr. Ray House, brought a small group of us into his office and told us that if we were willing to work hard, we could be anything we wanted to be. He said that we should go to college, but unless we aimed at being doctors or lawyers or going into some other profession, we needed to go only long enough to learn how to learn. Today, that is no longer true—a college degree is essential for most fields—but it is *still* true that learning is a lifelong process.

Back then, the idea of my going to college at all seemed an impossible dream. The recession was a hard reality in our town. My father was both police chief and fire chief, holding down two positions to have one small paycheck; I worked after school, and we made do the best we could, but there was nothing left over for the costs of college and no point in my worrying about it.

But one day everything changed. The Reverend Coy Muckle, the president of Wingate College, came to our home. He told my parents and me that he wanted me to attend Wingate. I, of course, was very flattered, but we quickly made it clear that there was no money in the Helms family budget for higher education.

That kind man said money didn't matter. I was the kind of student they wanted at Wingate, and they were willing to take a chance on me. This was an unexpected blessing, and I agreed to his offer—with the promise that someday I would find a way to repay this vote of confidence in my ability.

When the fall semester opened, I took my place in the freshman class at that feisty school. Founded by the local Baptist association in 1896, when there were no public schools in the rural areas, Wingate had become a junior college in the early 1920s. Philosophically, its operation was more often a matter of faith than funding, and that was never more true than in the years of the Depression. While other schools shuttered, the staff at Wingate pulled together and remained committed to their calling, even when their administration building burned down in 1932.

Following the example of their undaunted president, members of the faculty personally pledged to help finish individual rooms in the new building. They accepted barter as a significant part of their salaries in the leanest years. These dedicated people were no less committed to their students, and I was glad to be in their classes for that first year beyond high school.

While I was at Wingate, Professor Jasper Memory, a family friend from the nearby town of Marshville who was a professor at Wake Forest College, took an interest in me. He said that I had a sharp eye and would make a good copy editor, and that I should study journalism and continue my schooling at Wake Forest College.

I do not remember a time, since the day I walked into my hometown newspaper office, when I did not want to be a newspaperman. I was encouraged by Professor Memory's confidence in my ability to succeed in that field, and I was more than willing to transfer to Wake Forest if it was at all possible.

The issue of money was as daunting as it had been earlier, but this persistent gentleman found a job opening on campus writing sports publicity that would help me cover expenses, along with a job washing dishes at the boardinghouse where I would stay. The opportunity to learn more about journalism was too good to ignore, so I enrolled at Wake Forest.

One day, Mr. Frank Smethurst, the managing editor of the Raleigh *News & Observer*, spoke to our journalism class. After he was done, I went up to talk to him, and told him if an opening ever came up, I'd like to speak to him about it. He appreciated my comments, and he knew that I had worked on newspapers back home. I could proof and I could run line type. Not too many weeks after that, Mr. Smethurst called and offered me a job as the overnight proofreader.

In those days, Wake Forest College really was in Wake Forest, North Carolina, a small town outside of Raleigh. The school was close enough for me to travel by train the sixteen miles from the campus to the newspaper in Raleigh without being late to my job. But I had an early class every morning I was at Wake Forest. To make sure I wasn't late to my 8 a.m. classes, I was allowed to leave work at the paper a few minutes early, in time to run the two blocks to the train station, pay my twenty-five cents for a ticket, and arrive at school just in time.

My job in the Wake Forest sports publicity office paid $18.75 a month, and that salary was made possible by the National Youth Administration. My bosses were Walter Holton, the legendary football coach, "Peahead" Walker, and Murray Greason. In addition to my overnight job at the paper, my publicity job at the school, and a dishwashing job at Miss Lizzie's Boarding House, where I lived—which was better known as Ptomaine Lizzie's—I was also a news stringer (freelance reporter) for as many newspapers as were willing to pay me. Not too long ago, as I was recounting this story, my wife, Dot, asked me how on earth I went to school and held down four jobs at the same time. I hadn't really thought much about it because I had been going to school and working at least one job, usually more, since I was old enough to push a broom. I told Dot that in my college days I didn't need sleep as much as I needed money, and I enjoyed the chance to have a byline whenever I could.

Ironically, the Raleigh *News & Observer* was *not* a paper in which my byline appeared. I had talked to the sports editor, Anthony J. McKevlin, about stringing, but he wasn't interested in me. That changed abruptly the day I "scooped" him with an inside story about a Wake Forest game. Mr. McKevlin called me into his office and asked me why he had to read that story, with my byline, in the Charlotte paper. I told him there didn't seem to be an opening for me in the sports department. I don't remember the details of what happened after that, but a spot for a sports reporter turned up and they offered it to me.

Like I said, sometime during that busy school year, I realized that a lot of the lessons that were being taught in the classroom were ones I had already learned in the newsroom. Mr. Beasley, the editor in Monroe who had given me my first job, turned out to have been a great teacher also, allowing me to learn as I worked. The same thing was true about my situation at *The News & Observer*—I was able to learn and benefit from the correction and example of the editors and reporters around me.

Mr. R. F. Beasley and his brother G. M. Beasley opened *The Monroe Journal* in 1894, and R.F. was still hard at work editing his paper when I came along. Under his exacting eye, I developed enough skill to be permitted my own column, "Between the Lines," where I could report on local sports news and add the occasional note of commentary.

Mr. Beasley packed every page with news and features, laying it all out with a mix of ads from all the local merchants, including the Brewer-Sanders Mule

Company and Belk Brothers department store, where in 1939 a lady's dress for spring could be purchased for as little as $1.98.

There was truly something for everybody in that paper, even serialized novels, like *Rapture Beyond,* by Katharine Newlin Burt, and *The Feud at Single Shot,* by Luke Short. Like anyone who wanted to write, I also loved to read whenever I got the time. I didn't miss much in those newspapers, including the social happenings recounted by the paper's correspondents from the little communities surrounding Monroe.

It was one of those social items that led me to write a column in which I contemplated what it would be like if the reporting on weddings was done a little differently, something like this:

> [The groom's] neck was encircled with a collar around which a cravat of a mauve hue was loosely knotted so that it rose up under his left ear with that studied carelessness that marks supreme artistry in dress.

Mr. Beasley used his columns and editorials to talk about the great issues of the day, like Neville Chamberlain's quest to maintain peace in Europe and Mr. Beasley's own personal philosophy of life: that "except for personal bereavement through illness or death or other calamity, people can be happy when they try to be." That philosophy probably explained why jokes and cartoons were a regular part of the paper, and why he rarely missed the opportunity to publish stories that would give his readers a good laugh.

With the offer of the full-time job at *The News & Observer,* I had the opportunity to begin the career I had always wanted. I wouldn't just have a job at the paper, I would be a newspaperman. I accepted the offer without hesitation, thankful that my classes at both Wingate and Wake Forest had also helped prepare me for this break. Now it was time to see how much I knew—and how much I had to learn!

Young people are often surprised to discover that most people who grew up in the 1930s didn't go to college at all, and many who did left long before they would have graduated. My own purpose back then wasn't to get a diploma, it was to get the foundation needed for the jobs I wanted to have. My goal was to get started as a journalist. When I had that start in the form of the job at *The News & Observer,* it seemed wisest to concentrate on making the most of that opportunity, so that maybe one day I might own a small-town weekly paper of my own. Where could I get a better education for running a newspaper than as an employee of a successful one? Best of all, it was a job in the sports department, where I would work with the people whose writing I admired most. To my way of thinking, sportswriters were masters of the language, painting a picture and evoking emotion without an excess of words. That was the quality I wanted in my own writing.

Although I could never have anticipated it then, over the years I have received honorary doctorates from my alma mater, Wingate, as well as Bob Jones University, Grove City College, and Campbell University. Each of them meant a great deal to me.

Today, both Wingate and Wake Forest are fine universities with national reputations. Each year they graduate students who benefited as I did from what these institutions have to offer in the way of academics and personal encouragement. Each of them now counts one of my grandchildren among its successful alumni.

Wingate is particularly close to my heart, because the good folks there were so kind to this student who did not dare to dream of college. Over the years, I have made it my business to repay that kindness.

In 1988, there was a great deal of interest in the future location of my Congressional papers. Many schools, including one in the Ivy League, were asking for them. However, I had something else in mind.

One day, Dr. Paul Corts, who was then president of Wingate University, paid me a visit in my office in the Dirksen Senate Office Building. As Paul was leaving, I asked, "Paul, how would you like to have my Congressional papers for Wingate?" Dr. Corts was stunned that I would offer my papers to such a small school, but he was delighted and accepted on the spot.

As we began to contemplate sending my papers down to Wingate, one problem developed. It was obvious that the college did not have the space to store and preserve them adequately. It was then that Dr. Corts came up with the idea of having a building with special storage facilities where the papers could be shared with scholars and others who might be interested in the work of the Congress at the end of the twentieth century. He also envisioned making available to young people and the general public a collection of publications, seminars, and lectures to promote the conservative, free-enterprise principles on which I based my Senate career. Thus, the Jesse Helms Center was born. At first I was reluctant to have this center named after me, but when I realized that this was one way I could repay Wingate University for its faith in me so long ago, I was convinced.

CHAPTER 3

Meeting Dorothy

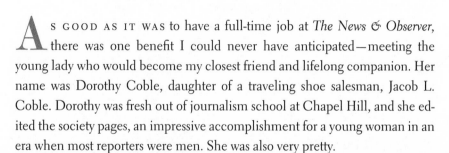

A S GOOD AS IT WAS to have a full-time job at *The News & Observer*, there was one benefit I could never have anticipated—meeting the young lady who would become my closest friend and lifelong companion. Her name was Dorothy Coble, daughter of a traveling shoe salesman, Jacob L. Coble. Dorothy was fresh out of journalism school at Chapel Hill, and she edited the society pages, an impressive accomplishment for a young woman in an era when most reporters were men. She was also very pretty.

The best path to my desk in the sports department was past Dot, and I made it my business to travel that path often. There was a little shop near the newspaper office, where you could get a cola and a small pack of peanuts for a dime. It seemed to me that Dorothy might enjoy some peanuts and a soda. I cultivated the habit of leaving a cola and peanuts on her desk whenever I went out for myself. That was the smartest habit I ever created.

Our first "date" was really a news assignment. Dorothy was supposed to cover a dance being held at North Carolina State University. Another reporter had assigned himself as her escort for the evening, but Dorothy decided she would prefer to include a "chaperone," and felt that I had the makings of an upright, well-mannered gentleman who would protect her from unwanted advances—which, of course, I did.

From then on, we formed a lasting friendship. On Friday nights, we both worked late helping to put the paper to bed for the weekend, and I could often persuade her to take time out for a steak dinner at the Hollywood Café about a block from the newspaper. We could buy a steak, a baked potato, a salad, and toasted biscuits, all for sixty-five cents.

It has been many years since those Friday-night dinners, but I must confess that no event, not even dinner at the White House, holds better memories for me than those evenings with Dot at the Hollywood Café.

The arrival of World War II accelerated our courtship plans. We scheduled our wedding to take place during my leave from the Navy, when I returned from training in San Diego. We married in Raleigh in late October—I've never forgotten our anniversary because it also happens to be Halloween.

Dot and I were married in a formal ceremony on Saturday afternoon, October 31, 1942, at four o'clock at the First Baptist Church in Raleigh. I wore my navy blue sailor suit and, I was told, looked like a beanpole (I was very thin during that time of my life). Dot picked the colors for her attendants' dresses, autumn green for her maid of honor and a dusty rose for her bridesmaids. (I remember the maid of honor kept referring to the color of her dress as olive drab.)

Dot's uncle, the Reverend Julius W. Whitley of Albemarle, was the officiating minister. My brother, Wriston A. Helms, was my best man. Dot's college roommate, Doris Goerch, who was the daughter of Carl Goerch, founder of *Our State* magazine, was her maid of honor, and her bridesmaids were her lifelong friend, Elizabeth Chamblee, and my sister, Mary Elizabeth. As Dot was escorted down the aisle by her father, it occurred to me that I was about to take an oath to love and cherish the loveliest young woman I'd ever seen. My memory replays that awesome moment often to remind me of the luckiest moment of my life.

In early October, while I was still away in training, Dorothy was honored with a bridal tea hosted at the Governor's Mansion by Mrs. Alice Broughton, the Governor's wife. A half-century later, Mrs. Broughton's grandson, Jimmy, would become a key member of my Senate staff, but no one could have imagined such a thing then.

We had a cake-cutting party at Dot's parents' home after the rehearsal the night before the wedding. Before the ceremony, Dot's aunts entertained the wedding party and all of our guests at a luncheon at the Carolina Hotel. We went home to our little furnished apartment after the ceremony, and that evening, after we had dinner at the Andrew Johnson Hotel, we caught the 11 p.m. train to New York City for our honeymoon. We stayed at the Hotel Taft and spent five days enjoying the sights and the shows, which included seeing Benny

Goodman's band perform in person and hearing a skinny young singer by the name of Frank Sinatra. Because of the frequent blackouts prevalent in the city during this era, it was very dark at night, but we didn't care.

One thing about wartime New York that made an indelible mark on Dot and me was the fact that no one would take our money. You see, I was in uniform, and shopkeepers and restaurant owners were so proud of the men of the service that this was their way of giving back. I was embarrassed, of course, because I felt that since I would be remaining stateside to work in a recruiting office, mine was the most unheroic service to the Navy.

I enjoyed my work at *The News & Observer*, but I was interested in doing more than just sports writing. When *The Raleigh Times* offered me a chance to be their city editor, I made the switch. I found the work interesting—I even earned an award for enterprising reporting—but, like most of my peers, my career plans were of no importance after the attack on Pearl Harbor. The day of that attack, I asked permission to put out an extra edition, and we sold $12,000 worth of those papers.

Soon after, I was on my way to the Naval Recruiting Office.

CHAPTER 4

In the Navy

IN THE YEARS LEADING UP to December 7, 1941, Americans watched events in Europe and in Asia with concern, but also with some detachment. On some level we knew that we might be called on to help our friends in Europe if Hitler persisted in claiming new territories, but many of us believed that the oceans separating us from trouble would also serve to keep us out of any conflicts. We wanted our country to be strong and our military to be prepared, but we were resistant to getting fully involved. My older brother, Wriston, had joined the Army, and of course we knew he was prepared to do his duty, no matter what the risks. So we hoped for the best and prepared for the worst—never imagining that the war would ever come to America's shore.

President Franklin Roosevelt had ordered an increase in military preparedness that started eighteen months before the Pearl Harbor attack, a decision that ultimately made it much easier for the country to move quickly into wartime production. The President had almost unanimous support, and he spoke eloquently of the determination of a united people to overcome a ruthless enemy. He said we were all in the war—every man, woman, and child— partners in "the most tremendous undertaking of our American history."

The nation responded. Back in Monroe, the chairman of the local defense council promised there was a job for everyone and began organizing volunteers to be plane observers and to assist police, fire, and emergency workers as well as public-works staff. The local Red Cross chapter announced its drive to raise $6,000 toward the $50,000,000 the national organization needed for its work in the war zones. We also learned that Monroe would be the site of Camp Sutton, one of many quickly established training facilities. It was operational by March of 1942, with a mission to train 18,759 soldiers.

Camp Sutton was named in honor of Frank Sutton, a young pilot who went to Canada in order to join the Royal Air Force before our country had entered the war. He was on duty over Northern Africa on December 7, 1941, when his life was lost. At age 24, this dedicated pilot was Monroe's very first casualty in the war.

In 1944, Camp Sutton was changed from a training facility to a German POW camp. The war had indeed come home.

WHILE MANY OF MY FRIENDS were serving overseas and aboard ships, it turned out that I spent my entire four-year hitch as a Navy recruiter. (Even while I was doing that, I applied more than once to be an officer trainee, but a slight hearing disability made that goal impossible.)

While not distinguished or heroic, my years as a U.S. Navy recruiter were, to me, both memorable and rewarding. They began with my friend Harry Gatton and me making a five-day train trip to San Diego, California for our basic training. They included hitches in Raleigh, Wilmington, and Ahoskie in North Carolina, and in Macon and Columbus, Georgia.

I'll never forget the morning of June 6, 1944. We were awakened at about five o'clock in the morning by the ringing of all of the church bells in Ahoskie. Dot gave a groan and started getting dressed, thinking there was a major fire somewhere and she needed to go. Then it hit us. It was D-day! Our troops had landed on Normandy Beach.

The young man who roomed across the hall from us was deaf. We didn't want him to miss out on the excitement, so I wrote the news on a slip of paper, woke him up, and showed it to him. He was as excited as we were.

I went about my stateside Navy duties somewhat reluctantly because I wanted to be where the battles were. Three different times I filed application papers for Navy training that would have led to my being assigned to an aircraft carrier, to interview Navy pilots immediately after they returned from bombing missions. But I was never transferred. My commander, Charles B. Neeley, who had been a General Motors executive before joining the naval reserve, chided me for even thinking about applying for sea duty. He liked having a publicity man around and asked me why, being a newlywed, I would want to leave—unless I was mad at somebody. I told him I wasn't mad at anybody, I just wanted to do my duty. Since he was the commanding officer and I was the petty officer first class, I stayed in Raleigh.

I appreciated the benefits of being so close to home and having Dot with me while I served, but I wanted to do all I could to secure freedom for our country and for our allies. I knew that what I was doing was valuable, but to me, it was not nearly as valuable as what my brother, who was stationed in Hawaii, and my friends were doing on the field of battle.

But, no matter what I had been assigned, I wanted to do it to the best of my ability. My first two years or more were spent in North Carolina, where I was a recruiter and then moved up to being petty officer in charge of the Navy recruiting office in Wilmington. Near the end of the war I was stationed in Columbus, Georgia (and briefly in Macon), where once again I was petty officer in charge of the recruiting station. Then, in December 1945, I was sent to Norfolk to be discharged.

Every one of my assignments allowed me to use what I had learned as a journalist to promote the Navy and boost recruiting.

One memorable summer, while stationed in Wilmington, I declared that August 8 would be New Hanover County Navy Day. Commander Neely came down from the Raleigh recruiting office and swore in more than a hundred young men. The ceremony was held in city hall with all the young recruits and their families and friends in attendance. Later, Commander Neely reprimanded me, saying I had no authority to declare the day New Hanover County Navy Day. It was, however, a special day for those young men and their families, and I don't regret doing it. I have often wondered about those young men and hoped that they all returned home from the war safely. They were mostly eighteen-year-old farm boys, and I'm sure they didn't realize what they were getting into. They simply loved their country and wanted to do their duty.

I developed friendships with the local newspaper editors and radio owners. The war had left them short-staffed so I was able to pick up some part-time work as my own responsibilities would allow. Dot, who had an impressive résumé of her own and was now the editor of three small-town weekly papers, shared my love of journalism. Our long-range dream was to someday own our own small-town weekly paper. We had no idea how we would ever afford such a thing, but we had both been taught that anything worth having was also worth the effort of working for. So we worked.

Early in 1945, I was transferred to the recruiting office in Columbus, Georgia. One night shortly after my arrival, I was at loose ends and I saw the lights on at *The Columbus Enquirer*. I went in and introduced myself to the editor, who was at his wit's end. All his male reporters had gone to war, and his only reporters were two or three military wives. He put me to work immediately, that night, and I worked at the *Enquirer* as long as I was in Columbus, covering everything from sports to international news. Of course, I had to get permission from my commanding officer, but he thought my working was good public relations for the Navy.

In early October of that year, I was in the recruiting station in Columbus when I got a message to go to the newspaper office right away. There was a telephone strike and service was limited, but a call had gotten through to the newspaper with an important message for me. There was a baby on the way in Raleigh, North Carolina, and I should try to get there as fast as I could.

It was midnight by the time I got the message, so there was great need for creativity. One of the folks at the newspaper knew a farmer who was headed toward Atlanta to get to the early-morning market, and he could drop me off at the airport. With the first leg of the trip taken care of, I was on my way. At the airport I told my story to a sympathetic ticket agent. She bumped an officer who was on his way to a football game and got me on the next flight to North Carolina. The plane wasn't going to Raleigh, but at least it was headed in the right direction. When the plane landed in Greensboro, I got on a bus and headed to Raleigh. After a sleepless night and a memorable trip, I arrived at the hospital to find that Jane Alexander Helms had gotten there somewhat ahead of me. Mother and daughter were both beautiful.

Shortly before Christmas, I was instructed to show up at the Navy base at Norfolk to be discharged. You can bet that I showed up on time, and my departure from the Navy was both quick and easy. The Lord be praised! I was going home to Dot and Baby Jane!

CHAPTER 5

Coming Back to Raleigh

W HEN THE WAR ENDED, I was glad to return to civilian life and to my post as city editor at *The Raleigh Times*. I thought we were settling down for a good long while.

Occasionally, when traveling for the Navy, I was authorized to take Dot along. During these travels around eastern North Carolina, I dealt with local newspapers and radio stations. At one such station, at Roanoke Rapids, I met and established a friendship with Ellis Crew, who, along with his brother, Winfield, owned a 250-watt radio station, WCBT.

To my surprise, very soon after I left the Navy and returned to my old job, Ellis Crew offered me a job as News Director of WCBT. I accepted because I was eager to see if small radio stations could prosper. It had been during my time with the Navy in that area that I became interested in broadcasting news. I believed that radio had real potential as a source for broader news coverage. Radio offered an immediacy that the best of newspapers could not. It captured the sounds of events and emotions in people's voices as they told their stories. Radio could reach places where the newspaper could not be delivered, or when the newspaper could not be delivered. Radio overcame barriers in literacy and provided a kind of companionship for people working solitary jobs. Radio had become a common accessory in trucks and automobiles. And no one could ignore the fact that radio had become a competitive option for advertisers who had previously spent all of their advertising money on newspapers and magazines.

When I was approached about the job at WCBT, I said, "If you let me come, can we emphasize news?" Ellis said, "That's the reason we want you to come." I was given full authority, and it paid off. Everybody in town listened to WCBT because of our news coverage. The "conventional wisdom" of the time said that all people wanted to hear was some soothing music and a little entertainment, with a short national newscast in the evening. We proved that wrong.

As much as I loved the newspaper, I recognized that we were becoming a much more mobile society, with little time for sitting and reading and less patience with waiting for hours or days to get details on the happenings in the world around us. If my earlier experience was something more than a wartime aberration, then the future growth of news delivery was in broadcasting. I was a newsman and I wanted to be connected to the part of my profession where the opportunity looked brightest.

I did not have a grand plan for the course of my career, and I certainly did not have any interest in public speaking. I did not then, and I do not to this day, consider myself an orator. If over the years people have wanted to hear me speak, it has been because they thought I might say something they wanted to hear, not because they were attracted to the sound of my voice or some style of delivery.

But I did have a sense that people wanted to know the news and would appreciate being able to get that news as they went about their day. I knew radios were turned on in barns and barbershops and kitchens all day long. I thought listeners would enjoy all kinds of news, from what was going on in the state capital to how the mayor and council were running their town. To me, the radio had far more to offer people than soft music and the national headlines once a night. I was willing to work hard to see if there was an audience for local news and maybe even news commentary. My goal was to deliver the news in the best format possible.

If I was wrong about broadcasting, there was plenty of time for me to return to newspapering. If I was right, I could be part of something nobody in my part of the country had taken seriously before. I had Dot's support, so I knew I was starting with at least an audience of one!

We moved our small family—Dorothy and me, and our toddler daughter, Jane—to Roanoke Rapids. Early every morning, I would go to work as the host of *Rise & Shine*; we went on the air at six o'clock. Later, I would go home for breakfast and then return to the station until our sundown sign-off.

While Dot, our baby, Jane, and I enjoyed life in Roanoke Rapids, I was on the lookout for a way to take radio news to a bigger city. I even approached the general manager of a large North Carolina station whose signal reached the entire eastern region of the country. He was very cordial as he told me, "Well, Jesse, you have to understand that we have a fifty-thousand-watt coverage, and the people way off as far as New York City and Florida don't have any interest in what goes on in North Carolina." I didn't agree with that assumption, but I didn't tell him I thought he was wrong! I knew the best way to prove I was right was to find an opportunity to try.

That chance came when I met a remarkable Raleigh gentleman, Mr. A. J. Fletcher. Mr. Fletcher was to become a father figure in my and Dot's life. Our association would profoundly shape the course of our lives.

Mr. A.J. owned a popular 250-watt Raleigh radio station, WRAL. The station was effectively managed by one of his sons, Fred Fletcher. Mr. A.J. offered me a job if I would come back to Raleigh to become News Director of WRAL and of two fledgling statewide radio networks operated by Capitol Broadcasting Company.

This was an attractive job offer that I viewed as having enormous possibilities. Moreover, Raleigh was Dot's hometown, and I knew she would welcome the opportunity to be closer to her family. So Mr. Fletcher and I quickly reached an agreement.

WRAL quickly allowed me to expand its news operation. We introduced a fifteen-minute news program called *The News of Raleigh* and ran it at 6:15 each evening—and after we had been on the air for four months and the audience ratings were released, our numbers were through the ceiling. We defeated the competition at every point. I wasn't any good as a broadcaster—I had a Southern accent that was thick as molasses—but I was convinced that local news with a personal emphasis had potential, and I enjoyed doing my job. People obviously liked what they heard, and the ratings showed that we could attract—and *keep*—an audience.

When the competition saw our success, they developed their own news operations, but WRAL had already learned how to bring in listeners—and that brought in advertisers, too. I felt that our experience in Roanoke Rapids had proved a point about listener interest. Local news would be useful and productive for any well-run radio station and, of course, for the communities served by them.

People responded to the personal aspect we added to the news. I remember one time there was a very personable young police officer working traffic duty on a hot summer day. Traffic was very heavy downtown, and cars were moving very slowly. I walked up to the officer with my portable tape recorder and asked how he was doing. To my amusement, he said, "I'm having fun. I can tell the temperature by the skirts of the ladies who drive by. When it's about eighty-five, they are down to here, and when it gets hotter, they get higher and higher. . . ."

That made a great little human-interest item, of course, but the chief of police laughingly reprimanded the officer. The listeners knew it was all in fun. They could hear not only what the officer said but how he said it—and that made all the difference.

The support I was given to do local news and to build a statewide radio network was just one example of the bold approach to business—and to life—that Mr. A.J. modeled. A. J. Fletcher was a man who made the most of the American Dream. His encouragement of me made all the difference in the world.

Mr. A.J. came from the humblest of circumstances, but with his brother's help he attended Wake Forest College and got a job as the editor of a weekly newspaper in rural Wake County. After he married, he and his wife saved until they could afford his tuition to law school. He stayed long enough to learn what he needed to to pass the bar, and then he opened a one-man office in the little town of Sparta, North Carolina. The Congressman for that district convinced Mr. A.J. to go to Washington and work on his staff, but he returned to North Carolina two years later to open both a law practice and a newspaper in Wake County. Within three years, he and his family moved to the county seat and state capital, Raleigh, where he expanded his business interests as well as his law firm. His interests ranged from the insurance industry to a local cemetery and the nearby nursery.

In 1939, Mr. A.J.'s son, Frank, an attorney in Washington, D.C., encouraged his father to apply for a broadcasting license for Capitol Broadcasting Company, the parent corporation of WRAL. In 1946, the Federal Communications Commission (FCC) granted Capitol Broadcasting Company a license to operate WRAL-FM, which became one of the most powerful pioneer FM radio stations in the country.

I joined the station in January 1948 and quickly developed a genuine love and respect for A. J. Fletcher. Perhaps it was his interest in public issues, perhaps it was our location in the state capital, but our news always included significant coverage of political activities, and Mr. A.J. strongly supported this emphasis. I was a regular at the State House and in the Governor's office—trying to get the lawmakers on tape (actually, it was "wire" in those early days) for our newscasts. We wanted our listeners to hear their officials themselves and to make up their own minds about issues.

CHAPTER 6

Learning About Politics

WHILE I CERTAINLY GREW UP with a strong interest in the news
of the day—an interest that had directed my career path, in both newspaper and radio—it was not until I got to know Dorothy's father, Jacob L.
Coble, that I really started to take an interest in political issues.

I admired Mr. Coble because he had pulled himself up by his bootstraps.
He made his living as a traveling shoe salesman and used his time away from
home to expand his knowledge. When he could, he invested some of what he
made in small rental properties. He had good business sense, and I was happy
to learn what I could from him. We lived in Raleigh with Dot's father for three
years after her mother died. It was during this time that I spent hours talking to
him about the issues of the day.

I grew up in a family that could be described as apolitical: My father and
mother, like the vast majority of the North Carolinians of their time, were
Democrats, and they voted, of course, but the issues and the candidates were
not discussed on a daily basis in our home as they were in Dot's. Her father had
very little formal education—as a child, he had gone to school perhaps three
months out of each year—but he was self-educated, and as an adult he managed to pass the business course at Massey Practical Business College in Rich-
mond, Virginia. Mr. Coble worked hard and was good at what he did; he was
the top salesman in his company. And he had no hobbies other than keeping
up with politics.

He was gone all week and was home on weekends. On Saturday he would work on his shoe orders, and on Sunday the family usually went to Sunday school and church, and maybe for a ride or to visit friends in the afternoon.

During the three years we lived with Dot's father, I, of course, was anxious to get on his good side, and he was glad to have a listener, so we discussed politics. Mr. Coble read avidly from news magazines, he listened to the news on radio, and he had very strong opinions, which he was happy to pass on to me.

I, too, began to think of the political impact of policies and events. I learned the important differences between conservative and liberal philosophies, and I began to think in political terms. I examined issues and made up my own mind about their potential good or harm for society. I started to understand how government decisions and public policies interconnected and how a seemingly inconsequential action could have a very large impact because of the precedent it might set. I'm sure those hours of discussions with Dot's father marked the beginning of my career as a conservative.

Mr. Coble challenged me to think through my political opinions. He didn't tell me what to think, but he urged me to know what I did believe about how government should work, and to stand up for those principles that mattered to me. Mr. Coble's example and our conversations on this topic helped me understand how the strength of the free-enterprise system is interwoven with the true strength of our democracy.

The more I paid attention to the issues, the more convinced I became that government works best when it intrudes least. That idea stands in opposition to the proposition that the government has a stake in every issue. Broadly speaking, people who think we need less government instead of more are called conservatives. Those who want as much government as they can get are called liberals. I'm a conservative, and I make no apology for it!

IN 1950, TWO FINE GENTLEMEN ran against each other for the opportunity to be the Democrats' nominee in the North Carolina race for a United States Senate seat. In this case the primary was more important than the general election because, as I said, no Republican had been elected from North Carolina since the days of Reconstruction. The winner of the primary was assured of winning in the general election. There were four candidates in that primary. One man, Dr. Frank Porter Graham, was the popular former president of the University of North Carolina at Chapel Hill, and he had been in the Senate for less than one year. The Governor, W. Kerr Scott, had appointed him to the Senate to fill out the unexpired term of Senator J. Melville Broughton, who had died in office in 1949.

Dr. Graham's main opponent was Willis Smith, a prominent Raleigh attorney who had served in the North Carolina legislature, on the board of trustees of his alma mater, Duke University, and as president of the American Bar Association.

The contest between these two men generated more continuing publicity than any other campaign in my memory at the time, and it went on while I was at WRAL Radio. Before the campaign was over, I had a much better idea of what it meant to be involved in a hard-fought election. The experience certainly did not leave me with any desire to ever be a candidate myself.

Willis Smith was a former law partner of A. J. Fletcher's. I liked and respected Mr. Smith, and he and I had similar conservative political philosophies.

On the other hand, "Dr. Frank," as Frank Porter Graham was affectionately called, was a beloved college president, particularly in my own house. My wife, Dorothy, a University of North Carolina alumna, was one of Dr. Frank's admirers. As students at UNC, Dot and her roommate, Doris Goerch, had attended many of Dr. and Mrs. Graham's "open houses," held for the students on Sunday afternoons. Sometimes there were only a few other students at the Grahams', so Dot and Doris got to know Dr. Frank on a personal basis. The downside for me was that, even for that day and time, Dr. Graham was very liberal in his thinking. I committed my personal support to Mr. Smith early on.

Our regular radio broadcasts and editorials about state government were pretty well known around Raleigh by this time. Although I never considered myself to be any kind of a public figure, it is possible that someone among Dr. Graham's advisors decided the best way to assure that I'd be positive about his campaign was to hire me to handle his press contacts, which would get me off the air.

That may be why early in the campaign I was summoned to Governor Scott's office. I did not know why I had been called until I arrived. The Governor was waiting for me with Dr. Graham. They asked me to become the publicist for Dr. Graham's campaign. In spite of my great respect for both men and the personal relationship I had with both, I had to decline because of my differences in political philosophy. I felt horrible, but Dr. Graham was very understanding and assured me that there would be no hard feelings. He continued to have my personal admiration for the many good things he had done for

North Carolina during his time as leader at Chapel Hill, and, of course, Dot remained steadfast in her affection for him. We had different philosophies about politics, but we were friends. It would have been unthinkable for me to do or allow to be done anything that assaulted that fine man's character.

The liberal news media resurrected the hard-fought Smith-Graham campaign during each of my five campaigns for the Senate, and each time falsely indicated that I had more of a role in that campaign than I did. Without personal knowledge or proper research, they have also created a false picture of Mr. Smith that is an insult to that fine man's life and record. He was not a racist. He had no such side. He was the kindest man imaginable. Willis Smith was a past president of the American Bar Association, and of the North Carolina Bar Association. His character was unassailable.

He had been Speaker of the North Carolina House of Representatives. He was at the top of his field, earning a really good living as a good lawyer, and everybody recognized that. His law firm was the strongest in the state, and he had become a successful businessman with a well-run textile mill. Nobody gave Willis Smith anything, and he didn't take anything. He did the best he could with what he had, and by the time he ran for the U.S. Senate, he had a lot with which to work. I am convinced that if he had lived long enough to do all he could have done for North Carolina and our country, he would be counted among our greatest Senators.

I had *no* official role in Mr. Smith's campaign when there were four candidates for the Democrat nomination, nor in his runoff campaign when the field had been narrowed to him and Dr. Graham. However, as head of the news department at WRAL, I did visit the campaign office every day to keep up with their news, and I sat in on some of the staff meetings as an observer.

I did get personally involved just before the end of the campaign. Dr. Graham had narrowly defeated Mr. Smith in the primary election but had not gotten a majority of the votes cast. The margin of victory was so close that Mr. Smith, as the first runner-up, had the option of calling for a runoff. He agonized for days over his decision, then decided to concede the primary to Dr. Graham.

The day before the filing deadline, Mr. Smith gave Hoover Adams, his publicity director, a telegram of congratulation to be sent to Dr. Graham. However, Hoover stuck the telegram in his pocket and delayed sending it.

The campaign staff members were devastated by Mr. Smith's decision, and many tears were shed. I was in the office when there was a meeting with

Charles Green of Louisburg, the campaign director, along with Alvin Wingfield, Hoover, and several others. I got into the discussion, and as a group we came up with an idea that we hoped would cause Mr. Smith to change his mind.

I contacted Mr. A.J. and asked for his permission to put a series of ten-second commercials on WRAL, at my expense if necessary, urging people to go to the Smith residence and encourage Mr. Smith to change his mind and run. That was the beginning and end of my involvement as a volunteer in the Smith campaign — one election was over and another had not yet been decided upon, but as an admirer of Mr. Smith's I hoped he could be persuaded to give the voters another chance.

When the report that Mr. Smith had decided not to run was not on the six o'clock news, Mr. Smith called Hoover Adams and asked him what had happened. Hoover told him that there had been a delay in sending the telegram and indicated it might be on a later newscast.

In the meantime, the commercials asking Mr. Smith to reconsider his decision went on the air. At about nine o'clock that night, Dot and I began to wonder whether the commercials had been effective. We decided to drive over to the Smith residence and find out. Every street anywhere near the Smith residence was congested with cars; the Smiths' yard was full of hundreds of people.

Mr. Smith repeatedly came to the front porch of his house in response to the chants of the people, thanking them for coming and for their support. Finally, he told the people that if they would go home and let him go to bed, he would run. Actually, what he said was: "If you all will go home and let me get some sleep, I will think about my decision, and I don't think you will be disappointed."

He filed for the runoff the next day, and as Paul Harvey would say, now you know the rest of the story. Mr. Smith was victorious in that runoff, winning with a clear majority. That November he was elected U.S. Senator from North Carolina. Unfortunately, he died in office about two years later.

One other point needs to be cleared up for the record. Not only was I not, as some have claimed, a member of the Smith campaign organization, but I also never was and never would have been involved in the alleged doctoring of a racist photograph that was circulated against Dr. Graham during the primaries. I never saw any such photo, and Willis Smith said he never saw any such photo either. I have always found such charges so repugnant that I chose not to give them the dignity of a response. I break that silence now so the record might be correct. Dr. Graham was a family friend. I would never have been a party to attacks on his character or supported a candidate who stooped to that level.

Beyond that, Mr. Smith was so opposed to that sort of tactic that he wanted to know if maybe one of his supporters, in a moment of zeal, had something to do with it—so he could put a stop to that kind of thing. He told me that he never found anybody who knew anything about it or who was supporting it. I could not vouch for the character of every individual who might have had motive to do such a thing, but I certainly could say without any question that it was not in Willis Smith's character to engage in this kind of reprehensible behavior or condone it on the part of others.

My friend Hoover Adams, who was on Mr. Smith's campaign staff, recently told me what happened the day after Mr. Smith learned of a particularly repugnant attack on Dr. Graham. Mr. Smith went into the office and specifically asked if any of that sort of material was coming from anyone in his employ. Hoover assured him it was not. However, Mr. Smith wanted to make sure there was no confusion about his rules. He told Hoover to make sure that everyone on his staff understood that if they stooped to such behavior, they would all be fired immediately and Mr. Smith would resign from the campaign.

In those days any anonymous person or so-called "committee" could create a flyer or even publish an ad for or against a candidate, without the opposing candidate's knowledge or permission, and without any connection to, or control by, the opposing candidate. Unfortunately, Dr. Graham had angered some people who cared more about unseating him than they did about doing what was right. And while they may have thought they were supporting Mr. Smith, they certainly failed to understand the high moral standards to which he subscribed and by which he expected others to live. He was offended by such tactics.

People have asked what made the Smith-Graham campaign so hard fought and so important. It was a classic and emotional battle between a candidate who was liberal in his philosophy and his goals and a candidate who believed in the principles and policies shaped by a conservative philosophy. There is rarely any apathy or middle ground when an election turns on issues rather than personality. This was such a race. Some voters, on both sides, saw it as a battle between good and evil.

Dr. Graham had been in the Senate for a brief time before the election, and in that time he had made decisions and cast votes that were not popular with many North Carolinians. Of particular concern were Dr. Graham's connections with a number of organizations that the Attorney General had on a list of suspected Communist groups. That perhaps naive willingness to be associated with people who possibly may not have been loyal to the country was troubling, as was the collection of liberal speakers who were welcomed on the UNC campus. When these controversial speakers declared themselves Graham supporters, it further strengthened his connection to liberal causes and a liberal agenda. In the first primary, more than half of the voters wanted someone other than Dr. Graham representing them. That is why there was so much clamor for a runoff.

In Willis Smith, conservative voters found someone who thought as they did and was loyal to the values that are bedrock to America. Smith's own story proved what they believed about the opportunity America offered anyone who was willing to work hard and not depend on someone else's effort. Smith's opponents tried to paint him as a friend of big business who would not look out for the concerns of the ordinary citizen, but his supporters knew better. They were confident that he would not vote against their interests.

After a vigorous campaign, Mr. Smith was nominated by the Democratic Party to replace Dr. Graham as North Carolina's junior U.S. Senator. At that time, achieving the Democratic Party's nomination to a statewide job was tantamount to election. In November 1950, the election was official. North Carolina was sending a conservative to Congress.

CHAPTER 7

In Washington with Mr. Smith

THERE WAS NO DOUBT ABOUT IT, Willis Smith had impressive political potential. He had challenged and beaten a popular appointed U.S.
Senator, and many people expected him to become one of our nation's top
conservative leaders. As a top-flight lawyer, he was in contact with the best legal
minds in the country, and I believed Senator Smith could help his country stay
true to the foundational principles of our founders in the creation of new laws
and policies.

While I was astonished when Mr. Smith invited me to join him in Washington as his administrative assistant, Dot and I together made the judgment that
we should go. With the blessing of Mr. Fletcher, I accepted Senator Smith's
offer.

By this time, there were four of us Helmses—Dot and me, our young daughter Jane, and her toddler-age sister, Nancy, who was born early in 1949. We
found an apartment to rent in Virginia and set off on a totally new adventure.

We found the Washington, D.C., area a thoroughly agreeable place to live
and soon found ourselves quite at home in an environment that, in those days,
was not so different from the pace of life in Raleigh. There was no ring of inter-
states, no proliferation of high-rise apartments, and compared to the crush of
traffic today, very few commuters heading into the capital each morning.

Serving as administrative assistant to a United States Senator is a true learning experience. It was especially so considering some of the interesting circumstances. For example, Senator Smith was assigned a three-room suite, number
345, in what was then the only Senate office building. Today, little more than

half a century later, there are three office buildings for just the Senate, and no
Senator's staff could begin to fit into just three offices. At that rate of growth, it
is hard to imagine how much space the Senate offices might fill up in the next
fifty years.

In 1951 there were ninety-six U.S. Senators representing the then forty-
eight states; today there are one hundred Senators representing the fifty states,
but I don't think those four extra Senators could be held accountable for two
extra office buildings!

One of those ninety-six Senators back then was a delightful young Republican Senator from California named Richard M. Nixon. I was impressed by his
intellect and his genuine interest in working with people who shared conservative principles without concern for their party tag. Senator Nixon had a solid
North Carolina connection because he was a graduate of the law school at
Duke University. As I mentioned, Senator Smith had been on the university's
board of trustees for some time and continued to be an active participant in the
affairs of his law school alma mater. There were many visits to Senator Smith's
office by the then President of Duke, Arthur Hollis Edens, and Senator Nixon
often stopped by to greet Dr. Edens. This Duke connection as fellow alumni
helped establish a solid friendship between Senator Nixon and Senator Smith.

The assignment of office space had put Mr. Nixon's offices between the
offices of Senator Smith and North Carolina's senior Senator, Clyde R. Hoey,
on one corner of the third floor of the Russell Senate Office Building. Each
suite had just three or four rooms apiece. Both Senator Hoey and Senator
Nixon worked well with Senator Smith, and they frequently met "in the middle" in Senator Smith's office.

Senator Nixon also came to my office frequently. Senator Smith usually
had a full calendar of visitors, so on a number of occasions Nixon had to wait,
and he sat there at my desk until he could get in to see Senator Smith.

We would banter together, and he tried to make it appear that all Southerners were racists. I said, "Neither Senator Smith nor I are at all racist!" and he
said, "Well, the way y'all treat blacks down in North Carolina, you don't know
how this Senator might treat blacks." I jokingly said, "I'm going to tell Senator
Smith what you said," and he said, "No, no, I know better than that." (Senator
Nixon knew that Senator Smith and I were not the least bit racist in our views
or our actions. He had seen the way we treated constituents and the people who
worked in and around the Capitol, and he certainly knew Senator Smith's
character, as well as his standards for the people who worked with him.) Sena-

tor Nixon looked at me and said, "But you've got to admit that there's a lot to be done on race relations in North Carolina." I said, "Well, that may be so, but I should tell you we treat our Chinese people very well." Senator Nixon acknowledged that a prejudice against people who were from China, or the children of parents who were, was certainly an issue in *his* home state of California. All of us had areas that needed improvement.

Senator Nixon would invite me for lunch every once in a while. I was just an administrative assistant for another Senator from another state, but I liked Senator Nixon and enjoyed our conversations. We had both grown up in modest circumstances, and we both had two young daughters who were very close in age, so we had much in common.

Based on what I had seen of the man during our frequent interaction, and his obvious intellectual abilities, I thought General Eisenhower made a good choice when he selected Nixon as his running mate in the 1952 Presidential campaign. Eisenhower was such a popular national figure that he could have chosen almost anyone as a running mate and not changed the margin of victory, but he made a wise choice by picking a man with considerable experience in Washington and a proven ability to win elections in California against formidable opponents. I expected that Mr. Nixon and I would have many opportunities to continue our friendship as he went about his duties as Vice President. I knew he would continue to maintain a good relationship with Senator Smith.

Then came the tragic summer of 1953. One Friday afternoon, Senator Smith told me that he wanted me to substitute for him at an event in Hickory the following Monday at noon. I recall his saying that he regretted to default on his commitment, but there had been a change in the Senate schedule and his vote was needed. So he suggested that I "get up" a speech over the weekend and fly down to North Carolina on Monday for that lunchtime civic-club appearance as his substitute.

I recall thinking how disappointed those folks were going to be when a young guy named Jesse Helms showed up as Senator Smith's substitute. But I put together a speech and arranged for a plane ticket, and on Monday, I headed for North Carolina by plane at about 10 a.m. Fortunately, I got along surprisingly well with the members of that disappointed civic club, and I was back on a plane not long after I was done.

When I finally reached our Washington office late Monday afternoon, I was greeted with the news that Senator Smith had suffered a heart attack and was at Bethesda Naval Hospital in serious condition. I went immediately to the hospital and to the Senator's bedside.

The Senator was pale and breathing gently when I reached his bedside at Bethesda. He was encased in a plastic cover. I saw his light breathing; he was asleep. I slipped my hand under the plastic and patted his hand gently.

He opened his eyes, saw me, smiled faintly, and said, "I know you received a nice fee for going and making the speech." Then he paused and managed a slight grin: "You and Dorothy ought to take a trip to spend it."

(He and I had joked many times about how often he was urged to go somewhere and make a speech, but no speaker's fee was ever offered, nor any reimbursement for travel. That was a little private joke between a great Senator, whom I loved dearly, and his young assistant, who had already learned a great deal from a very wise man.)

I wept quietly as I left him sleeping. I sensed what was going to happen. It did—the following Friday morning. To me, a giant had fallen.

Once again it fell to the Governor to appoint a North Carolina Senator. Governor William Umstead selected Alton A. Lennon for the post. I stayed on briefly in Washington to help Senator Lennon's transition, but we were back in Raleigh by the end of 1953, with no plans to ever become residents of metropolitan Washington again.

While I had no interest in joining their ranks, my experience in Washington provided me with a rare understanding of the responsibilities of United States Senators and the challenges they face. I learned to respect stalwart men like Senator Richard Russell, and I was pleased to accept a role in his brief campaign for the Presidential nomination in 1952.

We were settled back home in Raleigh before the Army–McCarthy hearings took the national stage. Senator Joseph McCarthy and his staff of investigators had started at a point where most Americans would have been supportive. His committee was asked to assess the possible presence of government employees who were in fact not loyal to our country. President Truman and his Cabinet, as well as the Congress, were concerned with the threat of Communism. Who would argue with the idea that enemies of the government shouldn't be on its payroll?

But from that initial mandate, Senator McCarthy expanded his area of investigation and broadened his definition of what constituted a threat and who might have engaged—or might be engaged—in threatening activity. The repercussions of the damage done when that committee violated its narrow parameters are with us yet.

Currently, opponents of some or all of the provisions of the USA PATRIOT Act point back to the excesses of the McCarthy era when they debate the value of increasing security at the cost of long-held freedoms. We may finally agree that no defensible level of expanded government power is too much if it rids us of terrorism, but we should not make that decision without a clear notion of what we may be sacrificing.

CHAPTER 8

The Tobacco Radio Network

W HEN WE RETURNED to Raleigh in 1953, I became the Executive Director of the North Carolina Bankers Association, a position I held until going back into broadcasting full-time in 1960. My position at the Bankers Association was one of the most enjoyable jobs of my life. I was the editor of *The Tarheel Banker* and responsible for its content—from editorials to news briefs.

The members of the Bankers Association were people who not only believed in the free-enterprise system, but also fueled the growth of new opportunities by their investments and their willingness to help people fulfill their own dreams—from home ownership to college educations or new business ventures.

I was glad to do what I could to promote this industry and was occasionally asked to talk to local civic clubs around the state. I used those times to remind people that their involvement as candidates, as voters, and as informed citizens was the best way for them to assure that our country remained a place of freedom and opportunity. I told them not to worry about whether or not they might win if they ran for office, because no one is ever so near to victory as when defeated in a good cause.

I was very comfortable issuing this challenge because by 1957 I had taken my own advice and won a seat on the Raleigh City Council. I served for two terms, from 1957 to 1961, and chaired the committee on law and finance. That experience eventually led me back to broadcasting.

While Dot and I were busy with the Bankers Association, A. J. Fletcher was continuing to expand his broadcasting operations. Since I had left WRAL in 1951, the company had grown to include WRAL-TV, Channel 5 in Raleigh. When the station applied for its VHF operating permit in 1953, it did not even have broadcast facilities—but it had a mission: to bring an independent voice to eastern North Carolina. The FCC agreed with that mission and awarded WRAL the license ahead of its very well equipped and very confident competitor, WPTF. When WRAL-TV first went on the air in 1957, it was using space in an old house on Hillsborough Street that had been converted into the headquarters of the National Opera Company.

But this was no fly-by-night operation, and Mr. A. J. Fletcher soon opened a new building that became the headquarters for all of Capitol Broadcasting's growing operations. WRAL-TV quickly found its audience and proved a success.

There was one fifteen-minute program on Sunday afternoons that I never expected to succeed, but somehow it did.

On the first Sunday in August 1958, *Facts of the Matter* made its debut, with me as its host. Some Sundays we would have a guest like the State Treasurer or a news columnist, or someone less well known but with an interesting story to tell. Other shows were mine to fill with news and commentary about things happening in Washington or in our own town, and how those things might impact life for all of us—from federal taxes to Southern sit-ins. It was a valuable way to let the people of Raleigh hear the full story about issues we had wrestled with in the City Council—rather than just the local paper's view on those issues.

We took a break before the campaign season for City Council seats so other candidates would not feel they were being treated unfairly by my access to the camera. I was happy to get back to discussing the issues when it was time to pick up the conversation, but I never ceased to be surprised when viewers took the time to send a letter commenting on the program or something I had said. Their interest was more a barometer of the fast-growing impact of television than it was a compliment to my style or delivery. I may have picked up some experience standing in front of audiences or sitting behind a microphone, but I certainly wasn't polished. If I had a style, it was unintentional. My goal was the same whether I was speaking or writing—to get to the point and not waste any words along the way.

In 1960, Mr. Fletcher began conversations with me about the possibility of joining the staff of WRAL-TV and Capitol Broadcasting full-time. Mr. Fletcher was concerned that the editorial content of the Raleigh *News & Observer* was the only view most people in the WRAL-TV viewing and listening area were exposed to. He wanted them to know there were sound arguments in opposition to many of the *The News & Observer*'s positions. He thought there should be a way to offer more information and commentary as an alternative to the newspaper.

I was in no rush to make a change from the Bankers Association, and finally said I would not consider a move unless I could do an on-the-air editorial on Channel 5 each day, Monday through Friday. This was a bold request. Editorials were very rare on television anywhere in the country, and the few that were aired were of the innocuous "support your local charities" variety. What I was proposing was to broadcast editorials on any topics we thought worthy of comment, even if they might be "controversial."

Mr. Fletcher agreed with my proposal and offered me the position of Executive Vice President for News Operations. The opportunity to do something innovative in broadcasting and the privilege of working with Mr. Fletcher again made it impossible to say no.

Not everyone at the station was comfortable with the decision to do editorials. There was a fear that inviting controversy might even cost the company its broadcast license. In a meeting that included his son Fred and other advisors and myself, Mr. Fletcher was challenged about the risk of losing WRAL-TV's license. Mr. Fletcher sat quietly for a while. He turned and looked out the window. Finally, he turned back and firmly said, "By God, if we lose it, we lose it."

With that vote of confidence, the decision was final. The station established an editorial board that approved every editorial before it was broadcast. It was chaired by Mr. A. J. Fletcher. The members of the board included myself as Executive Vice President of the station; Fred Fletcher, who was the President of Capitol Broadcasting; Aubrey H. Moore, an officer of the company; and Frank Fletcher, who was an important lawyer in Washington, D.C., whose clients included a number of radio and TV stations in many states.

It was shortly after the election of John F. Kennedy as President and Terry Sanford as Governor of North Carolina that I returned to the broadcast business. We called our editorial segment "Viewpoint," and the first topics we got into were the value of self-reliance, the virtue of limited government, and the danger of Communism.

With the freedom to inform, we were able to point out important facts that our friends at *The News & Observer* often overlooked.

It is impossible for me to overstate the power of facts. From the first day I was given the privilege to write for the little hometown paper, to this day, I have made it my business to have my facts right. Years ago a great hulk of a man stormed into our radio newsroom and backed me into a corner. He had the biggest fist I've ever seen.

But I didn't get hit that day because the man gave me a chance to ask him what was not correct about the news I had broadcast the night before. Finally, he acknowledged that the facts were correct. He simply objected to their being reported. I can assure you that I was delighted to be able to persuade him that hitting me wouldn't change the facts.

So we went out of our way to back any editorial opinion with fact. We were always ready to publicly report any error that was discovered. And we hoped that people who didn't like the facts wouldn't get mad enough to hit anybody.

On the evening of November 22, 1963, we had a brief local newscast, and in place of our planned Viewpoint, I tried to put how we all felt into words:

> Anguish alone will not suffice as the nation's proper reaction to the news of President Kennedy's assassination. All men of sanity and humanity feel a sense of revulsion at the act of the fanatical coward who hid in the attic of a building and fired down the shots that extinguished the life of a young man who, to us, seemed to possess not merely the quality of unbounded energy, but a sort of indestructibility as well.
>
> At this moment, of course, all Americans are united regardless of party, or philosophy, or ideals. Conservatism, liberalism, right wing, left wing—all these are meaningless semantics, no longer dividers, certainly not important unless and until we respond to the question of what happened to civilization in that dark moment in Dallas.
>
> So, in unity there is a helplessness that may assist us in groping for strength. One insane man with a high-powered rifle has exposed the incredible weakness of a nation. If we now understand it, some consolation may be found. Men have differed with Mr. Kennedy in his exuberant ideas about politics, government, and the quest for peace in a troubled world. But as he lies tonight in death, he has left more than a shocked and stunned nation. The manner of his death leaves America standing naked as a symbol of civilization mocked.

Every citizen will reflect upon Mr. Kennedy's life, and his death, in a personal way. Mr. Kennedy has become a part of America in a personal way. His harshest critics recognized his magnetism and persuasiveness which had drawn him into the inner circle of American life. He was not loved by everyone—still, no one doubted his courage or his stamina. He fought his political battles with every ounce of his strength. And he did it openly.

And this serves to emphasize the dastardly nature of his assassination. Jack Kennedy was killed by a coward.

As we sat alone minutes after the announcement of the President's death, a hundred images flowed through our minds. One little incident that we personally observed nearly eleven years ago came to mind as clearly as if it were yesterday. It was a cold, crisp January morning in 1953 and the quorum bells had just rung throughout the Capitol and the Senate Office Building in Washington. Members of the Senate, the old ones and the new ones, were scurrying to get to the Senate chamber. It was oath-of-office day for ten or twelve, including a tousled-haired young man from Massachusetts who had been elected to the Senate the previous November.

Senators were boarding the subway cars that connect the Capitol with the Senate Office Building by an underground route. Visitors and employees of the Senate were being repeatedly told by operators of the subway cars to stand aside for the Senators. They had priority.

Jack Kennedy arrived to take a seat on the subway car, but the operator waved him back. "Stand aside for the Senators, son," he said. Jack Kennedy stood aside with a grin—until an observer whispered to the operator: "He's a Senator, too." The embarrassed operator got only a pat on the back and a reassurance from Senator Kennedy.

An unimportant incident? Maybe! But it is one that we will remember always. No matter how much we might have disagreed with certain of the President's views and actions, the memory of that incident provided a sense of warmth and personal affection.

Millions of words will be written and spoken about this dark hour in America's history. Many days will pass before we can stand with pride and confidence, and say to the world that we are civilized. The cause of Communism has been served well by this tragedy. Freedom has suffered a telling blow. . . .

If our editorials at WRAL-TV had an editorial bias, it was one in favor of the conservative principles that were the bedrock beliefs enumerated by our founders. Those principles were the straight stick against which everything else could be measured. We stood against tyranny in government, and for liberty.

We dared to point out that it made little sense to let the federal government provide money for education when the money to create that bureaucracy had come out of our own pockets and was being returned to us at a rate of one dime back for every dollar sent from the state. We explained that the 26 million Americans in the United States in 1962 who belonged in the 13 percent tax bracket would automatically be bumped to the 20 percent bracket if they earned so much as $1.00 in a savings account, unless they remembered and knew how to fill out a quarterly form for the IRS—and that new layer of red tape (as well as the cost of administering it) was supposed to be for their benefit. We talked about the harm being done to relations among neighbors of different races by the militant intrusion of outsiders. We decried the hardening of attitudes about the war in Vietnam and the disrespect shown to those who had accepted their country's call to duty. We laid the blame for the farmers' growing problems where they belonged—at the door of the price supports and controls the government had imposed on their businesses. We warned that the price of big government programs in the sixties would produce debt that our children and grandchildren would spend their lives paying on our behalf.

We warned that there was not much that could be considered "great" in the grandiose programs of the Great Society. The night after Lyndon Johnson's State of the Union speech in January of 1968, we pointed out that

> He asked for a billion for the so-called "Model Cities" program, a venture that barely squeaked through the Congress in 1967. He wishes to inaugurate a program to build six million "low-cost" housing units in the next ten years—low-cost to those who occupy them, but "high-cost" for the taxpayers. He proposed legions of new investigators and prosecutors. All of this, and all of these, he said, will do wonders for the people. And, oh, yes, the Congress simply must enact a 10 percent increase in the tax bills of the American people. . . . The President adroitly sidestepped any discussion of the federal debt, and how his proposals would add to it. Such things had best go unmentioned in a State of the Union address, and especially in an election year. It is time for window dress-

ing, and Lyndon Johnson clearly had searched for every piece of political silk and satin in the shop, including the ones with frayed edges. . . .

There was a tremendous response to many of these editorials, and as expected, not all of it was positive. In his later years, Mr. A.J. was asked why he chose this course for WRAL-TV. He said, "I didn't start this thing for the money or any of the other reasons. I felt there was a compelling need to establish another means of presenting another side to the liberal positions advocated by so many of the state's newspapers. . . . I wanted the strongest voice I could get to present the other side, and I went out and got the strongest one I could find."

For twelve years, we had the privilege of delivering the news of our world and our communities and talking to the good people of North Carolina about the issues of the day. By the time I left the station, the mail responses to our editorials were delivered by the sackloads. In the years to come, I would meet many young constituents who would tell me that they grew up watching me. At their houses, everyone would gather around the television after dinner to hear the news and then the editorial from WRAL. This was a part of their family routine, and in many cases no one was allowed to speak until the editorial was finished. It would have made Mr. Fletcher smile to know that his bold decision to air editorials had impacted so many people and made such a lasting impression.

When he was first elected to office, my late friend Senator Paul Wellstone was particularly direct about his intent to go to Washington and oppose anything I was in favor of. To the casual observer, it may have seemed odd that this son of Minnesota would have singled out the senior Senator from North Carolina. Where could our paths have crossed? The answer to this was in Paul's resume. He was a graduate of the University of North Carolina, having earned both his undergraduate degree and his doctorate there. Paul, like most students and faculty on the UNC campus in the late sixties, was very liberal in his political philosophy. My WRAL-TV editorials got great ratings at Chapel Hill because I dared to point out the flaws in liberal philosophy. I was the local conservative liberals loved to hate, and I was content.

CHAPTER 9

Helms for Senate

BOTH DOT AND I WERE busily getting ready to attend a black-tie dinner one evening—I was busy with my tie; Dot was putting on her makeup—when she stopped abruptly and asked a question that changed the direction of our lives.

"Jesse, I can never, since I started voting, recall a candidate who was as conservative as I am. They sometimes *talk* conservative, but they are not obviously true conservatives." Then came her question:

"What do you suppose would happen if *you* did run for the Senate and gave the people a clear-cut choice?"

We had wrestled with that question for months, but in that moment, Dot made it clear that she believed that I *might* make a difference. Whether *we* won or lost, the people would have been given a clear choice. Dot's voice that evening disclosed a lot—including a healthy dose of optimism for the first time.

It was an interesting question that my best friend was raising. Since 1960, I had been in a job that brought me great satisfaction. I enjoyed being a part of the management of WRAL-TV, which had a goal to provide our station's audiences with more than entertainment.

It readily became obvious that WRAL television was meeting that goal. We had a strong news operation, and our editorials demonstrated that broadcasters *could* provide balance to the opinions of the liberal print media—*if*, that is, they would stand up against the liberal media and make clear that we had the courage of our convictions.

For years the station had offered a five-minute television editorial five evenings a week following our early evening news broadcast. Those editorials were repeated on our radio station the next day as well as on the Tobacco Radio Network, a group of independent AM stations and a growing number of FM stations across North Carolina. We had attracted an audience of people who wanted to hear the conservative view on the issues that were important to them.

By the early 1970s, my face and voice were familiar in many parts of the state as a result of my having written and delivered these editorials on behalf of WRAL-TV's editorial board each evening. Over the years, numerous people suggested now and then that I run for statewide office, but I never took those suggestions seriously. I had been elected to a couple of terms on the Raleigh City Council in 1957 and 1959 (I didn't seek a third term for the City Council because I had begun writing and delivering editorials on the air), but I just couldn't see myself as having any great personal appeal to the voters. Besides, I enjoyed my job at WRAL-TV and intended to spend the rest of my working life at it. However, in the fall of 1971, I was astonished when I was inundated with calls urging me to run for the U.S. Senate. At first, I dismissed the calls because I regarded the idea as preposterous.

But I had a great many friends who said the idea was *not* far-fetched. They insisted that I seriously consider becoming a candidate on the Republican ticket. By the way, our daughter Nancy was responsible for my becoming a Republican. Shortly after her eighteenth birthday, I escorted her to the Wake County Board of Elections, where she registered to vote. Nancy was carefully filling out the voting form, and I noticed that she marked the little box declaring herself to be a "Republican." I asked Nancy why she was registering Republican. She sharply responded, "Daddy, why do you stay a Democrat?"

I thought only a few seconds, then I asked a clerk at the board of elections office for a form to change my own registration.

Nancy, you see, made me realize that it didn't make sense for me to remain affiliated with a political party that didn't agree with many of my principles. (Nancy's challenge reminded me of the biblical passage ". . . and a little child shall lead them.")

So, by the end of 1971, Nancy and I were Republicans—and Dot Helms, on her own, had switched her registration as well.

My friend Tom Ellis was convinced that I would make a good conservative Republican candidate for the Senate. He had noted that when we had lunch at the Hudson-Belk cafeteria in Raleigh, a lot of people in the line took the time to speak to me. Tom recognized that these were the kind of people whom we call "salt of the earth"—those solid, hardworking people, Tom said, who don't make a fuss but take things like their liberty and exercising their right to vote pretty seriously.

Tom was, and is, a Raleigh attorney and very good at building a case. He kept after me, especially when several of us would go play cards with friends such as Pou Bailey. One night in late 1971, Tom was "after me" again, and I finally said I would *consider* running for the U.S. Senate—with some conditions.

First, I wanted Tom and others to talk with Mr. A.J. about the possibility. I wanted Mr. Fletcher to be in favor of the idea of my running, and I acknowledged that I wanted an assurance that I would have my job after the election. I might have been willing to run, but I didn't imagine I could win.

Second, I wanted to be assured that my running would not cause a problem with Congressman Jim Broyhill, who had been rumored as a possible candidate for the Senate.

Finally, assuming those two meetings went well, I would allow Tom to circulate a letter to friends asking them to write and/or send "seed money" to persuade me that I would have a good nucleus of support. When I agreed to that, I was nevertheless dubious that it would amount to anything. But three weeks later, the mail brought some fifteen thousand letters and about $20,000 in contributions (which I would return if I decided not to run).

All that support helped persuade me. It wasn't just the *volume* of the response, it was the *quality* of it. For example, there was one letter from an elderly lady in a nursing home. She sent one dollar, saying it was all she could spare, but she believed in me and hoped it would help. That really touched me—deeply.

But I was still reluctant. Becoming a candidate meant I would have to go off the air, and I felt I would be letting down the people at the station who had been so helpful to me.

In addition, I must confess that I didn't think I had a chance of winning even the Republican nomination, much less the general election, first, because I was a newcomer in the party, and second, because my major opponent for the Republican nomination, Jimmy Johnson, was already an attractive and articulate candidate.

Also, if I did become the Republican nominee, it would mean—or so I thought at the time—running against incumbent Senator B. Everett Jordan, a longtime friend. I certainly didn't relish that prospect.

Even before I made up my mind to run, I wrote a letter assuring the Senator of my continuing friendship and respect, and assuring him that any differences I might have with him would never be personal ones. I promised that I would never speak disparagingly of him as a man, or refer to his age or any physical infirmity (as one candidate had already done), or permit any of my supporters to do so.

Outside the coverage area of WRAL-TV in the eastern part of North Carolina, I was not certain that I was all that well known. The Piedmont and western sections of the state were where Republicans were strongest, and my name recognition there was poor. And, finally, another opponent in the primary, Bill Booe, was well known in the Charlotte area, where there were many more Republicans, and he was also a man whom I admired.

The results of the primary elections were a great surprise. I won the Republican nomination, and there was an upset among the Democrats. I had not expected that my friend Senator Jordan would be defeated by Congressman Nick Galifianakis. None of the experts thought I would win—I really had no idea I would win—but once the decision had been made by the voters, I was determined to do as well as I could.

The experience of the primary had demonstrated to me that there were a lot of people who felt the same as Dot did, and many of them told me that they wanted to have the choice of voting for someone who was as conservative as they were.

ALL CAMPAIGNS FOR a major office are hard and, I guess, more or less alike. As Dot often says, "Campaigning is my least favorite thing." It is no wonder that so many candidates have lost their voices by the end of their campaigns. They've lost sleep, used up energy, and talked constantly. It's exhausting, especially when you feel the need to see and meet as many voters as possible.

Now, as I look back on my five campaigns for the U.S. Senate, that first one was the only real doozy. We started from scratch, with scarcely anything but the notion. We had rented two rooms in the old Sir Walter Hotel in downtown Raleigh, and Mrs. Frances Jones, that great lady who had been my assistant at WRAL-TV, came on board to get things going—as did many dedicated women volunteers. Oddly enough, these dear ladies were not, at the beginning, personal friends. They had seen my editorial comments on TV, they agreed with my philosophy, and they just wanted to help. And indeed they did.

Next, we hired Harold Herring from Mount Olive in eastern North Carolina to be my campaign manager, and with him came his wife, Bev, who herself worked full-time on my campaign.

As things heated up, we rented a suite of rooms in a motel behind North Carolina State University, and lo and behold, along came five or six fine young men, members of the Young Americans for Freedom. They worked tirelessly as volunteers right up to Election Day. These young men slept on the floor of our offices. They got up early in the morning and took their showers and dressed for the day before anyone else arrived.

One of these young men was George Dunlop, who has remained my close associate to the present day. Another of those YAF volunteers was Charlie Black of Wilmington, who later worked in my Washington Senate office for a while before joining President Reagan's team. Charlie has become a respected and highly successful political consultant in Washington.

I can never adequately thank all of those who worked so hard. It was a totally exhausting experience—physically and mentally. In an interview after the 1972 campaign, I said that I believed campaigns then were too long and too expensive. I frankly admitted that there were times during my campaign when I was so dog-tired that I sometimes appeared at places not fully knowing where I was or what I was supposed to do. Other candidates have told me the same thing about their own experiences. Seeking high public office today is a brutal and debilitating task, and no relief seems to be in sight as campaigns get longer and the costs climb higher.

Certainly no one worked harder on that first campaign than Tom Ellis. Tom took a leave from his law practice to work on the campaign. He was my chauffeur during the early days of the campaign, driving me to speaking engagements and other functions. Often, even though we were a good distance from Raleigh, we came home for the night so as to save much-needed cash (and because I yearned to see my family). Mr. A. J. Fletcher had asked that I stay with the station through August, so the majority of those early campaign trips were to places we could get to by car on a Saturday. We'd start our return trip at ten o'clock or so, and I'd fall asleep while Tom drove. In some places the crowd was pretty slim. Tom likes to tell stories about those nights when we'd arrive to find three ladies and a plate of cookies waiting for us. But we kept on going.

Two experiences from that first campaign stand out. The first has to do with my good friend and colleague, the late Senator Strom Thurmond. Strom promised, years before I made the decision to run, that he would campaign for me if I ran, and he was as good as his word—in that first campaign and in every succeeding one.

One very hot day, the Senator came to make four different appearances for me. He gave a speech at each event, and it was a very long day. I remember wondering how I was going to stay awake for the fourth speech, to be given in a high school cafeteria somewhere (I'd lost track by then).

I got through my introduction, and Senator Thurmond bounded to the podium like it was his first speech of the day. When he was done, we stayed on until the last hand in the hall had been shaken. Finally, I climbed into the back of my car with Strom, grateful that we were very close to the hotel where we were spending the night. I was counting the minutes till I could go to sleep.

But not Senator Thurmond. With that unforgettable drawl of his, he said, "Jesse, when we get to the hotel, I want to call Nancy. She's in the family way, you know." (The baby that was on the way was Strom II.) "And then I want to go for a run. I thought I'd run downtown and back. Would you care to join me?"

Here was a seventy-year-old man who had given four speeches and driven for hours in the hot, sticky weather, ready for some brisk exercise before he turned in for the night. This exhausted fifty-year-old weakling was in awe. I told him that I was hoping I had energy enough to get to my room, and that I would see him at breakfast. Actually, I saw him again that night, when I looked out my window before I got into bed, and there he was, running past the hotel and on toward town.

The second experience was a defining moment for me, one that stands alone in its importance in shaping my goals as a U.S. Senator. It is not an over-statement to describe this event as a turning point in my life.

If it could be said in 1972 that I had a "stronghold" anywhere in North Car-olina, it would have been the part of the state known as "Down East." As vital as those voters are, no one can win a campaign without votes from everywhere, so it was important for me to win support in the western part of the state as well, where the Republican Party had been strong for some time.

A morning speaking engagement with business and party leaders in Ashe-ville was arranged. People on my staff worked hard to gather talking points, papers, information on economic issues of the day—the materials you would need to address such an influential group of people on topics about which they would have an interest.

I wasn't comfortable about speaking in Asheville. After all, I had been a Democrat all of my life until recently, and I was going to speak to a gathering of

Republicans in Asheville for the first time. Bear in mind, there had been two re-spected and longtime Republicans running against me in the primary. Now I needed the support of Republicans in the western part of the state, and they did not know me very well.

I had particularly hoped to get the support of Mr. Republican himself, the Honorable Charles Raper Jonas of Lincolnton. Mr. Jonas had been elected to the U.S. House of Representatives in ten consecutive elections since 1952, and had chosen to retire rather than run again in 1972. His opinion carried great weight, and I very much wanted his endorsement. Earlier, Mr. Jonas had been very cordial to me but told me that he made it a policy not to endorse anyone in a primary, a policy he recommended that I adopt if I was ever elected to office. He would be a part of the audience when I spoke, and his reaction would be carefully watched in that room.

I had been campaigning out on the coast, and the only way I could get to Asheville on time was to fly. Someone had gotten us a plane so we could fulfill all of our evening commitments and then fly west to Asheville for this breakfast meeting. George Dunlop was going along with me to do all those things that make it possible for the candidate to focus on speaking and shaking hands. Such assistance is indispensable, and I was grateful for George's company.

It was very early morning when we took off from the Raleigh–Durham air-port. The sky above us was still black, and you could see every star. Below, I could see the lights of all the little farmsteads and communities that make North Carolina so special. It was beautiful, and I was suddenly overwhelmed with the enormity of the responsibility I was seeking. How could I represent these good people? How could I make sure I paid attention to their concerns? Quietly I began to pray. A tear may have slipped down my cheek.

Suddenly it came to me. Do not talk to those people in Asheville about eco-nomics and give them a lot of facts and statistics. Talk from the heart. Tell them that we need for America to have a spiritual rebirth. Tell them that we need to get back to the roots of morality and to the faith in God that inspired our Founding Fathers to create this country in the first place.

The "vision," if you want to call it that, was so clear that I could not ignore it. I told George to put away his speech papers, that I would not need them.

When we got to Asheville, I had no specific idea as to what I was going to say to my audience. I knew that what I was going to do was against the advice of all of my political advisors. I also knew it was what I had to do. I spoke from my heart. You could hear a pin drop, and I thought surely I had blown it. But when I had finished, those people leapt to their feet and cheered and waved their napkins. I have never before or since received such an ovation.

Mr. Jonas did support me—strongly—in the fall election, and I have since come to suspect that he might also have given me some behind-the-scenes help during the primary.

Most importantly, I knew from that day on that the things that affected their families and the things they held most dear were the issues people really cared about. Those were the issues on which, with God's help, I would keep my focus.

The experts in these matters often cite this campaign as the first to make effective use of direct mail. This was not a secret strategy, but rather the logical outgrowth of the help of many supporters who told us they would be happy to contact members of their families or organizations on our behalf. As people responded to these mailings, we built a list of supporters whom we kept updated on the needs of the campaign.

These early supporters formed the nucleus of what eventually became, over the years, known as the National Congressional Club, through which literally millions of people across this country became involved in the political process. They were informed about issues that mattered to them and offered a way to keep their views in the public debate.

Throughout our 1972 campaign, Dot took the trouble to keep news clippings, campaign literature, and other mementos. Like me, she didn't expect that we'd be doing this a second time, and she wanted us to have a record of this once-in-a-lifetime effort. Little could we have imagined that there would be four more races before we came home to North Carolina in 2003.

It may not matter to our detractors, but the simple scrapbooks that Dot kept hold the facts about our campaign. We ran on the issues and where we stood. We certainly never wasted our resources on the kinds of attacks some people have suggested, including the false charge that we made our opponent's proud heritage an issue.

Congressman Nick Galifianakis was the first Greek-American to serve in the U.S. Congress. He was American by birth, the son of brave immigrants who came to this country because they wanted to be a part of the American Dream. He was elected to his seat in Congress five times, and he had had a long and distinguished career as an attorney. The difference between us was clear and easy to find: He was liberal in his approach to the issues, and I was conservative. I believed I could speak for the people, and in 1972 the majority of the voters agreed that I could.

If I owe my election to any one group, it is to those so-called "little people." They are the ones who put me in the Senate. They may be called "little people," but they're not "little" at all. They are the people who struggle to pay their taxes and raise their children, who never take a dime of welfare money and ask nothing of the government except to be left alone. They are the ones who care about character and want their democracy protected. They are the people whose homes I saw out the window of the plane that memorable morning as I flew to Asheville. They are the people of all creeds and backgrounds and races with whom I wished to identify in a billboard asking for their vote because "I was one of them." They are the people whom I was proud to serve.

If truth be told, there was only one person in our inner circle who was convinced that Jesse Helms was going to be elected to the U.S. Senate, and that was Dot's brother, Jack Coble. He traveled a lot for business, and he had talked to many people. He said to Dot and me, "You might as well pack; you're going to Washington."

I said, "Oh, come on."

He said, "No, you're going."

At 9:17 on election night, Walter Cronkite said, "Down in North Carolina, a fellow named Jesse Helms has been elected to the U.S. Senate."

I said out loud, "What am I going to do?" Then I went off by myself and got down on my knees and thanked God, and asked Him to lead the way.

My father was with me on election night. I told him I hadn't planned on winning and didn't quite know what to do. Once again, he gave me straightforward advice: "Just keep your promises." For the next thirty years, that's what I tried to do.

CHAPTER 10

At Home in Arlington

W E ARRIVED IN WASHINGTON and settled into our rented home in Arlington, Virginia. Not too long afterward, another house on that street was put up for sale. That became our home in Washington for the next thirty years, until Dot and I retired.

Our neighbors in Arlington were among our best friends. We got to know each other's pets, looked out for them and each other, and shared many milestones together. We were never even remotely attracted to the so-called "glamorous life" of receptions or seeing our names in the society section. We enjoyed the normal life of the neighborhood. As Dot often said, we just took our quiet Raleigh life to Arlington.

Early on I had made the decision to read every bill before I voted on it, and of course I wanted to know as much about each issue as I could. That meant long hours in my Senate office and stacks of material to read on the nights and weekends.

When Dot and I first arrived, there seemed to be at least one reception every evening to which we were invited, usually more than that, and I could not understand how a Senator could possibly keep up the pace and still do the work his constituents had hired him to do. My rule was to consider only the events that were related to North Carolina or North Carolina people, and those that would be helpful in strengthening the impact of conservatives in public policy. Even then, there were many events that I could not attend without taking time away from my first responsibility—making a difference in the Senate!

Most of these events, apart from those at the White House and the embassies, have blended together in memory, but there is one party that stands out. The occasion was a dinner to celebrate the publication of a book by Senator James Buckley, the conservative from New York. The location was a private home, where all of the beds had been removed from all the bedrooms in order to make room to seat all the guests for dinner. Dot and I *never* forgot that!

Senators have to have tuxedos in their closets, because you never know when you might be included on the guest list for an embassy reception, White House dinner, or some other formal occasion. Senator Chris Dodd and I were pretty proud of ourselves when we took advantage of a sale at a rental place and got very good deals on used tuxedos that we wore for a long time.

Dot's invitation situation was much the same as mine. As a Senate spouse, she was asked to attend all sorts of events. At first she tried to go everywhere that she was invited. She also wanted to be available to greet folks from North Carolina when they came to the capital, and she wanted to pursue her own interests, especially things related to history or working with the deaf.

Finally, Dot and Carol Laxalt, whose husband, Paul, came into the Senate around the same time I did and who was faced with the same question as Dot, asked veteran Senate wives Erma Byrd and Casey Ribicoff how *they* managed. They said, "You don't *have* to say yes to everything." In fact, they didn't need to say yes to *anything* other than what they enjoyed.

That good advice freed Dot to make time for the things that were most important to her. She met with the Senate wives' Red Cross chapter whenever her schedule allowed, and she became an active volunteer at Gallaudet University. There, she used her skill as a writer to produce profiles of deaf individuals who had overcome their challenges and could thereby serve as heroes and role models to deaf children and *their* families. Those stories turned into a research and book project on which Dot worked until 1979, when she turned the manuscripts over for publication.

The Senate wives did a lot of volunteer work on behalf of the Red Cross. Most of their meetings were strictly business, but once each year they invited the First Lady to join them for a luncheon at the Capitol and, in turn, each First Lady would invite *them* to a luncheon at the White House. These events were highlights of their club calendar.

Following the election of Barbara Boxer as a U.S. Senator from California, there was a move to make the club "inclusive," and the word "wives" was changed to "spouses."

It cannot have been easy for Dot to maintain a comfortable home in Raleigh and a comfortable home in Arlington, as well as our place for real peace and quiet, at Lake Gaston. But somehow she did it in a way that made each of those places truly home. At the same time, she maintained strong ties with each of our children, and with our grandchildren as they came along.

I can't speak for every Senator, but I do know that Dot Helms made sacrifices and rearranged her life without complaint, to enable me to concentrate on my work. No one who has ever met her could doubt that I married an incredible lady.

CHAPTER 11

Senator No

I T WAS NEW YEAR'S DAY 1973 when Dot and I officially moved to Washington, twenty years to the day after our first move there, but this time the girls were grown and our son, Charles, was in college. The two of us had truly turned a page.

January 3 was the day of my official swearing-in. This event took place in the Senate chamber, before the full Senate and a crowded gallery of guests. New and newly reelected Senators went up in groups of four to take the oath of office and be sworn in by Vice President Spiro Agnew. Senator Sam Ervin, the senior Senator from North Carolina and a man for whom I had the greatest respect and affection, escorted me when it was my turn to be sworn in. That moment was unforgettable. As I turned to retake my seat, I caught sight of my father in the gallery, along with Dot and the rest of the family. It was a proud moment for all of us, and a moving one.

My father had taught me much about life—so much that I felt free to go back to him for added wisdom whenever I needed to think through a decision or a course of action. I expected to be picking up the phone to call him often, but, sadly, that was not to be. His presence in that gallery to see me take my place as a United States Senator took on even more significance for me when he died just one year later.

We didn't have long to celebrate my swearing-in, because Dot and I immediately had to fly back to Raleigh to be present for the inauguration of Governor Jim Holshouser. We had a full schedule, including being part of the receiving line at one reception where we started greeting people at 7:30 p.m. and didn't stop until after midnight, after we'd shaken more than four thousand hands!

The next evening we had our own victory party with the people who had worked so hard in the Helms for Senate campaign. It was a genuine pleasure to greet those five hundred good friends, and to let them know that I had been elected because of *their* dedication, that my work in Washington would be for them and all the citizens of North Carolina—work that would not always be popular with the liberal opposition back home, especially with the major newspapers.

In 1978 the Raleigh *News & Observer* dubbed me "Senator No." It wasn't meant as a compliment, but I certainly took it as one. There was plenty to stand up and say "No!" to during my first term in the U.S. Senate. In fact, that was why had I run for the U.S. Senate—to try to derail the freight train of liberalism that was gaining speed toward its destination of "government-run" everything, paid for with big tax bills and record debt.

My goal, when Dot and I decided I would run for the Senate, was to stick to my principles and stand up for conservative ideals. I wasn't interested in a popularity contest and surely didn't care about anything the big newspapers called me. My experience with them extended over a lifetime.

I saw how they constantly ridiculed conservative ideas and conservative people. By some twist of logic they decided that the way to be "progressive" was to toss aside the underpinnings of our society. Anyone who thought differently was dismissed as "out of touch." I've been called a "troglodyte" on more than one occasion when I angered some writer or some group who wanted me to get out of *their* way and let them proceed with their unrestrained liberal agenda. (One of the earliest editorials I ever read written by editors who didn't like something I'd said or done was in response to a column I'd written in *The Tarheel Banker*. (*The Charlotte Observer* ran that editorial back in the late 1950s.)

Looking through their liberal glasses, the papers certainly presented a distorted view of reality. It had begun as early as my first Senate campaign, when the press took a look at my campaign and decided the slogan "He's One of Us" was some sort of attack on the nationality of my opponent's parents.

But as it turned out, the bad press back home was just the beginning of the fire I was to draw throughout my career. So aside from making a collection of all the political cartoons I could get my hands on, I quickly tuned out the criticism. A gentleman I knew back in Wingate often said that it wasn't a good idea to get in an argument with folks who bought ink by the barrel and paper by the ton, and I agreed with that.

I decided not to waste my time debating my critics. Over the years, I saved the U.S. Treasury a lot of money on press secretaries, until I eventually had to have one to deal with the deluge of media requests.

My staff, however, wasn't always as thick-skinned as I was. On one occasion I had to tell a new aide who was all set to fire off a response to a highly critical editorial, "Son, just so you understand: I don't care what *The New York Times* says about me. And nobody I care about cares what *The New York Times* says about me." As we worked together a while, the young fellow came to understand that I answer first to my Creator, then to my conscience. If that brought conflict or created some pressure, that was the price of doing business the way I thought was right.

Too many politicians think that the road to success lies in being "open." Too often that is simply another word for "hollow." I believe leaders must have principles, and must stand up for them.

I told my young staff that the way to be successful in politics and remain true to your principles is to know the distinction between your principles and your preferences. On your principles, you should never yield; you should be prepared to be defeated. Nobody likes to be defeated, but you should let everybody know in the most articulate and thoughtful and civil way you can (you don't go out and pick fights with people) that in certain matters that you define as matters of principle you *will not budge*, you *cannot* yield, you *will not* compromise. If you don't have the votes or the winning argument, then you stand to be defeated and rolled over, and you'll just have to come back another day.

But on circumstances that are your *preferences*, you'd better be prepared to compromise, because that's where you can demonstrate that you can engage with other people. Then you can, in fact, operate in the political realm.

So make a clear distinction anytime an issue arises—is this a point of principle or is this a point of preference? An awful lot of politicians never understand the difference. They compromise their principles and they fight to the death on their preferences. They end up, of course, being frustrated and unsuccessful—and failures at achieving their objectives.

When I took my seat in the Senate, there were forty-two Republicans, one Conservative, one Independent, and sixty Democrats. I probably was not much like many of those Republicans. They enjoyed being considered moderates, even liberal in their own politics. Plus, they were so outnumbered that they had become comfortable with the idea that they simply would never gain control of the U.S. Senate. Instead, they created a sort of gentlemen's club, for which I had no affinity. They didn't want to make any waves; I wanted to drain the swamp.

I believed then, and I believe now, that people who will not surrender their principles to assure their popularity can get things done. I did not have time to waste because there were critical issues facing us, not the least of which was the direction of the war in Vietnam and the negotiations for peace. I hoped to find a way for conservatives to work together without regard for their party labels, and to force change.

Thanks to Senator Jim Allen, I learned that my greatest ally in changing the Senate was the Senate itself. The rules of the Senate made it possible to bring to the floor issues that most Senators would just as soon have ignored. One of their revered traditions was to dispose quietly of almost any issue that they didn't want on their voting record. Controversial bills languished in committees or were disposed of in anonymous voice votes. Constituents often did not have the faintest idea that they were routinely reelecting people who voted in ways totally opposite to the way the constituents mistakenly assumed they were voting.

I believed then, and I still believe, that people, especially Senators, should have the courage of their convictions. I thought, and I will forever believe, that people should be "on record" about things that really matter to most Americans (e.g., for starters, school prayer, spending the people's money on obscenities, killing unborn children, raising taxes, giving aid to our country's enemies, protecting the Boy Scouts, and an end to a self-perpetuating welfare system, and so on and so on).

I thought then, and still think, that people want their Senators to fulfill their constitutional duty in international relations. The U.S. Senate had become ineffectual and left far too much in the hands of the staff of the State Department. Career diplomats had been given years of unfettered management; therefore and thereby, they had succeeded in creating an out-of-control bureaucracy that deserved its nickname, Foggy Bottom.

My staffers have laughingly but proudly told me that one of the most dreaded phrases on Capitol Hill was "Senator Helms has an amendment." Over the years I offered literally hundreds of them. Some, of course, did not pass, and my detractors, including newspaper editors, assumed that such losses were failures. In fact, they were small *victories* on the way to big ones.

I *wanted* Senators to take stands and do it publicly. I was willing to leave it to their constituents to decide what would happen next. When Senators were required, by circumstances, to stand up and vote so the people at home could see for themselves how they really felt about the issues, it rattled a lot of cages back in Washington. And when Senators had to run on their records instead of their rhetoric, things really began to change.

In 1973, when I went to the Senate, conservatives in Congress could have met comfortably in a phone booth. (There were actually more conservatives over on the Democratic side.) Senator Mike Mansfield was the Majority Leader and Senator Hugh Scott was the Republican Leader.

In those days, freshman Senators were to be seen and not heard. (That is not the case in today's Senate!) I knew that tradition was one more way of maintaining the status quo, so I rose to the Senate floor to make my first speech on January 11, just eight days after being sworn in. (It was a five-minute talk on an issue of great importance to North Carolina farmers: a defense of tobacco price supports as a part of the overall agricultural program.)

The first time I took the gavel to preside over the Senate was January 26. By October 10, I had presided over more than one hundred hours of deliberations and was presented with a gavel by the Senate pages, in a ceremony in the Vice President's Capitol office. I was the first Republican Senator ever to win that award.

The lessons I learned while presiding over the Senate were already being applied on the Senate floor. I knew the value of amendments and how to keep things from being caught up in committees. I knew when and how to make the call for a voice vote so Senators would have to attach their name to the issues they supported or chose not to support. I knew how to introduce substitute bills and how to recruit cosigners.

In April 1973, we helped sustain a veto on the flawed Vocational Rehabilitation Act by introducing a substitute bill that provided appropriate assistance to people who needed this sort of help. We were certain of White House approval after it had been passed by the Congress.

By November I was picking up steam. On the twenty-ninth I introduced three amendments to the Social Security Act and demanded a vote by the Senate. One of those amendments, calling for a balanced budget, was tabled by a vote of 46 to 43, but our little group of conservative Senators were very pleased by such a close vote on an amendment offered for the very first time, and by a freshman Senator.

From my arrival in the Senate, I worked closely with Jim Buckley, the Conservative Senator from New York, and I recall sitting on the floor with him on January 22, 1973—the day the Supreme Court ruled on *Roe v. Wade*. A page delivered the news report from the Associated Press wire just a few feet off the Senate floor. Jim and I immediately agreed to work together to do all we could to oppose this misguided and tragic decision.

That court decision also led all of the conservatives, regardless of party, to come together to form the Senate Steering Committee. I had noticed the way Ted Kennedy would come to the floor, with several Senators following, prepared to talk all afternoon. They were organized and had a plan.

Several of us thought that *we* needed to formally organize a response, so the Senate Steering Committee was started. Today the Senate Steering Committee is made up of about thirty-five conservative Senators (all Republican right now). They meet for lunch every Wednesday, to talk with each other and to hear from invited speakers who come to present important ideas.

By the 1994 midterm election, when Republicans took control of both the House and Senate, the conservative movement was growing stronger by the day. Its accomplishments became obvious. Some liberal Democrats even *tried* to sound like conservatives on those Sunday-morning talk shows. I enjoyed watching them struggle to explain away the decades of tax-and-spend that had finally caught up with them.

Snapshots from the Senate: My Staff

I WAS BLESSED SINCE MY FIRST DAY in the Senate with having the finest, hardest-working, most dedicated people working with me every moment I was a United States Senator. In whichever office they were assigned to—in Raleigh, in Hickory, in Washington—they were united in doing their jobs better than anyone could have expected, because they knew people were counting on them to make their government work the way it was supposed to work.

Those people—most of them young and all of them idealistic—joined with us because they were conservative, God-fearing, and genuinely willing to help everyone—especially those who in so many instances had desperate crises in their lives. In their difficult circumstances, constituents turned to my able staff and me for help, and we did all we could. These dedicated people often worked around the clock—indeed, in so many instances, they worked through the weekends—to help people who needed them. Their own comfort could be put aside if one more phone call might yield a passport so a son or daughter could quickly get to the bedside of a dying relative, or one more review of the facts might help resolve a disagreement over disability or retirement benefits. This network of public servants is still widely known as the Helms Senate family.

Write your Senator!

I am proud of—and grateful to—my staff for coping with the sheer volume of requests for our assistance. According to our records, more than seven hundred thousand North Carolinians—and hundreds of citizens from other states

—brought their problems to us. Each of them could count on being served promptly, with genuine dedication to making certain that the problems were solved if at all possible. It was discouraging to see how often those problems had resulted from dealings with a government bureaucracy that had lost sight of its responsibility to serve the very citizens who paid its salaries. We were often asked for help after constituents had exhausted themselves looking for the right path through a maze of paperwork, phone calls, and personal meetings. Complicated, contradictory regulations too often turned into roadblocks that people found impossible to remove, especially when they were dealing with the kind of hardships that brought them in contact with government agencies in the first place.

Our staff took the time to listen and to get involved. Relationships were built with people who knew how to cut red tape and who could see the human need behind the deluge of calls and letters. Overdue pensions were started, Medicare red tape was unsnarled, and passports were expedited. Our staff helped in emergencies and tragedies. Sometimes they simply got the attention of a department that needed a bit of a jump start to respond to what should have been a routine transaction. We made ourselves available, even keeping the office open on Saturdays so people who were not able to call during the week could still reach a person whose only purpose in being there was to be helpful.

As an example, I am reminded of an incident that happened in Raleigh. Herman F. (Rusty) Spain, a veteran, had passed away, and his widow, Mary Louise, was having a difficult time dealing with the Veterans Administration. One day, one of Mary Louise's neighbors asked her if she had gotten things worked out. When she replied in the negative, he said: "Well, I hate the son-of-a-bitch, but it's time for you to contact Jesse Helms."

Whatever these folks in my office did, they did with skill and courtesy. In the process they developed a reputation as people who cared. They were, therefore, one of the best staffs in the Capitol for constituent services. Did that make me proud of their work? You bet. But I was even prouder when I saw them take the time to show other Senators' staff members how to get the kind of results the Helms staff did. Helping citizens mattered more to them than competition or reputation.

Another group of staff members worked as legislative assistants, doing research and helping to prepare legislation and subsequently move it through the

Senate process. These people were knowledgeable both in their areas of specialization and in the layered process that takes a proposed bill through each step, moving it closer to law. This fine work brought them into contact with scores of people, inside and outside of government. Their understanding of these people, and the rapport they had as a result of working well with them, often gained us a high degree of cooperation that might otherwise have been impossible.

It may have been my background in journalism (and as a former staffer myself), but I made it a practice to stay close to the work of my folks. I had a policy of reading and approving even "form" letters, so as to make sure they were proper in both content and tone. Also, I insisted on seeing as much as possible of the deluge of mail coming to us. After all, people were writing to *me* and hearing from me. I wanted to know what was on their minds—and reading their letters helped me do that.

These letters provided important information on issues that really mattered to people. One example stands out in my mind, because it led to a change in federal policies, by exposing the absurdity of a policy that scores of people had allowed to flourish, and had even promoted.

A father from Plymouth, North Carolina, wrote to tell me about his family's struggle to put three children through college. He wasn't writing to ask me or his government for a handout, he just wanted us to be fair and logical about how we spent the money he earned and we didn't allow him to keep. Listen to his frustration:

Hon. Jesse Helms:

For the past 6 or so years we've been trying to get 3 children thru college. (At one point all 3 at the same time.) Now I found out there was an easy way to have accomplished this. I could have bought each one a gun and sent them out to commit a crime and their education probably would have been paid for. At the same time I learn of this, every governing body that affects us has either already raised our taxes or is in the process, claiming that they have cut all spending to the bare bone. The honest hard working taxpayer is being blasted from all sides while the criminal gets light sentences, early releases, lawyers paid for, air conditioned cells with color TV and carpet; plus a college education.

It is no wonder we're having a crime wave. The better it is made for
them, the more crime you're going to get.
    Please answer one question for me, Why?

This poor man had read an article in the local paper that had made him wonder if his family was approaching their problem the wrong way by working and saving for school. (If his children broke the law and got sent to prison, they would be eligible for Pell Grants and their educations would be free, just like they would be for the prisoners in the article.) This made the taxpayer mad, and he fired off a letter to his Senator, which set off a chain reaction because it exposed a foolish flaw in the administration of Pell Grants that was unnecessarily costing taxpayers more and more money each year.

It was never the intent of Congress for this sort of thing to happen, but liberal bureaucrats had allowed an entire industry of educational programs to go behind bars and sign up students who could never blame traffic for being late to class. If they had skipped the publicity, the practice might still be going on!

Our staff people researched the issue, and I took my constituent's letter to the Senate floor to share with my colleagues as I introduced an amendment to halt this practice. We had immediate success, and with the continued leadership of Senator Kay Bailey Hutchison, this practice was permanently ended. The full benefits of the Pell Grant have been returned to the students and families it was intended to assist.

The task of training prisoners has likewise been returned to the administrators responsible for prison management.

A great deal of good came from that one letter.

Just as we regarded *every* letter or card or call seriously, we took every citizen seriously, too. My office and my staff were in place to serve *all* the constituents. There is no place for political payback or special treatment in a Senator's office. Senators are sworn to serve *all* of the citizens, not just the ones who like us.

People who take the time to contact their Senators are entitled to a thoughtful, informative, and respectful response. Opinions may not always be changed, but the correspondent should know why his Senator is voting in a certain way, or why the provisions in a certain bill are beneficial or even harmful.

Interest groups frequently generate a flood of mail on particular issues. The temptation is to ignore these stacks of identical letters (especially when they are preprinted), but we regarded this as an opportunity to respond.

The Freedom of Choice Bill that was promoted by former Senator George Mitchell is a good example of that. The folks at NARAL, the National Abortion Rights Action League, targeted me and other Senators whom they expected would oppose the bill. NARAL asked thousands of people to send a postcard telling me they supported choice and wanted me to vote their way. The mailroom was a busy place for several days.

Our response to each and every postcard and letter on the subject was a letter thanking the sender for voicing his or her opinion, and detailing the provisions of the bill that made it impossible for me to support it. With *all* the facts in their hands, hundreds of people wrote back to say they had no idea the bill contained provisions like the ones we told them about, and they were no longer in favor of the bill. Even those who did not change their minds knew that my position was based on a study of the facts, not uninformed reaction.

My staff knew that nothing could undo our work faster than poor information or poor preparation. We had some basic rules. No one could suggest an amendment to a bill or a change to a law who had not thoroughly read the bill or the law itself. (And I always continued my personal rule: I never voted on a bill or amendment I hadn't taken the time to read for myself. Doing my homework may have cramped the Helmses' social life, but I know it kept me from making votes I would later regret.)

Information that we were to present as fact had to be correct in every detail. This meant checking and double-checking sources. It meant picking apart facts to expose weaknesses. It meant detailed research to assure that an opponent would have no surprises to spring. It meant being "bulletproof" so that no one could dismiss our position on the grounds that we hadn't properly supported it.

This was tough work, but my folks rose to the challenge. They took great satisfaction in their work because they knew we were making a difference, not just in policy but in people's lives.

Other Senators envied my staff and sometimes quietly sought their help. The opportunities for these young people came from every quarter. While I loved them and loved their loyalty, I never wanted any staffer to turn down greater challenges or bigger fields of service. We missed each one as he or she left, but welcomed new members to our family.

Just as there was a demand for people from my staff, there was a demand to become part of it. I loved the energy and enthusiasm these new people brought, and I didn't mind the chance to teach them a thing or two about avoiding split infinitives and making sure you knew where you stood on an issue and why you stood there. It gave me a great deal of pleasure to see these young people grow in their understanding of how government works, and in their determination to make it work better.

Over the years, the bond between staffers has grown even stronger. In 2002, they had an official reunion in Raleigh, and it thrilled Dot and me to see so many—and to hear about so many more—of the people who we always knew were the best of the best enjoying so much personal and professional success.

Among them are teachers, pastors, lawyers, a professor or two, business people, a sprinkling of politicians, foundation heads, a few mothers who have taken up careers as full-time homemakers, policy consultants, and a network of public servants in the White House, the Department of Defense, the State Department, at NATO, leading the staffs of Senators and Congressmen—and a happily retired grandma! What a blessing these people were to me, and now are to our country.

Dot and I have loved them all—and they have known it.

One day some of them might be tempted to write their stories from our years together. If they do, be sure you buy them, but remember *not* to believe a thing they say about the way I drove.

Richard Nixon

As I related earlier, I got to know Senator Richard Nixon well when I worked as Senator Willis Smith's administrative assistant in Washington. Our paths diverged when I left Washington and he became the Republican nominee for Vice President in the 1952 election. At that time I was working on the Presidential campaign of Senator Richard Russell, who was one of the candidates opposing Dwight Eisenhower for the Presidency.

Mr. Nixon and I met up again twenty years later when he was running for his second term as President and I was the unexpected Republican nominee for the U.S. Senate. I was glad to see him. He seemed little changed, still a very formal and dignified man, who seemed most comfortable in a suit and tie, no matter what the occasion.

While we had not been in close touch, I was certainly very much aware of President Nixon and his leadership. There had been decisions that I had spoken against, like the famous trip to China and the handling of the war in Vietnam, but I had no reason to think that Richard Nixon was anything other than the person I had known him to be when he was a Senator—a decent and honest man. When he appeared with Jim Holshouser and me on his whistle-stop tour in the final days before the election in 1972, we looked forward to working together in Washington. I wanted to support him whenever I could.

The day before my swearing-in as a Senator, I was visited by the South Vietnamese Ambassador. He was very concerned about the course of negotiations in Paris because our chief representative, Dr. Henry Kissinger, was not opposing a provision of the peace accords that would allow North Vietnamese troops to remain in South Vietnam. I shared the Ambassador's concern. I wanted Mr. Nixon to instruct Kissinger and others to seek better terms. Thousands, if not millions, of lives were at stake. I looked forward to offering the President my view and relating to him the Ambassador's fears as soon as that conversation would be appropriate.

Before that conversation could take place, the President announced that a peace agreement had been reached with the North Vietnamese, and he began the process of withdrawing U.S. troops. I could only wonder what would become of the many South Vietnamese whom we had worked with when the sixteen to eighteen divisions of North Vietnamese troops decided to take charge.

Although it was a wonderful sight to see the first POWs return to Clark Air Base in the Philippines less than a month later, I was sorry that their heroism and courage had been devalued by our unwillingness to repel Communists and foster a stable democracy. As a nation, we had not learned much about the pitfalls of leaving Communists in power. Without our troops, I felt the South Vietnamese were unlikely to maintain their freedom for long, and, unfortunately, history proved me correct.

The antiwar crowd may have thought they had done a good thing, but I was afraid they had set the country up for future trouble. I hoped as we moved forward that I could be a voice for what America had always stood for—freedom and loyalty to our friends. I certainly wanted to keep attention focused on the South Vietnamese who had fought with us and now needed our protection and support as they tried to make new lives for themselves. And, of course, I was committed to do all I could to make sure that the families of all the MIAs would learn the fate of their loved ones.

It is impossible to talk about anything involving President Nixon and his decisions during this time without discussing Watergate.

Based on what I personally knew of Richard Nixon from those days in the early 1950s, I felt sure that the ongoing attention paid to the Watergate break-in after it was first reported was overkill. The burglary seemed to have been a foolish campaign dirty trick and the work of people acting on their own. I could not imagine how the President of the United States would have been involved in any way in such an event or any activity connected to it.

From my first day in the Senate I stood ready to defend the President and was prepared to do so publicly, as well as to urge him to protect our allies in South Vietnam, in my first full speech in the Senate. That speech was never delivered because it was set for the twenty-second of January, the day Lyndon

Johnson died. On January 24, the peace plan was announced and the speech was obsolete.

The interest in the Watergate break-in and the questions about the President's connection had increased throughout the spring and early summer of 1973. On July 11, I was one of a group of nine Senators invited for an informal talk with the President. Our appointment was set for 6 p.m. Dot and I were going to another engagement immediately after this meeting, so she went along with me, was given a tour of the White House, and then settled into the Map Room with a book she had tucked in her purse before leaving home.

The President told the other Senators and me that while it was hard for him not to worry about the situation, which most recently had produced the resignations of his top aides, Bob Haldeman and John Ehrlichman, and the firing of John Dean, he felt everything would turn out all right. He said the distraction was preventing him from doing some of the things he needed to do as President. Immediately after the staff shake-up, the White House issued a statement indicating that it was John Dean's activity in an effort to cover up knowledge of Watergate that had made him the author of the current crisis.

The President told our small group that one particular point that bothered him was the failure of the press to give him credit for having enough sense not to allow any cover-up, had he known about it. He said a cover-up was stupid and unnecessary. So, there I had it, the President of the United States had offered, without prompting, his assurance that he had no involvement in any aspect of the scandal.

When the meeting wrapped up, the President told me to give his best wishes to Dot, and when I indicated that she was elsewhere in the White House waiting for me, he insisted on going with me to greet her himself. Dot was quite startled to see the President when she looked up from her book. She was impressed by his graciousness.

We left the White House with me firmly in the President's corner on the Watergate situation. I could tell anyone who should ask me exactly what I had been told. President Nixon had stated as fact that he had no connection to the break-in and would not have allowed a cover-up.

On October 10, Vice President Spiro Agnew, who had campaigned for me and who had in 1970 so aptly described the unrelenting critics of the Nixon administration as "nattering nabobs of negativism," resigned from office. He had been charged with accepting bribes and falsifying federal tax returns while serving as Governor of Maryland. It was a disappointing moment for me. It was also a loss for our country because as citizens we genuinely desire that our leaders always remain above any form of misbehavior.

President Nixon acted quickly to name a replacement for Mr. Agnew and announced on October 13 that Representative Gerald Ford was his choice for Vice President. After the brief distraction of the change in Vice Presidents, the focus of the media immediately shifted back to the President—and to the scandal.

Dot and I were able to get out of Washington for a few days. We looked forward to seeing the family and celebrating my birthday at our Lake Gaston cottage. We were anxious for the peace and quiet of a long weekend away.

But there was no "getting away" from Watergate. On October 19, it was announced that the President had agreed to provide a summary of the so-called Watergate tapes to the Senate Watergate Committee and to ask Senator John Stennis to listen to those tapes so he could vouch for the summary. I thought that sounded like a good idea and hoped that it would help wrap up the controversy.

The next day, Saturday, October 20, the President demanded the firing of Special Watergate Prosecutor Archibald Cox and the abolishment of his task force. Attorney General Elliot Richardson and his deputy, William Ruckelshaus, refused to comply and resigned. The President then ordered the acting Attorney General, Robert Bork, to officially inform Mr. Cox that his services were no longer wanted.

The President's critics were inflamed. I remained convinced that the press was overplaying this whole situation, but calls for impeachment were growing stronger. Under this pressure, the President agreed on October 23 to turn tapes of Oval Office conversations over to federal judge John Sirica.

In mid-November the President began a series of meetings with all of the Republican Senators and Representatives to discuss what had become known as the Saturday Night Massacre. We went in alphabetical order and were given the opportunity to ask questions and resolve any doubts about Watergate and the President's handling of the crisis. Certainly we wanted assurances that he had no part in the activities for which others were now facing prison.

Knowing Richard Nixon as I did, I knew this private and dignified man must have found these meetings demeaning. In our session, in response to a direct question, the President indicated that Elliot Richardson had agreed that Mr. Cox had to be fired, but at the last minute had backed down from taking action, thus forcing the President to act himself.

When I left that meeting with the President, I was once again feeling that he was doing his best to improve his image and put the nation's focus where it needed to be—on fuel shortages, inflation, and the Arab-Israeli conflict. I still wanted to help him do what he had been elected to do, and I was frustrated that he had invested so much time and energy in Watergate-related issues.

In March 1974, the Watergate grand jury formally indicted seven individuals from the President's inner circle on conspiracy charges. The President was named as an unindicted coconspirator. On March 18, Senator Jim Buckley called to tell me that he would hold a press conference the next day to urge the President to resign. I was shocked by this and felt that Jim was making a mistake by withdrawing his support for the President.

Shortly after Senator Buckley's announcement, I put out a statement noting my disagreement with his position and asking, "What if President Nixon is innocent?" Under our system of law, every person, even the President of the United States, should be considered innocent until he is proven guilty. Guilt or innocence should be determined by the process of law and under the rules set out in the Constitution.

If President Nixon could be hounded out of office by the news media or by critics, could not future Presidents?

The House Judiciary Committee took up the issue of possible impeachment in the spring of 1974. In early June things seemed to look a little better for the President, and I hoped the matter could be put to rest once the facts were in front of the committee.

The President himself was in the Middle East. In Alexandria, Egypt, he was greeted by a million cheering people, but the press implied that the crowd was assembled to take America's mind off Watergate. They were so committed to the President's downfall that they could not acknowledge any good that he had done for the cause of peace—or that he was held in high regard in other world capitals.

On July 24, the U.S. Supreme Court ordered the President to release the tapes that Judge Sirica had subpoenaed, and the House Judiciary Committee opened its debate to live television coverage.

I still believed what the President had told me in early 1973 about his ignorance of any plans for a burglary or any cover-up; I still believed in his veracity. But by now, after month after month of revelation, I could certainly fault him for his selection of senior staff members, and for the foolishness of having a recording system in his office.

Yet, if he were a guilty man, why would he be so confident that those tapes would exonerate him?

On August 5, I appeared before the Senate Rules Committee in an effort to ensure that the President would be given a fair trial. I was still convinced that the facts would show that he personally had done nothing wrong. I had no way of knowing that while I was speaking on his behalf in the Capitol building, the President himself was making an announcement that changed everything.

At the insistence of his personal lawyer, the President admitted that he did have a hand in the Watergate cover-up. The evidence of his involvement was in the tapes he had turned over to Judge Sirica. This development assured his impeachment by the House of Representatives.

With knowledge of these facts, I now realized that I would cast a vote against the President on article one of the impeachment. Clearly, as indicated in his own statement, he had obstructed justice. This man of great strength was also a man of great weakness.

I hoped that the President would resign and spare the country the pain of the impeachment process.

On August 8, the President asked a group of thirty-four Senators and Congressmen to meet with him at the White House. The time of that appointment was 7:30 p.m. He had called us together for a farewell.

We waited for the President in the Cabinet Room. When he entered, his appearance was so different from what we had been used to seeing for so many years. The stoic was gone, and in his place was a man weighed down by the enormity of the cost of his actions. The sadness in that room was unlike any I had ever seen. The President moved around the room, stopping to talk with each one of us. When he came to where I sat, I rose to greet him, and he looked at me and said, "I am so sorry. I am so sorry. I am so sorry."

Finally, he tried to gather himself and address us together. He said he had failed us. Then he burst into tears. We wept with him and for him. When he left the room, he walked with his head bowed and his hand covering his face — broken by the realization of all he had lost.

It was an unbearably emotional meeting, one that none of us could have imagined less than two years before, when the President had been elected with more than 60 percent of the vote. I was astonished that I was witness to the downfall of an American President.

At nine that night, the President spoke to the nation and said that he would resign, effective at noon the next day. But still he could not quite believe that he had no other choice if he wished to spare the nation further turmoil. At 1 a.m. he called Senator Harry Byrd and asked if resigning had been the right decision. Senator Byrd assured him that he had done what was best.

The next morning, after an emotional farewell to his staff, the President and his family lifted off in the helicopter and began their trip to San Clemente. Watching this man, who had devoted his entire career to public service from the moment he went to work as an attorney in the Office of Emergency Management in Washington, D.C., to this day thirty-seven years later when his own actions forced him to relinquish the most powerful office in the world, was almost too painful.

Richard Nixon's story did not end here. The great strengths that carried him to the most powerful office in the world now kept him from sinking under the weight of his mistakes.

To his credit, Richard Nixon found new ways to be of service. His successors sought his counsel on foreign policy matters, and he became a respected elder statesman. He traveled for as long as his health allowed, and met with world leaders to further peaceful partnerships.

His memoirs and other books reflected his brilliant mind. His party remembered the promise fulfilled and moments of triumph like his famous encounter with Nikita Khrushchev. Even the media pulled their cameras back from the flaw so that they could observe the whole of the man.

We kept in touch from time to time until his death. He knew I had forgiven him for what had happened and that I wanted him to get back on his feet. On one occasion he sent me a copy of a book his daughter Julie had written, along with a note telling me that he thought it was very good and that wasn't just his fatherly opinion. He was right. She had inherited his skills.

In their retirement, Pat and Dick Nixon drew closer, and the President was a gentle caregiver after Pat's stroke. Her death was an enormous loss, even though Julie and her sister, Tricia, and their families stayed close to the President, encouraging him to stay active.

I sadly but proudly took my place as a part of the Senate delegation at his funeral in 1994. On that occasion all five of his successors—Gerald Ford, Jimmy Carter, George H. W. Bush, Ronald Reagan, and Bill Clinton—came to remember what was good in this man's life. It was the first time in history that so many U.S. Presidents had assembled together. Their presence was an acknowledgment that history will speak favorably about Richard Nixon and his contributions to his country.

From this distance, some thirty years after the Nixon resignation, after the books detailing the Watergate scandal have been written by those who were involved, after all the tapes have been released for our hearing and all the facts are before us, some may ask why I defended the President throughout the investigation when so few remained convinced of his innocence.

I do not think of myself as naive, but perhaps in those first months after my election, I had not made the adjustment from North Carolina to Washington. I was raised to believe that a man's word was his bond. I was taught to tell the truth in every circumstance, even when that truth might not be pleasant or might get me into trouble. My experience back home never caused me to doubt that all decent people lived by those rules.

The President of the United States—whom I knew twenty years earlier as an honorable gentleman—told me he had no knowledge of a burglary and that he was not a party to any cover-up. *The President of the United States gave me his word.*

I assumed he was telling the truth.

CHAPTER 14

My Early Focus on Foreign Relations

I T OFTEN SURPRISED PEOPLE that a Senator from North Carolina would have an avid interest in foreign policy. They could understand agriculture, even banking, as the state's power as a financial center grew, and certainly it would have made sense to have an interest in the armed services, with North Carolina's major military installations. But foreign relations seemed a far less obvious choice to them. It did not seem that way to me.

I believed when I arrived in the Senate in 1973, and I believe even more now, that there was no committee whose work has more impact on the welfare of North Carolina than the Foreign Relations Committee of the United States Senate. I was delighted to receive my requested seat on the Senate Foreign Relations Committee in my freshman year, and even more pleased when I was selected for the subcommittee that had the Americas as its specific area of responsibility.

North Carolina has long been a state with myriad international connections. In 2001, the state exported more than $16.7 billion in products to more than two hundred countries. In 2003 we were number one among states with the highest percentage increase in foreign workers. Eight of the Fortune 500 companies, all with multinational business links and an international workforce and client base, call North Carolina home.

Our industries include leaders in banking and finance, pharmaceuticals, research, and agriculture. Our young people are deployed across the world in military service. We are a state that welcomes the world, while at the same time wanting to preserve all that we love, all that makes North Carolina great.

We are not an isolationist state. Our first settlers were immigrants, and our exports have always been welcome far beyond our borders. Our bases have long prepared the best of our nation's young people to serve in posts on every continent. To my way of thinking, Foreign Relations is *the* most appropriate committee for a Senator from North Carolina, and certainly every bit as appropriate as the traditional assignments.

The war in Vietnam was not the only international war being waged when I arrived in Congress. On every continent, Communists were attempting to establish or strengthen their hold on national governments. I did not have to wait for a committee assignment or someone's "permission" before I could get involved in *this* war.

The Ambassador to South Vietnam made no mistake by stopping by to see me on my first day in the office. I had no intention of waiting until I had "enough seniority" before I spoke up in favor of freedom—and against Communism, wherever it was found.

In August 1973, Dot and I traveled to London, where I spoke at a Peace Through Freedom rally and met with leaders from countries on every continent who shared my concerns about the threat of Communism. For many of these people such a threat could not be dismissed as overreaction or partisan politics. They had seen the ruthless tactics of the guerrillas and knew that Communist governments lie their way into power and then simply do away with the opposition.

I believed that we had a dual responsibility, first to make sure that Communism did not and could not get so much as a toehold in our own country and then to make sure that we worked against it every way we could in other countries.

The opponents of Communism in some countries were not always flawless themselves. However, neither were they trying to open branch offices of an international totalitarian philosophy with support from the Union of Soviet Socialist Republics.

Following my London trip, I made it a point to meet as often as possible with leaders in the anti-Communist movement, both here in the United States and at gatherings in other parts of the world, like the one in London. I was honored to meet with and address groups from every continent, and I took the time to meet as many individuals as I could.

I met famous people, like the Dalai Lama; Aleksandr Solzhenitsyn; and Dr. Charles Malik, former Foreign Minister of Lebanon, who was a leader in the

United Nations, along with scores of Ambassadors and Foreign Ministers, and many heads of state.

My door was always open to those who were in the news, like His Holiness the Dalai Lama, who knows well what the cost of standing up for freedom may be. I met this distinguished and beloved spiritual leader not too long after I had arrived in Washington. I was captivated first by his warm and generous smile, and after I had visited with him at various official Senate meetings I realized that this was a wonderful and unique man. We have been friends now for many years. Likewise, Aleksandr Solzhenitsyn visited me in Washington beginning in the mid-seventies. He said, "Cannot your people perceive the advancing tide of Communism? Can they not somehow be led to act, before it is too late?"

But I was just as glad to meet with the people the press never notices—refugees who had escaped from Communism and the relatives of people who were imprisoned or had been killed because of their quest for freedom. I wanted those people to know that they had at least one ally in Washington.

In the Americas, there were other enemies gaining power, not as champions of a political ideology but in pursuit of riches. These enemies promote death in the guise of pleasure; they are the drug cartels. In spite of a series of well-intentioned "wars," these predators remain a threat. They work in the shadows, where they are too easily overlooked, and they prey on the poorest of their countrymen to risk their lives for the promise of a share of the profits. They intimidate those they cannot buy off, and dare us to battle them.

Drug trafficking poses a particularly ominous threat to the people of North Carolina. Both our geography and our economy make us an attractive target for those who make their money from human misery. We have a vested interest in ending the demand for drugs and drying up the sources.

When I served as the Chairman of the Subcommittee on Western Hemispheric Affairs, our concerns included the flood of refugees who were fleeing political upheaval, and the Latin American connection to the drug smuggling and drug trafficking in the United States. It remains an appalling situation, in spite of the millions of dollars earmarked annually for drug interdiction and for programs that were supposed to dry up production. Drug trafficking today is an insidious and pervasive element in our society. Not only does it create corruption, but it also corrodes respect for law, inciting crimes of violence and leading to the breakup of families.

In a speech to law enforcement officials back in 1981, I described as a "staggering amount," the 30 to 60 metric tons of cocaine smuggled into the United

States in 1980. (I had no idea then that twenty years into the future that figure would top *six hundred metric tons* per year.)

The multiplication in the availability of marijuana is just as dramatic. It is hardly news when local law-enforcement officers discover a tractor-trailer load of marijuana harvested in Mexico or elsewhere in Latin America and driven across the border with little fear of detection. (The occasional loss of a single shipment is simply the price of doing business for the drug lords, who have grown rich and powerful—and seemingly untouchable in spite of the manpower invested in breaking up the traffic.)

For many North Carolinians—indeed, for most Americans—the jungles and mountains of South America, the deserts of the Middle East, and the crowded cities and isolated villages of Asia seem very far away, very remote. That is a fiction. Our history and the front page of today's newspaper show the reality. What happens in any part of our world, no matter how inconsequential it may appear at the moment, inevitably has a strong impact on our country.

From my first day as a United States Senator, I believed and acted on the belief that we cannot be passive observers who watch without comment when events in other countries put our own at risk—or when they call out for our compassion.

Nor can we care only about our own welfare. This great United States of America must chart a course that is marked by both our willingness to be good neighbors *and* our commitment to protect our people and all we hold dear.

Pursuing such a course will never be easy, but it will always be worth our effort.

CHAPTER 15

Gerald Ford

WHEN I TOOK MY SEAT in the Senate, Representative Gerald Ford was the Minority Leader in the House of Representatives. Mr. Ford had a reputation for being a steady, hardworking legislator who did a good job of bringing people to the middle ground. In 1964, when the party was being torn by the rivalry of the Goldwater and Rockefeller wings, Ford backed his friend George Romney as a consensus Presidential candidate. As a leader in the House, he worked in the same way, believing that the time would come when the GOP would have the majority of votes in the House of Representatives and the power to better shape policy.

Gerald Ford's political goal was to be Speaker of the House. He was both well known and well liked, a frequent speaker at Lincoln Day and at state party events around the country.

In both 1960 and 1968 there had been talk of his selection as a running mate when Richard Nixon won the Presidential nomination, but nothing came of those rumors, just as Congressman Ford refused to pursue a run for the Senate or as Governor of Michigan.

But when Vice President Spiro Agnew resigned, President Nixon needed to choose a man with whom people already had some familiarity and confidence, one who did not have any blemishes on his record or a collection of opponents who might fight his selection. He was in no position to push through a controversial choice, or to pick someone without solid experience. On October 13, he announced that Gerald Ford was his nominee. Earlier that same day I had been a guest for lunch with Ronald and Nancy Reagan. During our meeting, I told the Governor that if he were ever to decide to run for the Presidency he could count on my enthusiastic support.

Representative Ford had gained a national reputation for his skill as a member of the Warren Commission and his leadership in the House. He and the President had a good personal relationship and had even served together in the House of Representatives in 1949. Ford's confirmation process moved quickly. It was claimed at the time that Mr. Ford had had the most thorough background check in the history of the FBI prior to his affirmation.

The day after his nomination, Congressman Ford and his family were guests, along with Dot and me and our children, for a Sunday worship service at the White House. We all had a brief chance to meet and talk. I came away from that meeting feeling comfortable about the choice and confidently cast my vote in favor of his nomination.

I continued to spend as much time as I could presiding over the Senate, so the Vice President and I met often. I enjoyed getting to know him, and at one point told Dot that I believed that at his core Gerald Ford was a conservative.

Gerald Ford became President of the United States on August 9, 1974, barely ten months after he took the oath as Vice President. He took his oath in the East Room and quickly addressed the country, assuring us, and people around the world, that our constitutional form of government works, no matter what the challenge.

He spoke again to a joint session of the Congress on August 12. The following day, August 13, was the deadline for the names of possible Vice Presidential nominees to be submitted to the President. I was honored that several individuals and groups, including Senator Thurmond, formally submitted my name for consideration, but I had no expectation that those suggestions would be taken seriously. Nevertheless, it was flattering.

On August 20, the President announced Governor Nelson Rockefeller as his choice. This was good news for the liberal wing of the party, but certainly not my first choice. (I had recommended that the President choose Senator Goldwater.)

The Governor and I met privately, at his request, in the Vice Presidential Chambers in the Senate on August 22. I assured the Governor that any differences between us would be philosophical and not personal. The Governor then assured me that he and I were the same, philosophically. I didn't want to argue at that moment, but I knew we had many differences. I also knew this appointment would set the tone for the Ford presidency. This was going to be a more liberal administration than I would have hoped for. For the first time in our history, we had an un-elected President and an un-elected Vice President in office.

On September 8, President Ford announced that he was issuing a full pardon to Richard Nixon for any possible crimes, known and unknown. This was a wise decision and I supported President Ford fully, because we needed to get back to the issues that had been neglected while the Watergate drama played out.

But the decision was not a popular one. The enemies of Richard Nixon wanted a public spectacle. The pardon took away their opportunity to jeer. The anger was transferred to President Ford and to the Republicans. First, in the 1974 elections, Republicans who would have been sure of reelection were turned out. Then, in 1976, the best decision Gerald Ford ever made became one of the factors that cost him the opportunity to be elected President of the United States.

While Gerald Ford and I have always gotten along, and I like him very much personally, we had our differences over important issues.

Vice President Rockefeller had proven himself to be every bit as liberal as I thought he was. In February 1975, he was presiding over the Senate during a debate to sustain President Ford's veto of a bill related to a per-barrel tax on oil imports. After a ruling that was flagrantly in favor of the liberals who were attempting to defeat the veto, Senator Russell Long told the Vice President that he did not "own this body," by which he meant the Senate, and then went on to imply that the unelected Vice President was attempting to take over. At that point, eleven other Senators rose to their feet to object to the Vice President's ruling, and he attempted to debate with them from his seat as President of the Senate — a violation of parliamentary procedure. Senator Allen actually grabbed three microphones, shouting into them, "Mr. President, a point of order . . ."

In April, I went to the White House on Department of Agriculture business. When that meeting wrapped up, President Ford asked me to stay on for a private meeting. He wanted to know more about an idea of mine that I had first brought up in February during a speech to a group of activists, in which I had suggested that the two political parties in America should be Conservative and Liberal, not Democrat and Republican. The speech got a lot of coverage in the press, and the President wanted to know what I was doing. Was I trying to form another party or move the GOP to conservative control?

These conversations were always more than a little frustrating because the President would talk to me like he was a conservative, then promptly act like a liberal.

Certainly that was true of his reliance on the advice of Dr. Henry Kissinger as Secretary of State. It was under Secretary Kissinger's leadership that the Ford administration announced plans to begin the surrender of U.S. sovereignty in the Panama Canal Zone, in open defiance of the wishes of the Congress.

Then, in June, on the advice of Secretary Kissinger, the President refused to meet formally with Aleksandr Solzhenitsyn at the White House. Senator Scoop Jackson hosted a reception in the Caucus Room of the Russell Building, which was attended by many Senators and covered by the press. The President tried to get around the problem he had created by inviting Senator Thurmond and me to bring Mr. Solzhenitsyn to meet him. But Solzhenitsyn refused to go to the White House without a personal invitation.

Dot and I were guests of the President and Mrs. Ford in late July for an evening on the Presidential yacht, the *Sequoia*. It was a delightful evening with a dozen Senators and several of President Ford's assistants and their wives, but it didn't narrow our political gap.

Two days after our sail down the Potomac, I was back in Raleigh, waiting for Governor Reagan's plane to land. It was our first big event in his bid to gain the GOP nomination for President. In order to succeed, he would have to beat Gerald Ford in the primaries.

When I had made my promise to Ron Reagan in 1973, there had been no way of knowing that supporting him would mean not supporting a sitting President from my own party. My situation was awkward, but the truth of the matter was that while I very much liked Gerald Ford the man, and applauded some of his decisions, he was not leading the country in the direction I thought we needed to go.

In Ron Reagan, we had a candidate with an appreciation of conservative values, a record of leadership as Governor, and a contagious energy that attracted voters. I did not regret giving him my pledge of support—even though he faced a much harder challenge in getting the nomination than we had foreseen.

In September, Dot and I were enjoying our evening at the Vice President's newly decorated home, as guests of the Rockefellers, for an open house with a buffet and dancing in a tent set up on the lawn, when word came that an attempt had been made on President Ford's life while he was in San Francisco. It was deeply disturbing to realize that we had come so close to another loss.

In early November, President Ford announced a major shake-up in the Cabinet that included the firing of James Schlesinger as Secretary of Defense. Mr. Ford said his reason for the dismissal was that he wanted to surround himself with his own team. I was convinced that it was because Secretary Schlesinger was a hardliner when it came to Russia, and that that annoyed Henry Kissinger. Dr. Kissinger and I are good friends now and agree in most of our current policy stands, but that was certainly not the case during the Nixon and Ford years.

The new Secretary of Defense was to be Donald Rumsfeld. I cast my vote against his confirmation to protest his predecessor's removal. The nomination was approved, but I had succeeded in drawing attention to the issue.

At the same time the Cabinet changes were announced, Vice President Rockefeller announced that he did not want to be considered as a Vice Presidential nominee in 1976. At least that was good news for conservatives who had made it clear that they did not want him on the ticket.

In November, Dot and I were once again aboard Air Force One. This time we were headed to Raleigh, where the President was to speak at a luncheon. We stayed on in Raleigh to take part in the state GOP convention the next day. I made a speech there in support of Governor Reagan, and our own Governor, Jim Holshouser, made one in support of President Ford.

Whatever else might be going wrong in our country at any given moment, it is a tribute to our democracy that our political battles are usually over issues and philosophy.

As the primary season got under way in 1976, President Ford's speeches began to sound more and more conservative. He was tacitly acknowledging the strength of Ronald Reagan's appeal. For his part, Reagan was learning how hard it is to win against an incumbent.

After a string of defeats, we were able to help Ronald Reagan win his first Presidential primary in North Carolina. That victory kept him in contention and kept the President tied to more conservative themes, even though his campaign promises had liberal price tags tied to them.

We went into the August convention with the nomination still in doubt. While it appeared that President Ford had enough votes to win on the first ballot, there was a very good chance Reagan would win on a second ballot. We never got to find out. The Ford forces had the necessary number of votes in the first round.

President Ford immediately announced that Senator Bob Dole was his choice as running mate. My name was placed in nomination, too, but I asked that it be removed. It was time to unite around the ticket.

In September, the President signed the New River Bill, which I had authored. I was invited to the White House for that ceremony, and any ice that may have formed between the President and me leading up to the convention was broken.

I was disappointed in November when Jimmy Carter defeated the President. While we did not agree on many issues, I will always be grateful for Gerald Ford's strength of character and steady hand during those difficult days in 1974 when he became our President.

CHAPTER 16

The Rise of Conservatism

ONSERVATIVE POLITICAL IDEALS are as old as America itself. America's Founders recognized the worth and strength of free men and women and their inalienable rights. So, not surprisingly, it was conservatives who encouraged the initiative of individual free citizens and groups while creating a free environment where benevolence prospered—along with the fortunes of those who believed in the ideal that hard work cleared the path to prosperity, no matter what the doubting Thomases said.

It was our conservative Founders who flatly refused to pay unwarranted taxes. It was those same conservative Founders who recognized, first of all, God's sovereignty over the nation's affairs, and with it each individual's freedom to worship in his or her own way and without interference.

For many generations this new nation called America enjoyed a foundation that remained rock solid. Leaders who made law and set policies based on the principles of conservatism guided us. But inevitably the fires dampened and liberalism began to emerge.

It started off purely as a desire to let the government do what people would no longer do for themselves, but it gained a powerful strength when special interests saw the power of the government as a means to shape society to their liking.

Self-sufficiency and philanthropy were overrun by government programs that stripped people of their confidence in themselves and robbed others of the understanding that had been gained by extending a hand to a neighbor. Then states' rights and personal rights were subordinated to court decisions having the force to and therefore the result of rewriting the Constitution itself.

Like a boulder gaining speed as it heads toward the bottom of a mountain, the liberal approach to government relentlessly escalated from offering small and fragile solutions to limited problems, to creating a pervasive reliance on the federal government, which in turn pushes its controls into every segment of society.

Lyndon Johnson's dream, which he grandly referred to as the "Great Society" (one shaped and run by the federal government), was a genuine nightmare for conservatives. They finally understood, however, that Thomas Jefferson was speaking to them when he said, "The price of freedom is eternal vigilance."

Individuals and small groups spoke up to protest, but they lacked the strength to be effective in their opposition. The most effective conservative of the Johnson years was Senator Barry Goldwater, and even he, while he did gain the Republican Party's nomination in 1964, never had unified support. (We must never forget that Barry Goldwater's political opponents managed to stereotype him as "too aggressive" to be Commander in Chief.)

Goldwater and his supporters, including the then Governor of California, Ronald Reagan, were powerful speakers, but relatively few, as we look back on it, were truly listening. The experts in such things described those leaders' appeal as personality-based—certainly not a response to their antiliberal philosophy.

Among the Democrats, the conservatives were treated like an embarrassment. Giants like my friend Senator Jim Allen of Alabama were ignored by the liberal coalition that confined itself to shaping bigger and bigger programs designed to hand out tax money.

Like the Republicans, the leaders of the Democratic Party saw no need to consider the decidedly minority opinion of their dwindling conservative membership.

The situation was so bad, it would have been easy to think there was no hope for the conservative movement. But, in fact, it was just such a crisis that galvanized a consortium of leaders into action.

Together, they began what would be known later as a revolution. The sum of the parts multiplied the efforts of the individuals and small organizations. When conservatives spoke up together, they could no longer be ignored!

When I ran for election in 1972, young men who were members of Young Americans for Freedom formed the backbone of my strictly volunteer corps.

For them the challenge was not about getting an individual elected, it was about adding one more conservative vote to the Senate. YAF started with sixty young people meeting at the Buckley family home in New York in the early 1960s. They helped with the Goldwater Presidential campaign and with the Governor's campaign in California, where Ronald Reagan confounded the Left.

These young people did not have "clout" and they certainly did not have funds, but they were more than willing to invest what they did have in energy and dedication. Their enthusiasm for conservatism was a real encouragement.

When I got my bearings in the Senate after the first few months of 1973, I observed one important difference between the way liberals and conservatives went about their business in the Senate. The liberals were organized. They planned their offensives and knew how to get what they wanted.

By comparison, the conservatives worked independently. Therefore, they appeared weak and ineffectual simply because they did not make use of the power they might have had together.

Jim Buckley and I agreed that we should organize those Senators who were conservative—regardless of their party affiliation—and begin to meet together regularly. At first there was just a handful, but one by one we gained in number.

We also gained in our ability to make an impact on legislation. That did not mean that we often won votes, but our victories came in small but steady increments that finally changed the way our colleagues responded to our concerns.

During the 1972 elections, there were frequent references to the "silent majority." That was not an inaccurate description. Small groups were active around Washington and around the country, but there was no unity in their efforts and no great call for others to get involved.

All that changed in 1979 when a group of men, well known in conservative circles but not beyond, came together with a plan to invite the Reverend Jerry Falwell to create a national organization to get the silent majority involved in political issues.

That group (which included Howard Phillips, Richard Viguerie, Paul Weyrich, and others) convinced the Reverend Mr. Falwell to form a separate organization known as the "Moral Majority." The organization's purpose would be to prompt the millions of people who watched his religious programs on several hundred TV stations across the country to become active in the political arena.

This was a radical and controversial idea at the time. Church people had focused their energies on church issues and family life. They had separated themselves to the extent that many did not even bother to vote, and most did not voice an opinion to their elected officials.

The Reverend Mr. Falwell challenged this disengagement and declared that God expected His people to influence every part of their world, including the government. He used biblical illustrations in his sermons to demonstrate that it was God's plan for His people to give themselves to public service and at a minimum to end their silence on the issues that mattered most to them.

So, taking a lesson from the success of Jesse Jackson's Rainbow Coalition, the Moral Majority set up voter-registration tables in churches. Starting in North Carolina, they successfully registered thousands of voters and developed a strategy that added millions of voters to the rolls nationwide.

But that was just the beginning. As a part of their voter-education efforts, the Moral Majority taught these newly aware voters how to get involved in the decision-making process. They learned how to gain power in the political caucuses and how to organize support for candidates who agreed with their principles.

As the group grew, other groups were formed with an emphasis on specific issues. Each of these groups learned from the others, building strength as they gained experience. By the late 1980s the Moral Majority organization had fulfilled its original purpose, and its leaders wisely disbanded it so they could turn their attention to other challenges.

Our own National Congressional Club was formally organized in North Carolina in 1973. The original members of the club had been among my supporters in the 1972 election. These people wanted to stay informed and stay involved in politics, and the Congressional Club gave them that opportunity through regular newsletters and events, and through opportunities to support those who shared a conservative political philosophy.

The membership of the Congressional Club grew year by year as people responded to our letters of encouragement. People have said that our organization was a pioneer in the successful use of direct mail across the country, and that may be true. I do know that our contacts grew into a national force that, on one occasion, helped to generate a quarter of a million letters to CBS over the issue of accuracy and fairness in news coverage.

Just as the Moral Majority learned about voter registration in churches by watching the Rainbow Coalition, many conservative organizations learned about the effectiveness of direct mail by seeing how it was done at the Congressional Club. Starting with their own contacts and adding the names of people who had shown an interest in similar areas, these groups built strong organizations of their own. That strength quickly became apparent to members of Congress and other elected officials when conservative organizations rallied their supporters to comment on an issue.

A plea to contact members of Congress in support or opposition to a particular bill or nomination can still produce an avalanche of letters, phone calls, and e-mails.

One other lesson was well learned—the power of coalition. Today the conservative movement is represented by a host of institutions, foundations, political action committees, schools, politicians, professors, and even publications. Each is unique, but all are wise enough to stay connected so they are ready to stand together when needed.

In my three decades as a member of the United States Senate, I was invited many times to take part in the meetings of the group that best exemplified that spirit of cooperation: CPAC, the Conservative Political Action Conference.

In 1974, there were four hundred people at the conference. But in 2002, the last time I attended as a sitting Senator, there were four thousand registrants.

That impressive growth and the promise it holds for the future of this great country encourages this conservative more than you can imagine.

CHAPTER 17

Ronald Reagan, 1976

W HO COULD EVER FORGET the first time they met Ronald Reagan? He was a handsome, reserved, smiling, and confident gentleman, who, thank the Lord, was twice elected President of the United States.

Our first meeting came just as the sixties began. The encounter was business-centered and pleasant, but seemingly unremarkable at the time. Ron Reagan was guest host of *General Electric Theater*, and I was executive vice president of WRAL-TV in Raleigh. As part of his contract with General Electric, Ron toured the country speaking to groups of GE employees and doing public-relations tours to the stations that carried their program.

When the smiling, soft-spoken actor and host stopped by WRAL, he was recognized by everyone as "the movie star." I was delighted that he had stopped by—and so was my staff!

Ron and I talked awhile about Hollywood and the media, and about edi-torializing—some time earlier, WRAL had begun televising editorials; it was only the second TV station in the country to do so—and, of course, we talked about politics. Ron knew before he stopped by that I had served for a while in Washington for Senator Willis Smith.

I was aware that Ron had become increasingly active in political circles, first through his experience as head of the Screen Actors Guild and more re-cently as a result of his own concern for the direction liberal policies were tak-ing the country. (Not too long after his visit, GE asked Ron to back away from the political involvement, and he refused. GE canceled his contract. It was some months before Ron was selected as host and frequent lead of *Death Val-ley Days*.)

Ron Reagan suggested at the outset that he be called "Ron," not Mr. Reagan. We then agreed to first-name each other—and then, out of the blue, with that inimitable smile and those twinkling eyes, he asked:

"Are you going to run for office one of these days?"

I said no, I didn't have any plans to do that—but that I sure hoped *he* would.

After a moment of reflection, he said, "I'm thinking about it."

Well, thank the Lord he *did* think about it.

In 1964, the GOP was split between what were known as the Goldwater and Rockefeller wings. Ron was a Goldwater supporter, and his nominating speech for Goldwater was the highlight of the 1964 convention. He said it was "time to choose," describing the situation this way:

> This is the issue of this election: Whether we believe in our capacity for self-government or whether we abandon the American Revolution and confess that a little intellectual elite in a far-distant capital can plan our lives for us better than we can plan them ourselves.
>
> You and I are told we must choose between a left or right, but I suggest there is no such thing as a left or right. There is only an up or down. Up to man's age-old dream—the maximum of individual freedom consistent with order—or down to the ant heap of totalitarianism.

In October, Ron did an extended-length commercial in support of Senator Goldwater that created a national stir because it made the case for conservatism in a way most people had never heard—and it made sense to them.

Barry Goldwater was outspent and outmaneuvered in his run for the Presidency. He was able to post more than 27 million votes and carried six states, but that accounted for just 9.7 percent of the electoral vote. It was a lopsided loss, but the Goldwater campaign had helped conservatives around the country "discover" a future star in Ron Reagan.

It wasn't too long after that '64 election that we conservatives learned that the actor-turned-political-activist was now about to turn candidate. In 1965, Ron announced that he was going to challenge two-term incumbent Governor Pat Brown's reelection in California.

The Brown forces had a great time making fun of candidate Reagan. Their plan was to make a joke of the idea of an actor dealing with real life. Ron ignored the taunts and focused on the issues. The voters in California, especially the thousands who made their living because of the motion-picture industry, liked what Reagan said and decided to take him up on his offer to turn California in a different direction.

In 1966, Reagan was elected Governor of California, and he immediately set about returning the state's college campuses to their intended use as places for learning (not sit-ins), and bringing fiscal responsibility back to Sacramento's government offices. This led him to be reelected with a healthy majority in 1970.

We kept in touch, and in 1972, when I decided to run for the U.S. Senate (knowing that I could not possibly be elected), Ron Reagan supported me. He even did a TV message that endorsed my candidacy.

So there we were, a widely known and respected Governor of California and I, the first Republican ever to be elected to the U.S. Senate by the people of North Carolina. The liberal media were, of course, already lambasting this Governor of California for being "too conservative." They predicted that I would be a one-term Senator and described me as "one of those right-wing nuts."

At the same time, they dismissed Mr. Reagan's entry into politics and hung on to the "Reagan the actor" dismissal of his accomplishments—and growing national popularity.

Well, that actor showed them—and with the rest of the country, I watched the career of Ronald Reagan blossom.

It was in mid-October 1973 that I made my commitment to help Governor Reagan if and when he decided to run for President. I was in San Francisco to speak at the annual banquet of the Association of American Physicians and Surgeons when a call came from the Governor suggesting that I fly down to Los Angeles for lunch with him and Nancy at their private home. Needless to say, I did.

As we enjoyed our lunch that day, the Reagans impressed me with both their sincerity and their decency. They had a deep concern for their country. I brought up the topic of his running one day for President, and as I recall, the Governor was less than enthusiastic about the possibility. I dropped the subject, saying, "Well, if you ever decide to run for President, and if you feel that I can be helpful, count me in. I'll be honored to do anything I can."

Of course, we could not have imagined that Congressman Gerald Ford, who—the very same day as my lunch at the Reagans'—had been named Richard Nixon's Vice President, would in less than one year become President of the United States and himself a candidate for the 1976 nomination.

I held Gerald Ford in great affection then, as I do now, but I had given my word that I would support my friend Ronald Reagan, and when Ron asked for my help I was ready to get involved. Among our Senate colleagues, only Senator Paul Laxalt and I publicly supported the Reagan campaign.

Taking on a sitting president of one's own party is not easy, but Ronald Reagan gave it his best shot. In New Hampshire the vote was 50.2 percent for Ford and 49.8 percent for Reagan—shocking the Ford campaign into trying to make their candidate seem a little more conservative before the next primary.

They were able to hold off the Reagan campaign with narrow victories in five consecutive primaries, and it looked like the Reagan campaign was just about over as they came into the North Carolina primary. Ron was in a difficult position.

The media people declared him finished; the Ford people cranked up the pressure for Ron to get out of the race. Nine of his fellow Republican governors issued a statement calling on Ron to withdraw, and even some of his own advisors were telling him to throw in the towel. But Ron wouldn't give up—and if *he* wasn't giving up, we sure as heck weren't about to give up on *him*.

Tom Ellis and his colleagues at the Congressional Club went all out for Ron and his wife, Nancy. They put together a travel schedule across North Carolina and got Dot and me involved as their hosts and supporters. Nancy and Dot went east; Ron and I went west. Jimmy Stewart came to North Carolina and barnstormed all over North Carolina for his friend.

The North Carolina campaign people also raised some money for media. They bought an hour of radio time so that Ron's speech at the North Carolina Fairgrounds could be heard by a much bigger audience. When the Reagan staff people balked at the sight of the station's sound truck, the North Carolina team refused to budge—explaining that they had purchased the time, the mikes were set up, and that speech was going on the air.

They spent some more money to buy TV time to air a thirty-minute program that had originally been put together in Florida, tailoring it for the North Carolina audience by cutting off the pictures of palm trees that appeared at the end of the tape. When the Reagan staff people dragged their heels in making the tape available, Tom Ellis cut through the red tape and took his case directly to Nancy Reagan. The tape arrived without any more delay!

Sam Donaldson was on hand among the Washington reporters covering the race in North Carolina. At just about every campaign stop, Donaldson would bellow in his familiar way: "Governor! Governor Reagan! When are you getting out?" And in a ritual that later became familiar to just about everybody, Ron would smile, cup his hand to his ear to pretend he couldn't quite make out what Sam was saying, and keep on walking with a smile on his face. Ronald Reagan campaigned his heart out, and he left North Carolina tired—and convinced he was going to lose.

But he didn't! He carried North Carolina by 52 percent to 46 percent. It was the first time in a quarter-century that a sitting President had been defeated in a primary. A week or so later, Ron went on to Texas—and won again. The Reagan campaign was on a roll; suddenly there was a real race.

In late June, following an overwhelming convention victory for the Reagan slate of national convention delegates at our North Carolina state convention, I received this handwritten note from my friend:

Dear Jesse,

Just off the plane from Mississippi, Minnesota, Wyoming, Montana & Idaho in that order & in three days. I'm delighted about your convention and the result. Believe me, our victories are not all that complete. I've never been so disgusted in my life.

In every convention the W.H. gang are there manipulating, trying to get the rules changed, etc. In Minnesota, they were successful to the extent of perhaps a half dozen delegates. We were outnumbered however on the floor of that convention.

In Montana they were taking an exact opposite tack aimed at getting themselves seven delegates. I don't know the outcome as I write this but our people are in the majority there so maybe we'll win one. Don't get me wrong, I still think we'll take him. But Jesse it almost seems as if they are out to win a convention instead of an election. They have created a great deal of bitterness with their high handed ways.

Give my thanks and regards to Tom. Nancy sends her best and
we hope we'll see you soon.

Sincerely,

Ron

What turned the tide in North Carolina and Texas in 1976? The answer to
that is simple: Ronald Reagan simply campaigned on principles. He made
clear where he stood—and North Carolina stood with him and loved doing it.

Prior to his North Carolina victory, an armada of self-declared experts had
respectfully warned that Ron Reagan should tone down his conservatism and
make himself appear more "mainstream"—and thereby acceptable to Middle
America. That strategy lost him five states in a row, and coming into North Carolina, thank the Lord, the time had come to let Reagan be Reagan!

Ron Reagan rejected the Ford–Kissinger détente policy with the Soviet
Union. Ron's honesty and his refusal to be a phony led him to sense that the
American people feared that America was losing the Cold War. They *saw*
country after country fall to Communism, as American resolve faltered and the
Soviets pulled ahead of us in the race for military superiority.

In short, Ronald Reagan made his case to the American people: We should
stand up for freedom, he said over and over again, instead of seeking "peaceful
coexistence" with Soviet tyranny. He called for rebuilding America's defense
capabilities. He declared that "peace does not come from weakness or from retreat. It comes from the restoration of American military superiority."

As the Kansas City convention neared, there was still hope for the Reagan
candidacy.

Strategy meetings were held in person and by telephone as the opening of
the convention neared. If the nomination process went to a second ballot, it
was quite possible that Ronald Reagan could prevail. There were several delegations whose members were bound by their state party rules or election laws to
vote as instructed on the first ballot, but they would not have to support Mr.
Ford on succeeding ballots.

One way to expose the differences between the two candidates was to make
sure the party platform took a stand on issues that mattered to conservatives.
One of those issues was morality in foreign policy.

It was our goal to insist that the plank lay out the issues that Ron had discussed in his campaign. He had condemned immoral agreements—for exam-

ple, the Helsinki Accord, in which, Ron declared, the Ford administration had put America's "stamp of approval on Russia's enslavement of the captive nations [and had given] away the freedom of millions of people—freedom that was not ours to give." He called for an end to "balance-of-power" diplomacy and said that our battle with Soviet Communism was not simply a struggle between rival powers but rather a battle between right and wrong, between good and evil.

Henry Kissinger and others disagreed vehemently. Kissinger called Ron "trigger-happy" and said that he was "inciting hawkish audiences with his demagoguery." But the American people were responding positively.

On their behalf, Reagan insisted (over the objections of the Ford forces) that the GOP platform declare that henceforth "the goal of Republican foreign policy is the achievement of liberty under law and a just and lasting peace in the world."

The platform forthrightly stated that "we must face the world with no illusions about the nature of tyranny" and that the United States must not conclude agreements with the Soviets that "take away from those who do not have freedom, the hope of one day gaining it" (a direct repudiation of the Helsinki Accord).

Unfortunately, winning the platform battle meant we had lost an opportunity to wage a floor fight on the Moral Foreign Policy plank that would have exposed the depth of the pro-Reagan support. The proceedings were under the tight control of the Ford forces, led by the convention chairman, Congressman John Rhodes of Arizona. Representative Rhodes decided anything contentious by voice vote, and, of course, he always knew which side had the majority. As good as his hearing was on these voice votes, it seemed to fail him completely when delegates tried to get his attention from the floor.

With this kind of support, it was inevitable that Gerald Ford would gain the nomination and the opportunity to be elected President. I was honored to see my own name put in nomination for Vice President, but I asked that it be removed so Mr. Ford could make his own selection. I certainly applauded his choice of Bob Dole.

In the days leading up to this selection, Ron Reagan did make one decision that was very hard for his conservative supporters to understand. I do not know all the details of the process that led up to the decision, or who among his advisors advocated it, but I can only assume they were the same advisors who tried so hard to keep Ronald Reagan from being himself at the start of his '76 campaign.

What was this decision? It was the announcement that if he secured the Republican Presidential nomination, Ronald Reagan would choose Senator Richard Schweiker of Pennsylvania as his running mate. I knew the Senator and liked him personally, but I also knew he was no conservative.

The evening the announcement was made, Ron called me at about midnight and said, "Jess, you know where my heart is. . . . It's all right." I certainly hoped it would be all right, but the fact was, Richard Schweiker had one of the most liberal voting records on the Republican side of the Senate, and he was no friend of the principles Ron Reagan had campaigned on, like morality in foreign policy.

To make matters worse, it was soon clear that the choice had been made without soliciting the advice of any of the conservative leaders who had worked so hard for Reagan during the primaries and in the weeks leading up to the convention. Someone decided it was more important to barter for some possible Pennsylvania delegates than it was to maintain loyalty to the principles that had garnered all those other delegates.

A pragmatic political professional wouldn't have thought twice about choosing to go for the votes instead of opting for a compatible conservative, but the people who got behind Ronald Reagan because they thought he was a conservative who would not abandon his principles felt betrayed.

For my part, I left the convention wondering if the time had not finally come to form a truly conservative political party.

For his part, Ron Reagan left Kansas City with the cheers of the convention letting him know he had gained many new supporters for any future campaign. His strong showing staked his claim as the front-runner for the nomination in 1980. With his speech and his support of the strong platform plank on foreign relations, Ron Reagan had laid down a marker that the era of coddling Soviet tyranny was coming to an end.

CHAPTER 18

Jimmy Carter

PRESIDENT JIMMY CARTER AND I rarely found ourselves in agreement, much to the surprise of those who assumed two sons of the South would be mirror images. On paper it might have seemed that we would do well together while Mr. Carter was in the White House. I certainly would have preferred that to having to continually fight against his policies that I knew were wrong for our country.

We did have geography and much more in common, which might have helped to forge a good working relationship. Both of us grew up in small towns. We were both raised as Southern Baptists. We both served in the Navy. In fact, my last duty station in the Navy was in Columbus, Georgia, less than sixty miles from Mr. Carter's hometown of Plains. Both of us have October birthdays (I'm three years older).

There was even a story circulating that claimed we were distant cousins. But a careful tracing of the family trees disclosed that while it is possible he had ancestors who were neighbors to ancestors of mine in rural North Carolina, we are absolutely *not* related.

It hasn't always been clear which one of us would have been less enthusiastic to see the other guy show up at a family reunion, or who was more relieved to learn conclusively that we are not even the most distant of cousins. I know there were many days when it was probably me—especially during the months when we clashed over policy decisions on Taiwan and the Panama Canal.

Over the years, Jimmy Carter and I have demonstrated that people can start from similar places and arrive at very different destinations.

For his part, President Carter embraced an egalitarian philosophy that manifested itself in foreign policy, most dramatically in a desire to redistribute United States assets to other countries, and internally with policies that put more value on perceived equality than personal achievement.

President Carter believes that strength produces bullies, while I believe that strength provides the capacity to act benevolently. President Carter believes that those who succeed have an obligation to hand over what they have earned; I believe they have a responsibility to offer a hand up so others can gain the pride of earning their own success.

Our most significant clashes were over foreign policy. On one occasion in 1979, Secretary of State Cyrus Vance claimed the British government had complained that two of my aides were interfering with its negotiations with Rhodesia. I was sure that was not the case, but to make certain, I called my friend Maggie Thatcher, who was, after all, the Prime Minister and would know if there was a problem. She told me she didn't know anything about the matter (I'm certain she would have called me directly if she had) and as far as she was concerned there was no such problem. I conveyed the essence of my telephone call to Secretary Vance and that was the last we heard of that particular charge.

But there were many other battles to be waged, particularly over Carter administration policies toward Panama and Taiwan.

The Carter plan to give away the Panama Canal got under way shortly after he was sworn in. The administration began a public-relations war to change the public's perception that the handover was a "loss" for America. Colonial governments were treated as though they were all brutal enemies of the native populations, and we were told that we were operating a "colonial outpost" of our own in Panama.

Of course, most sensible Americans never bought that nonsense, but to our great harm, enough liberal politicians did.

The betrayal of our friends in Taiwan began with President Carter's decision to terminate the mutual defense treaty with Taiwan that Congress had ratified in 1954. My friend Barry Goldwater immediately sued to upset the President's action, based on the fact that any treaty action by the United States of America requires the agreement of two-thirds of the members of the Senate. The Supreme Court refused to hear the case, saying it was not "ripe" for their review because the Senate had not acted to preserve its constitutional prerogatives.

Fortunately, in April 1979, Congress codified the United States' support for the brave people of the Republic of China with the passage of the Taiwan Relations Act. This gave our friends the cover to develop the vibrant economy and flourishing democracy we see today and prevented them from being overrun by the same tyrants who are now in the process of eradicating democracy in Hong Kong.

In spite of our differences, Mr. Carter and I have always been cordial. I was frustrated by what often seemed like his isolation, and I believe his administration would have been less troubled if he had listened to more conservatives. I made it my business, when called to the White House or during our phone calls, to offer whatever support I might give for the good of the country. Whatever our disagreements, neither of us wanted anything but good for our citizens.

The thing for which Jimmy Carter is most admired is the way he gave himself to philanthropic work and the cause of peace after he left the White House. His life has been a model for retirees who want to do more than relax and rust out in their retirement years. It is hard to imagine Jimmy Carter turning aside the opportunity to help Habitat for Humanity or travel the world to help a country hold an honest election. He has lived out his faith in big ways and small.

We last traveled together in 1995 as a part of the official United States delegation to attend the funeral of Israel's Prime Minister Yitzhak Rabin. The makeup of that delegation—men and women from both parties, liberals and conservatives, former and current political opponents—provided an opportunity on this sad occasion to show the world that people of goodwill do not need to fear those who differ with them, that, in fact, if they choose, they can dwell in peace.

CHAPTER 19

The Panama Canal

THE FRAMERS OF THE U.S. Constitution were particularly wise when they decided that the United States could enter into treaty agreements only with the concurrence of the President and two-thirds of the U.S. Senate.

Requiring a two-thirds vote instead of a simple majority assures bipartisan involvement in these often-crucial issues and painstaking evaluations. It does not mean that *every* treaty agreement we enter into will be right, but it does weed out the vast majority of the ones to which we should never be a party.

Not very long after I was elected to the Senate, the issue of rewriting the Panama Canal treaty of 1936 took center stage. That treaty was actually a replacement of the 1903 treaty between the Republic of Panama and the United States of America. That 1903 treaty set forth the terms for the construction and operation of the Panama Canal *and* the sovereign rights of the United States to a band of land ten miles wide—which encompasses the Canal itself—across the country, in return for cash payments and a guarantee of the independence of the republic. The 1936 treaty increased the amount of the annual payments and, at the request of the Panamanians, ended our guarantee of their independence.

In 1959 the amount of the annual payment was increased once again, and the railroad yards in Panama City were turned over to the country at no cost. In 1962, the United States built a high-level bridge over the Pacific entrance to the Canal and agreed to fly U.S. and Panamanian flags jointly over those parts of the Canal that were under civilian authority.

By 1973 we were paying the government of Panama $2.33 million per year—a significant increase over the $250,000 per year in our original agreement (plus a $10 million one-time fee, *plus* purchasing the rights of the French builders who had gone bankrupt, *plus* paying private landholders the asking price for their property within the Canal Zone).

In the mid-seventies, under pressure from the Carter administration, Congress jointly brought up the issue of a new series of treaties with Panama that would include turning control of the Panama Canal over to whatever government of theirs was in power in the year 2000. It was then, and remains now, a flawed agreement that millions of Americans opposed. The validity of those concerns became appallingly obvious in the years following the treaties' ratification.

But, for some inexplicable reason, the Carter administration decided that instead of being the benefactors of the people of Panama, we were their colonizers—and that we should now give away the strategic route from the east coast to the west coast of the North American continent that we had built, paid money to own, and fully supported in its operation for the use of all nations. It was a dumb idea and most Americans knew it. Those of us who opposed turning over control of the Panama Canal, including then-Governor Ronald Reagan, who was running for the GOP Presidential nomination in 1976, recognized the strategic importance of this passage for both U.S. commerce and defense.

We were concerned about the realities of potentially unfriendly governments in Panama, including the one then headed by General Torrijos. We were concerned about the inability, or unwillingness, of the Panamanians to maintain the Canal, and about the risk of the control of the Canal falling to an unfriendly or potentially unfriendly third-party country—even though the treaties would supposedly guarantee permanent neutrality to the Canal.

Of course, many of my concerns came to fruition soon thereafter, when the corrupt and morally bankrupt regime of Manuel Noriega came to power in Panama in the 1980s. When it became apparent that Noriega was deeply involved in drug smuggling, gun running, and money laundering, even many in the liberal media concluded that he had to go. In December 1989, President George H. W. Bush ordered twenty thousand American troops to liberate Panama from Noriega and his thugs. Of course, this was readily accomplished, but unfortunately at the cost of twenty-three dead American servicemen.

However, in 1978, there were not nearly enough U.S. Senators willing to consider the risks we would be assuming with this change in ownership, even though the majority of their constituents could see them. A two-thirds majority of the Senate bought the idea that giving away the Panama Canal would cement harmonious relations with all of the governments of Central and South America—as if Marxists would suddenly *stop* hating freedom.

The Senators were willing to risk U.S. security for U.S. popularity. Besides, in 1977, when the U.S. signed the new series of treaties, the year 2000 was far in the future. (The Panamanians ratified the treaties in October 1977, and the Congress ratified them in April 1978.)

It seems that the American people agreed with me: Within four short years, twenty-nine of the Senators who had voted for the Panama Canal treaties were out of office, many attributing their downfall to their vote to give away the Canal. (No wonder some Senators were squirming like a worm on a hot brick when we debated the issue.) In 1980, Republicans gained control of the Senate and Ronald Reagan was elected President, launching the Reagan Revolution. Senators who had voted for the treaties found out that many voters did remember in November.

The new Panama Canal treaties dramatically increased our payments to the government of Panama, with a fixed annuity of $10 million per year and a net ton fee for every U.S. shipment. In 1995 that tonnage fee alone was more than $80 million.

Unfortunately for the American taxpayer, the Clinton administration was in office in 2000 when the time finally came to hand over the Canal. Just in case we hadn't already paid for the Canal a million times over, the administration arranged for a going-away check of $160 million to be paid to the Panamanian government. The media quoted one of my staffers at the time saying, "Look, it's one thing, if I buy a used car, to give me the gas that's in the tank. It's another thing altogether to let me siphon from the tank of the previous owner's car."

Since the final handover, we have watched the Panamanian government reach deeper and deeper into funds intended for the upkeep of the Canal to prop up their general treasury, and we have seen them willingly negotiate with companies under the authority of the People's Republic of China for services that would give *them* physical control of the Canal itself. Based on what we have already experienced since 1978, who knows what kind of turmoil we have created for decades ahead because of this series of treaties that should *never* have been ratified by the United States Senate.

CHAPTER 20

Running for Reelection

THE PART OF BEING a United States Senator I liked least was the time and energy spent in long campaigns. Election campaigns cost far too much money and too often get tangled in topics having little to do with the issues most important to citizens.

My campaigns also seemed to bring out the best or worst in what some of my friends call the "Looney Left"—from ACT UP to People for the American Way, they all had to get their best shots in on me every six years. Sometimes their attacks were so virulent that even my opponents didn't want them going after me, as in the case of Harvey Gantt's staff wishing NARAL (the National Abortion Rights Action League) would stop trying to "help" his campaign. Fortunately, the actions of these groups often highlighted why I was in Washington in the first place.

Truly, if regular campaigns are legally sanctioned war, then my campaigns were often the equivalent of nuclear war.

In order to serve for thirty years, I had to win four reelection campaigns. None of them was easy. No two of them were alike. But all of them boiled down to the same thing: I was a conservative and liberals wanted me out—and in North Carolina, the registered Democrats significantly outnumber the registered Republicans. Therefore, I had to receive substantial Democrat support each election if I was to have any hope of winning.

In 1978 the Democrats had a wide-open primary, with Luther Hodges Jr. favored as the winner. Luther had the support of the party leadership, and they were surprised when the top vote-getter was the state's Insurance Commissioner, John R. Ingram. Ingram had a difficult time raising sufficient money for his campaign, but he got support from two sources that were important to him: the president of North Carolina's AFL-CIO and President Jimmy Carter.

The union boss was angry with me because I had opposed legislation that would have forced millions of Americans to join unions in order to get or keep jobs that they were fully qualified to hold. President Carter was hoping for my defeat because I had been vocal in saying Mr. Carter had been wrong to give away the Panama Canal.

My supporters were a little more colorful: Baseball star Catfish Hunter joined my team; and Albert Long Jr., a standout four-letter man at the University of North Carolina, did a thirty-minute TV spot on my behalf.

Dot was a faithful campaigner who went to as many grand openings of campaign headquarters or ladies' luncheons as my folks could schedule. Perhaps because she empathized with their work, she cooperated with the newspaper reporters from the big dailies and small-town weeklies in every part of the state. She also got her first taste of doing television interviews, which she did very well.

Everyone in the family joined us at some point or other, even the grandchildren. We worked hard to make sure people could meet us and know we were committed to their best interests.

But it was the unknown volunteers who always made the difference. These people knocked on doors and made phone calls; they put signs in their yards or a few dollars in an envelope to help pay for a TV ad. These are the ones who really win elections. They wanted me to keep on representing them, and I wasn't about to disappoint them.

This time around, I also had a record to run on—and fortunately, most of the voters thought I was doing okay. When the votes were tallied, I had 54.5 percent of the total, even though President Carter himself spent a full day that fall in western North Carolina, campaigning and raising money for Commissioner Ingram.

The polls closed at 7:30 p.m. on November 7, and by 7:45 p.m., ABC declared that I had won. Our hard work had paid off. Best of all as far as Dot was concerned, there wouldn't be any more talk about my '72 victory being a "fluke" (as some in the media had claimed) based on riding someone else's coattails.

CHAPTER 21

President Ronald Reagan

It's no secret that Ronald Reagan was my favorite President. In fact, I am confident that most fair-minded people will acknowledge that he was the greatest twentieth-century President of the United States—indeed, one of the truly great Presidents in our nation's history.

Since finishing his second term as President, no honor has come to Ronald Reagan that he did not deserve—from roads, schools, and federal buildings bearing his name to the Ronald Reagan Washington National Airport that serves our nation's capital. No honor has been more appropriate than the great United States Navy ship, the USS *Ronald Reagan*. I was among the throngs celebrating at Newport News in March 2001 when the remarkable nuclear aircraft carrier was christened by Nancy Reagan. Commissioned for service in 2003, this symbol of America's commitment to the cause of freedom will be a part of our proud armada long into the twenty-first century.

As Nancy Reagan said, when this great ship sailed for the first time into its home port in San Diego in July 2004, Ron Reagan must have been smiling down on the scene. This great ship's motto sums up the goal this President set for his country, "Peace Through Strength."

It was our mutual commitment to the principle that the United States must use its strength to further the causes of freedom and peace, and our mutual belief that this country must never retreat from that which made us great, that kept us personal friends and political allies for many decades, even when we had differences over specific issues.

Certainly one of those issues on which we differed was whether it was best for conservatives to form their own national party or to stay within the Republican Party.

As I have mentioned, I was disappointed with the Reagan campaign staff's urging Ron to announce that he would select Dick Schweiker as his running mate if he were to win the presidential nomination in 1976. And I was dismayed that Ron agreed with that plan, even though he called me and personally reassured me that it would not impact any of his stands on issues that matter to conservatives.

Deal-making like this might be okay for people who care more about having power than advancing principles, but it was *not* okay with the millions of people who were tired of voting for people who said they stood for values that mattered to those people when in reality they didn't care enough to fight for them. And it certainly was not okay with me.

My musings about the possibility of a new party had been widely publicized and sparked a great deal of debate in 1975. Governor Reagan had expressed his conviction that it would be better to remain within the Republican Party. He wanted conservatives to stay and build a majority. Clearly, the issue needed to be resolved. Conservative leaders gathered at the Conservative Political Action Conference's annual meeting in Washington that year asked me to form the Committee on Conservative Alternatives (COCA), and I agreed. I also suggested that if a Committee on Liberal Alternatives (COLA) were formed by that other crowd, we could refer to our groups jointly as Coca-Cola.

Our committee came to the conclusion that we could better advance our conservative goals by working hard to reform the Republican Party. We agreed that the path to change started at the grassroots level and certainly included unified support for the election of conservative candidates, even when it meant primary opposition to incumbents or well-known candidates within the party who were known to hold views contrary to conservative voters.

Needless to say, the choice we made meant we were agreeing to engage in a long-term battle, one that in many ways continues to this day in the precincts and in state and national primaries. It may surprise those who are not active in party politics to know that sometimes these battles are internal and take place in unexpected quarters, including among a candidate's closest advisors. This is a genuine problem when campaign professionals gain authority to set priorities or formulate policy decisions based solely on what the professionals think will gain the best press or most votes.

The circle of advisors around Ronald Reagan in the late 1970s included a few people who were more interested in power than principle. They wanted to compromise and soften the Reagan message into a toothless shadow of what it had been in the late sixties and early seventies. They were nervous when Ronald Reagan spoke from his heart about the conservative principles he believed in, and they made it their business to move him to the mushy middle.

As long as those people were in charge, I withheld my support. Finally, after the New Hampshire primary in February 1980, there was a change in the Reagan campaign leadership and I had a personal assurance that Ronald Reagan was going to emphasize the issues that conservatives considered "nonnegotiables," while his chief rival, George Bush, was less committed to conservative policies.

By April, I was engaged in the Reagan campaign and working on behalf of other conservative candidates around the country. When there were breaks in the Senate schedule, I was happy to speak to voters and encourage them to elect as many conservatives as possible to the Congress.

The night in Detroit when Ronald Reagan was formally nominated held, for me, a very special significance. Conservatives had demonstrated an ability to come together for an important cause. Together we had persevered, and now we had an opportunity to have as our President someone who believed in the principles of conservatism and would lead our country in a different direction. The following evening, when Governor Reagan formally accepted the nomination, I was sitting in the CBS television booth with Walter Cronkite, Jack Kilpatrick, Bill Moyers, and others. Together we watched Ron Reagan speak to the American people.

It was a good speech, but Ron had already proven that he could be eloquent. He had formed a coast-to-coast love affair with millions of Americans, and he loved America and its impact around the world.

I found myself remembering the message Ron had delivered in Kansas City in 1976, when he had encouraged his supporters to stick with their principles. He pleaded with them not to give up. There are millions of Americans "out there," he said, who want the same things that you want, who want America to become, once again, "a shining city on a hill."

To me, Ronald Reagan's willingness to believe the best about America and his forthright stand for a foreign policy based on principle not only won him that North Carolina primary back in 1976—ultimately, it won the Cold War as well.

We left that 1980 convention united around our Presidential candidate but less than enthused about his choice for Vice President. Once again the people around Ronald Reagan, who were afraid of conservatism, had pushed their view that it was essential that he "balance" the ticket. Without consulting the conservative leaders who had helped assure his candidacy, Ronald Reagan announced that he had asked George Herbert Walker Bush to run as Vice President. I got this surprise news as I sat in the CBS broadcast booth with Walter Cronkite. The best word to describe my reaction is "flabbergasted."

When I got back to my room that evening, I discovered that Ronald Reagan had tried several times to reach me by phone. I didn't call him back. At that point, I was not ready to talk to Ron.

Conservative leaders met through the night to decide how they might respond to the Bush choice. There was strong sentiment in favor of putting my name into nomination to oppose the Bush candidacy, but finally it was decided that I should address the convention to send a message to conservatives across the country that (1) we supported Ronald Reagan and (2) we supported the party platform.

The draft of the speech was hammered out and reshaped until the very last minute. Our final version was whisked away to be typed and delivered to me after I had already stepped to the podium. We made our point.

The convention ended and the campaign began with much to celebrate, as well as some concerns. Finally we had a Republican candidate for President who was strong on important issues like the defeat of Communism and strong national defense. He supported the right to life and opposed federal solutions to local problems. But the very agreeableness and positive attitude that made Ronald Reagan so likable made him susceptible to arguments in favor of compromise.

What battles might we have with him as President? It was now clear that we would have to be cautious—and be willing to disagree when necessary.

November 4, 1980, was a banner day for me. Not only was Ronald Reagan elected President, but enough conservative Republicans were elected along with him to give the Republicans a majority in the United States Senate. Some of the Senate's most famous liberals were sent home, including Birch Bayh, George McGovern, John Culver, Frank Church, and Gaylord Nelson.

There was quite a celebration later that month, when the Republican Senators hosted a dinner at the Library of Congress to honor President-elect Reagan and Nancy. The President-elect and I met privately before the dinner, and both he and Nancy recognized Dot and me in their remarks. I was pleased that Dot was applauded for her work and for her patience as I was flying from one state to another for so many months.

At that dinner, Ronald Reagan reminded us that tough times would be ahead, and he encouraged us to stick together. I intended to do my best, with the understanding that I could not compromise principle—even for friendship. I determined that I'd try to stay to the President's right and make it easier for Reagan to be Reagan.

I was tested early on with a handful of appointments I could not confirm, but President Reagan and I kept our line of communication open. He knew I wanted him to do well, especially in the task of reshaping our foreign policy.

Early on, I demonstrated my willingness to work with him by voting in favor of his request to raise the federal debt ceiling, for which I am sure there are conservatives somewhere who, to this day, have yet to forgive me. Nevertheless, I remained determined that on most issues I would stay to the right of the President.

SUCCESS, IT IS SAID, has many fathers. And America's victory in the Cold War has innumerable claims of paternity. It did not take long following the fall of the Berlin Wall before everyone in Washington began claiming to have been "on the right side" of the battle for freedom, and claiming that back then "we all agreed" on the need to confront and defeat Soviet Communism.

That, needless to say, is hogwash.

Things were *not* easy during the Cold War, and we did *not* all agree. The left wing howled (led by Ted Kennedy and company) when Ronald Reagan declared the Soviet Union an "evil empire," which, of course, it was. Their blood curdled when Mr. Reagan declared his intent to leave Communism on the "ash heap of history."

The libs opposed his efforts to build the Strategic Defense Initiative (SDI); they opposed his efforts to rebuild our nation's military; they opposed his efforts to support freedom fighters seeking to overthrow Communist regimes in our hemisphere—and around the world, for that matter. They fought him tooth and nail every step of the way.

But President Reagan himself put it best in 1992, when he addressed the Republican National Convention for the final time: "I heard those speakers at that other [Democrat] convention saying, 'We won the Cold War,'" Reagan said. "And I couldn't help wondering . . . just who exactly do they mean by 'we'?"

Make no mistake; it was, of course, Ronald Reagan who won the Cold War. But his victory in the Cold War was merely the first of many instances in which his detractors sought to associate themselves with his successes and to co-opt his ideas.

I AM OBLIGED TO MAKE the record clear: While President Reagan and I agreed on most things, there were some topics on which I felt obliged to publicly state my opposition. Not all of Ronald Reagan's appointments, especially for some international posts, would have been *my* choices, and I said so.

At one point, I publicly speculated that some of the nominations that I had found most troubling were those sent forward while the President was recovering from the attempt on his life during his first year in office. Critics who thought I gave Presidential nominees from the Clinton administration a hard time might have been heartened to recall my opposition to nominees back then.

On the other hand, I wanted to be fair when I found no clear reason to cast a negative vote. When President Reagan nominated Sandra Day O'Connor as a Supreme Court Justice, I studied all of the information, took the time to ask my own questions, and finally voted in favor of her confirmation—even though there were well-meaning people opposed to her appointment.

Another significant area where I both publicly and privately urged Ronald Reagan to modify his policies involved federal spending. I have always contended that the federal government—or any government, for that matter—should not operate in the red. While I applauded Ronald Reagan's tax cuts and his many programs that successfully stimulated the U.S. economy, I stood in opposition to budgets that were not balanced.

The Reagan administration took a pragmatic approach, hoping that it might set a course for restrained spending and increased revenues from and by a thriving economy. This to me was wishful political posturing in the face of liberal Democrats who supported more and more government programs for their pet subsidies and regulatory boards.

I have always readily acknowledged that Ron and I were not mirror images in all of our opinions (most notably on issues like the General Agreement on

Tariffs and Trade and disarmament treaties), but Ronald Reagan holds my undiminished admiration for all that he accomplished and the course he set for America's future. By the strength of his conviction and the generosity of his spirit, he won critical battles that turned us away from overbearing government and, in the process, once again encouraged us to reach for the best and do our best to succeed.

I don't believe it's possible to overstate how much President Reagan changed —and continues to change—the political landscape of America. Indeed, the Reagan Presidency produced changes of seismic proportions—a shift in the tectonic plates of American politics that impacts even the details of the way our Presidents since Ronald Reagan have done business.

For example, recognizing his unique ability to articulate conservative principles, my good friend Tom Ellis and others wanted to encourage the President to initiate a series of "Fireside Chats" to help all of our citizens, young and old, understand topics like the miracle of free enterprise.

I set up a meeting, and the idea was well received by the President—and deemed "worth considering" by the White House advisors sitting in on the meeting.

Very soon after, the President was shot, and I was quite sure the idea for the programs was swept away in the ensuing changes in his office. To my surprise, Nancy Reagan herself wrote to Tom to say that the President would begin a regular weekly radio address as soon as he could. That weekly address has grown in importance year by year, and is now an important means by which the White House can get out its message without having the media reshape it in any way.

It has been said that Ronald Reagan made the Clinton Presidency possible. This is not to besmirch the memory of our dear friend President Reagan but to demonstrate instead just how fundamentally the Reagan principles altered the ground rules of American politics.

When President Clinton assumed office in 1992, his and Hillary's first major project was their effort to nationalize American health care. It was an old-style, left-wing, big-government project—and it was a colossal failure! The American people wanted nothing to do with a return to big-government liberalism.

And to make sure that President Clinton got the message, the American people went to the polls in 1994, turned out the Democrat Congress, and elected a Republican majority—a stinging, personal repudiation of Bill Clinton.

Bill Clinton got the message. By 1996 he was standing before a Republican

Congress declaring: "We know big government does not have all the answers. We know there is not a program for every problem. . . . The era of big government is over."

I remember that evening, and I recall thinking that with that one statement, Mr. Clinton was conceding Ronald Reagan's victory in the war of ideas; with that statement, Mr. Clinton acknowledged that, thanks to the Reagan Revolution, a Democrat President could no longer govern the nation on the basis of the Democrat orthodoxy of big-government liberalism.

That orthodoxy had been repudiated by Ronald Reagan and rejected by the American people. And the only way a Democrat President could govern and expect to be reelected was to do his best to imitate Ronald Reagan!

Mr. Clinton did his best to borrow pages from the Reagan playbook. And when the history books mention the Clinton years, surely it will be obvious that Clinton ran a couple of successful plays from the Gipper's game plan: the passage of welfare reform and the expansion of the NATO alliance to include the former "captive nations" of the Warsaw Pact. If they are honest, historians will note that both of these accomplishments, among others, were lifted from the agenda of Ronald Wilson Reagan. Publicly, Clinton tried calling his approach the "Third Way." Privately, the term was "triangulation." But whatever he chose to call it, it was nothing more than a smoke screen behind which a Democrat President sought to hide the fact that he was stealing ideas from Ronald Reagan.

With the election of George W. Bush, the White House returned to the true way forged by Reagan. We had a President of whom we could again be proud — a President who was not reluctant to embrace the enduring legacy of his ideological predecessor.

In a speech at the Reagan Library in 1999, then Governor George W. Bush declared: "We live in the nation President Reagan restored, and the world he helped to save." That was an appropriate assessment, for so much of what President Bush is seeking to accomplish for America is in fact a continuation of the Reagan Revolution — the completion of its unfinished agenda.

At the Reagan Library, President Bush rejected isolationism as a "shortcut to chaos . . . an approach that abandons our allies, and our ideals . . . [whose] result, in the long run, would be a stagnant America and a savage world."

Some in the media declared that those statements were a tactical shift back to the center, an effort by then-candidate Bush to distance himself from the conservative wing of the Republican Party. Nothing could be further from the truth. In point of fact, President Bush was calling on Americans to heed the call of Ronald Reagan, who exhorted us in his farewell address at the Houston convention to reject the "new isolationists [who] claim that the American people don't care about how or why we prevailed in the great defining struggle of our age . . . [and] who insist that our triumph is yesterday's news, part of a past that holds no lessons for the future."

But the consensus for vigorous, "distinctly American" leadership on the world stage is only the beginning of Ronald Reagan's legacy. There are so many things that we take for granted in American political life today that would never have happened were it not for the leadership of President Reagan.

For example, take missile defense. In 1983, when Ronald Reagan declared America's intent to build and deploy strategic missile defenses, the liberals ridiculed it as science fiction — "Star Wars," they called it. That was *then*.

In 1999, after eight wasted years under Bill Clinton, Congress enacted into law the National Missile Defense Act, which mandated the deployment of missile defenses.

This act of Congress was bipartisan, passed by a veto-proof majority.

There is a consensus in Washington today on the need for a defense to protect the American people from ballistic missile attack. President Bush has declared that building and deploying missile defenses is a significant national-security priority.

As for the economy, when Ronald Reagan argued twenty years ago that the way to get the economy moving again was to cut taxes to spur economic growth, the Left howled its rage. The liberal media sought to make "Reaganomics" a bad word.

That was then. But today, after two decades of the almost-uninterrupted economic expansion that Ronald Reagan set in motion, when the economy slows, most everyone in Washington agrees that a tax cut is needed to spur economic growth.

Consider: The Democrats voted to cut taxes! They dared not vote any other way. The Republicans want to cut taxes more, and there are indeed disagreements over the numbers, but the consensus in Washington is on the need for tax cuts. No one in the political mainstream today contests the principle that cutting marginal rates is the key to economic growth.

That is the legacy of Ronald Reagan at work.

How about "compassionate conservatism"? Was not Ronald Reagan the original "compassionate conservative"? Listen to the commission President Reagan gave us in Houston in his valedictory speech to the Republican Party, when he called for conservatives to declare war on poverty the same way we declared war on Soviet Communism:

> Just as we have led the crusade for democracy beyond our shores, we have a great task to do together in our own home. . . . With each sunrise we are reminded that millions of our citizens have yet to share in the abundance of American prosperity. Many languish in neighborhoods riddled with drugs and bereft of hope. Still others hesitate to venture out onto the streets for fear of criminal violence. Let us pledge ourselves to a new beginning for them.

How do we do that?

Start with education, President Reagan told us: "Let us apply our ingenuity and remarkable spirit to revolutionize education in America so that every one among us will have the mental tools to build a better life." (Or, as President Bush might say, let's make certain that "no child is left behind.")

President Reagan then told us that we must make sure that the engine of economic growth touches every American community: "Let us harness the competitive energy that built America into rebuilding our inner cities," President Reagan said, "so that real jobs can be created for those who live there and real hope can rise out of despair." (Or, as President Bush has put it, we must have "prosperity with a purpose.")

And let us never forget, President Reagan declared, that the American Dream must be open to every American: "Whether we are Afro-American or Irish-American, Christian or Jewish, from big cities or small towns, we are all equal in the eyes of God. . . . In America, our origins matter less than our destinations, and that is what democracy is all about."

So the Reagan agenda is still our agenda today: principled American leadership on the world stage; a commitment to freedom under God as the organizing bedrock of our foreign policy; unmatched military might and concrete defenses for the American people; limited government and growth-oriented tax cuts that keep our prosperity going; and a commitment to give every one of our citizens a shot at the American Dream.

Millions of Americans remind themselves that while Ronald Reagan's voice has been silenced, his vision and his principled leadership will forever continue to speak to our future.

Before he left us for that long journey that led him "into the sunset of [his] life," President Reagan laid out a parting vision for the Republican Party and the conservative movement. It is a vision that I believe is shared, in the most heartfelt way, by George W. Bush. I know Ronald Reagan would be proud of this man—and would be pleased to see that a courageous leader so worthy of the office is once again sitting at his desk.

When we remembered and honored President Reagan at his death, we were not merely commemorating past glories. Rather, we were renewing our commitment to a living revolution, an ongoing and unfinished agenda, and the lasting leadership of Ronald Reagan.

His kindness and thoughtfulness were ingrained, not programmed for public occasions. On more than one occasion he took time to support me while I was running for reelection. I remember one particular occasion when he came to North Carolina to attend a campaign event in Greensboro. President Reagan spoke, then spent the night at a hotel before an early flight out.

At six the next morning, there was a knock at the door of our room. I opened it, and there stood Ronald Reagan, the fortieth President of the United States, saying he wanted to thank us for the good visit he'd had in our state. Imagine, I thought: This remarkable friend was thanking *me*.

I said, "Let me thank *you*, sir, for every night. Have a good trip, sir."

One of the last notes I received from this great friend was on my seventieth birthday. He was at home in California, but he took time to remember the birthday of a longtime friend.

Dear Jesse,

It is with great pleasure that Nancy and I send our warmest congratulations on this happy occasion of the 31st anniversary of your 39th birthday!

These occasions cause us to reflect and, as you review the years past, you can do so with enormous pride and a real sense of accomplishment. On a personal note, I'll never forget what you did for me in 1976. I shudder to think how things would have turned out had North

Carolina not gambled on this guy. Your friendship and support have
meant so much to me and Nancy over these many years.

Happy Birthday! Nancy and I send our best wishes. May God bless
you and keep you.

Sincerely,
Ron

It was entirely true that what you saw was exactly what you got with President Reagan. During that sad week in June 2004, when America said its loving good-bye to my friend, I heard so many others who worked closely with him, and with us, in the campaigns and in the White House years, describe precisely the man I knew.

He was warm and friendly, and his cheerful good humor made all of our meetings a pleasure, even when we had difficult topics to discuss. He loved stories, and I never came back from a meeting at the White House without a joke to tell Dot that night at dinner. (I liked this story enough to "borrow" it for a speech or two myself: A Soviet farmer told a visiting commissar that the harvest from his collective was going to be so bountiful that it would "stretch to touch the foot of God." The loyal commissar reminded the farmer that in the USSR there was no God. The farmer replied, "That's okay, there's no crop to harvest either.")

President Reagan was always glad to share a bit of news or hear the latest story from Capitol Hill, but at his core, he was a private man, who was much more interested in the business of the day than in its gossip. He kept us at a comfortable distance with his charm, choosing to share his deepest thoughts and greatest friendship only with his beloved Nancy. The depth of their commitment to each other was obvious to everyone who knew them, and certainly obvious to all of America as Nancy Reagan led us in mourning for her Ronnie. Who will ever forget the sight of her leaning close to that flag-draped casket to whisper her love one last time.

It is often said of great men and women that we will not see their kind again. I believe that because Ronald Reagan led this great country from the state-mandated sameness of liberalism to a new respect for the worth of every individual—which is the hallmark of conservatism—we can indeed expect to see a new generation of leaders whose lives have been shaped by the ideals Ronald Reagan espoused. Young people across this country revere his model of public service. They, too, are a part of his legacy.

As for me, I will always be grateful to have known this great and good man, who reawakened our pride in the shining city on a hill. America will never forget Ronald Reagan, nor shall I.

I CANNOT CLOSE this chapter—and President Reagan would not forgive my omission—without talking about our good friend and ally Lady Margaret Thatcher. I first encountered this indomitable woman when she came to Washington many years ago to meet with our small group of conservative Senators. From the beginning I knew she would be a leader like few the world has seen.

Early on, when she was a minority member of the House of Commons, I offered her the use of a desk in my office whenever she came to the United States. I little imagined that one day I would be visiting her office at 10 Downing Street.

Her election as Prime Minister could not have been at a more fortuitous time in history. As a team, President Reagan and Prime Minister Thatcher accomplished more than either one could have alone.

I was glad to lend support to each of them whenever I could.

CHAPTER 22

Hot-Button Issues

FAIRNESS IN MEDIA

A S A PROFESSIONAL JOURNALIST and broadcaster for more than thirty years before becoming a United States Senator, I do not take on this topic without a clear understanding of the issues. Freedom of the press is a part of our great heritage, and I applaud those who have made the search for truth and reporting the truth their life work.

Their work, and their profession, should never be debased by those who attempt to hijack printing presses and broadcast media for their own purposes. Too many of our news outlets and best-known "journalists" have misused their positions of trust to promote personal or political agendas disguised as honest reporting.

This is not a new phenomenon. The problem was with us in 1975, in 1985, in 1995, and, sadly, it is still an issue in 2005.

Let me use a few personal examples, beginning with *The Washington Post.*

On the morning of October 23, 1983, *The Washington Post* confidently published one of its famous political analyses: "Jesse Helms Has a Problem— He's Destined to Lose." Well, I think *The Washington Post* has a problem: It can't count.

From the time of my arrival in Washington, the *Post* constantly identified me as the *right-wing* Senator from North Carolina. Moreover, during my first term, the *Post* never missed an opportunity to make clear that my election in

1972 was a fluke, that the people of North Carolina didn't know what they were doing, and that they would surely correct their grievous error come 1978.

But in 1978, they were dismayed again by *another* "fluke."

And then, in November 1984, the *Post* was dismayed a third time.

I felt it was reasonable to suggest to *The Washington Post* and its fellow travelers in the major media: *Three flukes, fellows, and you're out!*

The same was true of "news" reports about Ronald Reagan. The major media proclaimed that the Republicans had better not nominate such a wild man, because he could never get elected. He was too extreme, too far to the right, too much of an ideologue.

In 1980 they could find solace in the fact that he carried only forty-four states, and in 1984 they could point to Minnesota and the District of Columbia as proof that Reagan couldn't win everywhere.

Why do the media elite have such a hard time acknowledging the successes of conservatives and conservative initiatives in government and society? I am convinced it is because for the most part they operate out of a philosophy that is at odds with our core values as Americans and our great national traditions.

The longer I live, the more convinced I become that God didn't direct the creation of America in a moment of idle indifference. I believe God had a purpose for America. He gave us a meaning and a destiny. And if we now discard the Miracle of America, if we now fade into the pack, the future of all that we hold dear will be lost.

There are forces around the world today, just as there have been for decades, that are eager to see America swept into the dustbin of nations that lost their way, lost their courage, lost their principles, and lost their purpose.

In the 1980s we faced the confrontation between tyranny and freedom, between spirituality and atheism, between justice and brutality. Back then, the opinion-makers in our land—the major news media—attempted to lead us to believe that Communism is just another philosophy, just another political system. They would still have us believe that today—about Cuba and China and North Korea—and they would have us believe that brutal regimes cloaked as religion-based governments like the Taliban are the cultural choices of all the citizens. Tell that to the women of Afghanistan or Iran.

There is such a babble of voices today, a cacophony of exhortations by cunningly false prophets. There are overwhelming efforts to dictate what our people shall think and say and do. And it's so difficult for so many to sort out their priorities.

I sometimes wonder whether I'm on the same planet as the reporters and editors who put our best-known newspapers and network news broadcasts together. I know from firsthand knowledge that events I saw in the Senate and elsewhere were frequently described in their reports in a way that had nothing to do with reality.

Let me use this example. In 1995, Governor Jim Hunt and others proposed that the Ambassadors of the countries that were then members of the Association of Southeast Asian Nations (ASEAN) be invited to tour North Carolina and learn more about how the businesses of our state might provide goods and services for their governments and their citizens. I thought this was a wonderful way to promote our free-enterprise system and expand our exports. The two-day tour would take the Ambassadors to farms, factories, banking centers, and research universities. And while they were in the Piedmont region of the state, we would provide a brief tour of the Jesse Helms Center, and the Center would host a luncheon at nearby Wingate University, so students and Ambassadors might enjoy getting to know one another.

Between the time the invitation was extended and the detailed plans were put in place, ASEAN voted to enlarge its membership by inviting the country of Vietnam to join their organization.

While I might not have participated in hosting the tour if I had known in advance about this change in membership, I had no interest in insulting all of the other nations of ASEAN by taking back my invitation or suggesting that the Helms Center change its plans.

On the day of the Ambassadors' arrival, there was a generous contingent of the press, including NBC reporter Andrea Mitchell. Ms. Mitchell interviewed me and planned to attend the luncheon and do a report about the Ambassadors' visit for the evening news. As a part of that package the NBC camera crew shot many scenes, including my greeting all the Ambassadors, including the representative of the government of Vietnam.

Just before lunch, Ms. Mitchell's cell phone rang. It was NBC News headquarters telling her that Secretary of Commerce Ron Brown, traveling with a group on a trade mission in Croatia, had been killed in an airplane accident.

Andrea, who had recently returned from Croatia, was told to return immediately to her headquarters to work on the Ron Brown story.

The story about the Ambassadors had been "spiked," as they say in the business. That was understandable, even though the members of the Governor's staff who had worked so hard on the trip were disappointed at the missed opportunity to brag about North Carolina's many benefits for business.

I thought no more of the situation until that summer.

NBC News decided that it was time for them once again to set their sights on the tobacco industry with a week of "in-depth" features. (I'm sure it's a coincidence that the networks seem most likely to attack businesses that do not have advertising contracts with them.)

Imagine my surprise when footage of my greeting the Ambassador from Vietnam during that ASEAN tour suddenly appeared on the screen, accompanied by the "reporter's" assertion that I was so blindly tied to tobacco interests that I would even try to sell tobacco to Vietnam.

It was an astoundingly out-of-context misuse of the photo images, the real story, and my own motives and behavior. We complained, of course, but no one cared. The network had their story, and didn't much care about the facts they had ignored in the process of crafting it.

I could fill this book with stories just like this. Stories that are blatantly false or deceptively nuanced are too often the order of the day. Even worse, when the errors are exposed—as the allegations of Ambassador Joseph Wilson that the Bush administration lied about Saddam Hussein's attempts to buy uranium in Africa were exposed, by no less than the investigative staff of the 9/11 Commission—the newscasters and pundits who bought and headlined the false allegations compound their misbehavior by burying the proof that they were the ones who spread the story to begin with.

How can the major media be so wrong so often? The answer is obvious: They are profoundly out of sympathy with the ideals and goals of the American people. Of course, there are sound and honest journalists in all parts of the country. But the elite media—and you know who they are—are overwhelmingly produced by men and women who certainly have a smug contempt for American ideals and principles.

I agree with the observers who track and analyze these things. The major media automatically blame America first. They reject many of the goals and aspirations of ordinary Americans, they reject most of the moral and ethical values ordinary Americans hold, they reject the success that America has achieved, and they condemn many of the political and economic institutions that are the foundation of that success. They even reject their own personal success and affluence.

In the mid-eighties, surveys and studies conducted by Stanley Rothman and S. Robert Lichter based on interviews conducted with hundreds of journalists from the elite media found:

- *52 percent thought government should substantially reduce the income gap between rich and poor (as if government could!)*
- *54 percent thought the government should guarantee jobs (as if government should!)*
- *58 percent saw no wrong in adultery*
- *76 percent saw no wrong in homosexuality*
- *90 percent favored abortion on demand*
- *45 percent said that the United States causes third-world poverty*

Nothing in my experience gives me reason to think views like these have done anything but increase in the last twenty years. In fact, the most recent report of the Pew Research Center in 2004 indicated that among the national media:

- *42 percent believe government should* guarantee *that no one is in need, no matter how an individual might mishandle his own or his family's personal resources*
- *88 percent now see no wrong in promoting the homosexual lifestyle*
- *93 percent describe themselves as moderate, liberal, or very liberal*
- *64 percent acknowledge a blurring of the line between reporting and commentary*
- *91 percent believe it is not necessary to have a belief in God in order to be moral*

The members of the liberal media have made a god of government and devalued Godly wisdom about human conduct. They do not comprehend that the federal government cannot solve the problems of society—because the federal government too often *is* the problem.

The problem goes far beyond their political bias or a philosophical orientation. Many in the media have expressed puzzlement at the deep distrust of the media by the American people.

I would ask you to consider this question: Is this not a major issue for us to confront?

Should not the people of this country be able to know the truth about the news of the day—undiluted, uncontrived, and unburdened by the biases of the media elite?

Should we not, at the very minimum, be informed that the typical twisted and opinionated films from Michael Moore in which he chooses himself as producer, director, and star are no more "documentaries" than are *War of the Worlds* and *King Kong*? Instead, we see him repeat his lies on every major news outlet without so much as a halfhearted challenge over the most obvious errors that Moore typically serves up with a belligerence he wants his audience to take for honesty.

We need to face up to the fact that the nation's freedom has been put in danger by the very people who claim to uphold it, with their claim that freedom of speech gives them license to say anything—or do anything—because they are simply being "informative."

We know very well the terrorist threats we face, and the threat created by the rejection of social mores everywhere in the world. But the real threat to our personal freedom, to freedom of speech, and to our constitutional system is paraded on our TV screens every evening—and on the front pages of some of the nation's most powerful newspapers every day.

If we ever lose our freedom in this country, can the elite news media be absolved of a large share of the blame? Can we absolve them of a share of the blame for real-life behavior held up as exemplary by their approving coverage of even the coarsest and most violent behaviors?

Our constitutional government is a government of checks and balances and the separation of powers. Our Founding Fathers intended that the federal government would be balanced by the power of the state governments, and that within the federal government the powers of the three branches should be in a rough balance.

But they never expected the news media to become a fourth branch of government. They never expected that this country could be ruled by a power that is unchecked, unbalanced, unelected, unreliable, and undemocratic. They never thought that the day would come when the press was no longer free and no longer responsible.

Among the powers that today's news media have unjustly claimed for themselves, there are three that stand out as most alarming to me.

First, the power of character assassination: This is the power to undermine government without constructing; to destroy without evidence; to exceed the truth without fear of retaliation. Who can forget the question first asked by Ronald Reagan's Secretary of Labor, Ray Donovan, after he was fully exonerated of false charges of corruption: "Where do I go to get my reputation back?"

How many more people must have wondered that same thing after *they* were caught up in supposed "investigative" reports fueled by people with personal vendettas and spread by stations with a thirst for ratings?

Second, the power to set the agenda for public priorities and principles: The media today has the power to set our national agenda, to determine the limits of debate, and to discipline those who refuse to follow the agenda set by the media. The joke slogan, "It's news only if we *say* it's news," is no joke in newsrooms all over the country, where stories are blocked out of broadcasts because the managers of the broadcast simply don't want to cover them.

If you could have been with me in private meetings in the Senate, or the conferences with the House, you would know how Congress is constantly reacting to issues and events created by the media. Even the President himself frequently feels obliged to react to the media's agenda.

Third, the power of psychological warfare against the American people: It is not enough that the character of the nation's leadership be assassinated; it is not enough that our national agenda is managed by the media; the people themselves are the real target.

How many times have you seen TV programs telling you that the United States, and not our sworn enemies, is the real threat to peace? How many times have you heard from our best-known reporters and commentators that our supposed cultural insensitivity is the reason for beheadings and bombings? How many times have you heard that our diligence and the prosperity it has produced are unfair to those who prefer to blow up their own pipelines and power plants?

How many times have you heard that our brave military personnel, the people who by the hundreds of thousands risked their very lives to bring freedom to those who could not free themselves—America's bravest young people—are an *impediment* to peace?

Have we reached the point that the elite media in the United States are no longer defenders of democracy? Are they not instead a *threat* to democracy?

How do the media persist in the kinds of behaviors that have been exposed in libel trials and in the insider books of those who can no longer be silent about what passes for journalism in our elite media operations? How and why can they escape judgment?

At least one reason is the long-lasting impact of a 1964 U.S. Supreme Court decision that set up an impossible standard of justice for victims of libel who happen to be public figures. The case was *New York Times Co. v. Sullivan*. The *Sullivan* case was a turning point for the media in the United States. Before *Sullivan*, those of us who were working in the media had a healthy fear of a libel suit. We knew that we could not publish anything that was both defamatory and false. We knew that the publication of a defamatory falsehood could bring an end not only to our personal careers but to the newspaper or broadcast station itself. But after *Sullivan*, journalists did not have to worry, so long as it could be argued that the victim was a public figure. There was no longer any check, any worry, any cold sweat until the proof was under lock and key.

What *Sullivan* did was add a third element to the traditional elements of defamation and falsehood. If the victim happened to be a public figure, he had to prove "actual malice," that is, he had to prove not only that the material was defamatory and false, but that the attacker knew it was false or acted in reckless disregard of the truth.

There is not, of course, a federal common law of libel. But the Court argued that the First Amendment was incorporated by the Fourteenth into state libel law in the case of public figures because the state court was an instrument of government. If the state court set an excessive judgment, said the Supreme Court, it was interfering with the First Amendment.

It turned on its head the traditional doctrine that the First Amendment was intended to protect freedom of the press from legislative restraints by the federal government. What the Court said was that falsehood against public figures was protected by the First Amendment. None of the framers of the First Amendment, nor the Fourteenth, for that matter, had any intention whatsoever of upsetting this mechanism for protecting good reputations and encouraging responsible journalism. But this did not inhibit the Supreme Court in 1964. In the *Sullivan* case, the justices in effect said that, despite the fact that we never noticed it before, the First Amendment does not allow recovery for libel under state law by a public figure unless he can show that the defamatory falsehood was published with "actual malice." The justices then defined "actual malice" in such a way that it is virtually impossible to prove.

Look at the result of that decision. Checkout counters at just about every grocery store in the nation are lined with magazines and newsweeklies claiming to have the inside story on the lives of entertainers, persons in the news, and public figures. Cable and broadcast channels have filled their schedules with programs whose sole purpose is to get to the dirt and dig it out fastest. The fine line between responsible journalism and what used to be disparaged as "tabloid" journalism has been blurred beyond recognition.

The public deserves protection against the presently unchecked excesses of the media. I know that any attempt, no matter how well intentioned, to regulate the behavior of news organizations would immediately be attacked as an attempt to abridge the constitutional rights delineated in the First Amendment. Therefore, in 1985, I was very supportive of a different and uniquely American approach to foster responsibility.

An organization known as Fairness in Media was put together by my friend Tom Ellis and others, with a goal to encourage people who were tired of biased reporting to take control of an entire broadcasting operation and change its management.

Their idea was to purchase a sufficient number of shares of CBS stock to gain a voice in the company's policies. There was certainly nothing revolutionary about this. Wall Street opens its doors every day to people who want to invest in private business, and some of those people want to have enough of an investment to have a say in the way the business should be run. It is even a recognized and common practice for individuals who are not able to purchase enough stock on their own to gain a measure of control by joining with others and voting as a block of like-minded stockholders.

But apparently it never occurred to the people who ran the news organizations that such an ordinary right of ownership and influence might extend itself to people who held views other than the ones the liberal media supports so vigorously. They went on a diet of fingernails at the prospect of a board of directors at CBS that would insist on objectivity and fairness. There was mass handwringing and more than a few cartoons lampooning the idea that somehow a change in the ownership and management of CBS would put me in charge. My favorite cartoon put a pair of my eyeglasses on the well-known CBS "eye" logo. As silly as it was, I'm sure it was an image that must have filled Dan Rather and the denizens of his newsroom with some foreboding. At least it put them on notice that the elite media could no longer assume that their shaping of stories and selective use or misuse of the facts would proceed without challenge.

While the attempt to purchase CBS never came to fruition and the battle for fairness continues to this minute, there is a measure of good news. Without much notice the old AM radio stations around the country—all but abandoned by those who assumed (just as they wrongly did in the 1940s when I got my start doing news on the radio) that the only thing people cared about hearing was music in an FM format—started letting people talk.

Those talk shows needed content, and that content often included guests who had firsthand knowledge of the news of the day. In this new format, people could question guests, and program hosts had time to gather details about the issues. The number of listeners grew. Some of the best radio hosts became syndicated, and an entirely new source of news, provided in a format that invited discussion, became a force within the broadcast industry. Worse yet, in the view of the elites, it was a conservative source, where the facts mattered more than the message, and the audience was trusted to come to its own conclusions once it had all the facts.

The rise of the cable news channels has also expanded the opportunities to at least get conservative views heard, even though there is nothing approaching parity on that front. C-Span provides a public service by letting every American see its legislative bodies at work. Beyond that, only C-Span provides gavel-to-gavel coverage of the national political conventions with no cutaways, no partisan commentaries, and no sugarcoating of what is being said or done.

Now the Internet is providing the ultimate in freedom of speech—no wonder it is so tightly regulated and feared in countries like Cuba and China. Unfettered access to the Internet means that no one is restricted to dependence on the local paper or the big network's version of what is happening each day. Anyone who really wants the facts can find them on the Internet—twenty-four hours a day. There has never been an information tool that can compare to this source of both immediate information and in-depth research.

No longer can a political candidate or his spokesperson demand that an unflattering photo be removed from public circulation—or claim that the photo was unauthorized. The photo is archived a thousand times over on the Internet, and the organization or individual responsible for taking the picture can also freely post the facts surrounding its existence and its distribution on its own web site.

It will take a while for the old-line liberals in the media to realize they have lost their power, but their day is over. Real fairness in media has arrived in a form they would have never suspected—but it has arrived, and we will all be the better for it.

THE NEA AND ARTS FUNDING

The average American may not realize that it required an act of Congress to prevent the federal government's sending taxpayers' money to people who feel obliged to coat themselves with chocolate and/or submerge a crucifix in urine, and call *that* art.

But it did happen, and it required a protracted fight to prevent the taxpayers' money from being spent in connection with such absurdities. On July 26, 1989, I responded in the Senate to the concerns of millions of Americans who were offended and outraged by the kinds of images and performances that were receiving tax funds from the federal government through the National Endowment for the Arts.

I brought the concerns of these good Americans to the attention of the United States Senate. Sensible citizens, and many of their elected representatives, had been expressing their disapproval directly to the NEA for some time. Sad to say, their opinions were brushed aside while many of the federal officials who should have been listening to them approved more and more such outrageous requests—and did it in the name of "free expression."

Such expressions, of course, were anything but free. It certainly was not "free" to the taxpayers whose hard-earned money was being spent on such foolishness. More importantly, it carried a high cost for families who wanted their children and other impressionable young people to be shielded from such absurdities and obscenity. Sensible Americans were put in the difficult position of protecting their children from the materials their government was promoting.

Since the NEA refused to acknowledge the unfairness of its policy, the only solution was to provide it with rules that it could not violate without breaking the law and facing arrest for having done so.

To the surprise of almost no one—certainly not me—the people whose work we were trying to defund were furious. They depicted me as a "prude with no knowledge of the arts" and proclaimed that I had no inclination to permit anyone to see or hear something that I happened not to like. I got many good laughs out of the political cartoons generated by these attacks, but I marveled at the deliberate obscuring of the real problem.

The issue was *not* censorship—in America all of us are free to pursue any form of expression within the law—it was about *federally funding* such nonsense. Instead of artists seeking support from those who knew and encouraged their pursuits, they lined up for *government* checks. They demanded funds without acknowledging the government's responsibility to *know* for what the government was spending "the taxpayers'" money. And they did so under the false pretense that it was on behalf of the American people.

What was involved in this episode was far more than credible debate about the allocation of $170 million of the taxpayers' money for the NEA in the following fiscal year. The NEA was already in line to receive that much—or more—for each of the next several years. The NEA had nearly $1 billion available to be wasted in whatever manner the NEA chose to waste it. It had already demonstrated that it had little concern about how the taxpayers' money was spent.

The funds involved may be regarded by some as trivial. I did not consider it "trivial," though I did acknowledge that the federal government was spending far more than that amount in a few hours on any given day.

No, what was really at stake was whether America would allow the cultural high ground in this nation to sink slowly into an abyss just to satisfy people who clearly seek (or are at least willing) to destroy the traditional foundations of this Republic.

Let us lay to rest once and for all the nonsense about censorship somehow being involved when the federal government refuses to automatically grant funds to self-proclaimed artists. There is a great deal of difference between censorship and sponsorship.

Censorship is when the government bans the production, distribution, or display of materials in both the private and the public sector. That is censorship.

Self-proclaimed artists whose minds are in a gutter are free, of course, to do whatever they please with their own money. People who want to scrawl dirty words on men's-room walls are free to do so—as long as they provide the walls and their own crayons. But this crowd wants the government (that is to say, the American taxpayers) to pay for that sort of thing. This Senator had to say no.

What we are talking about is a question of sponsorship. It has nothing to do with banning anything. It has only to do with whether the federal government should finance art to which millions of taxpayers object—and do so with their money! That is absolutely out of the question.

I have insisted that when the government refuses to pay for the production and distribution or exhibition of certain obscene materials, it is refusing to sponsor such sleaze. This refusal is exactly what the vast majority of taxpayers want.

The government has no obligation whatsoever to require taxpayers to subsidize projects that are so far beyond the applicability of constitutional protection that the federal government in my opinion *could* legally ban their dissemination. The government's refusal to pay does not prevent people from displaying or selling such materials at their own expense in the private sector.

Let there be no misunderstanding—the issue we faced in 1989 wasn't over trivialities or musical tastes. We were in a battle over whether the government should fund work that the average citizen would find shocking and offensive. How can I say that with such authority? Let me share some of the "behind the scenes" aspects of this story:

The day I first went onto the Senate floor to bring to the Senate's attention the clear evidence that a war was being waged against America's basic values by a gaggle of self-proclaimed "artists" and that these "artists" were being funded by the National Endowment for the Arts, I carried with me *examples* of the so-called "art" that the American taxpayers were being forced to subsidize (and thus reward). The senior Senator from West Virginia, my distinguished and longtime friend Robert Byrd, was the manager of the Department of the Interior appropriations for the fiscal year 1990. I showed the Senator some of the so-called "art." Senator Byrd took one look at it, shook his head, and said, "Good golly, I will support your amendment!" And that is when the battle began.

After my amendment prohibiting the NEA from using the taxpayers' money to sponsor obscenity was approved, I was showered with hoots and jeers from the liberal media all across this country. And I welcomed every syllable of it.

The media made fools of themselves on this issue. They did not persuade any American that people who produce such rotten material are entitled to have any funds allocated to them from the federal treasury. Just the same, the media spared no effort in promoting the absurd claim by radical fringe artists that my amendment somehow "censored" artists. But not once was the "mainstream" media willing to broadcast or publish, for example, the photographs that I brought to the Senate floor that day in 1989. The media knew the uproar that publication of this kind of thing would cause.

It is fair to say that various elements of the major news media engaged in a deliberate cover-up. There were instances in which various newspapers published carefully selected, noncontroversial pictures, implying that Jesse Helms was concerned about art depicting floral scenes, beautiful little pictures, and paintings. This fell squarely into the category of journalistic falsehood. They knew what I was talking about, but they were unwilling to make it clear to their readers and their viewers.

Let's be very clear about this: The so-called "art"—and please take note of the quotation marks around the word "art"—that I opposed is so rotten, crude, disgusting, and filthy that it turns the stomach of normal people. That was the kind of material that so many newspapers and magazines refused even to *describe* to their readers—while charging that it was censorship for me to oppose forcing the taxpayers to promote such rotten material with their own money.

I challenged the major newspapers directly. I wrote and called to say, "Just publish one or two of the pictures that we are talking about so that the people can understand what I think is so offensive." To make sure they could not use the excuse of not having any of the pictures to publish, I enclosed one or two of the pictures for each edition (and the editors unanimously ignored them!).

I was not at all surprised by the reaction of what we called the "big-city editors" in North Carolina. One ridiculed me as being a "purist." Another described me as being an "ignoramus" because of my failure to "appreciate modern art." All implied that I was engaging in censorship.

Yet no North Carolina reporter was assigned to come by my office to take a look at all of this art. Several Senators did view it in order to understand the depth of the problem, then promptly added their support to our initiative.

I was determined that all of these editors should have a chance to inspect this "art" personally in the privacy of their own offices. I arranged to have the Senate's print shop make copies of all of the repulsive and revolting photographs in question. My first plan was to send a package of photos to each of the editors by registered mail, but it occurred to me that one or more of those editors might accuse me of sending "indecent material through the mail." Therefore, I made arrangements to have the packages delivered by hand.

I also asked each editor to make this "art" available for inspection at each respective newspaper. I specified that the photographs should be seen only by adults who asked to see them, and, finally, that mention be made by each of the papers that the photos would be available at the newspapers for inspection *only by male adults*.

Guess what? There was absolute silence for several days. I tried to reach each of the "big-city editors" by telephone to learn how the public reacted. Only one was "available," and none ever called me back. The one whom I finally reached responded with an obscenity and a strange declaration that he was "running a newspaper—not a blankety-blank lending library."

But the editorials barely slowed. The papers continued to mislead their readers with inane suggestions that it was somehow "censorship" for Senator Helms to oppose using federal government tax money to subsidize and/or promote "art" that was just too rotten for the papers to publish or the television stations to broadcast.

I must not forget the television stations. They refused to show the pictures because the Federal Communications Commission would jerk their licenses in an instant; they claimed that showing those photos would have been a "blatant violation of the FCC broadcast standards." Not one of those television and radio stations dared to broadcast or otherwise show the shocking photos, including the infamous work of Robert Mapplethorpe, but still they denounced those of us who opposed the NEA's practice of paying for this rotten material. I was even denounced by one or two stations for proposing that the federal government apply exactly the same standard to the NEA publicly funded "art" that the Federal Communications Commission applies to television stations broadcasting over the public airwaves.

The assault on America's basic values by self-proclaimed, self-appointed "artists," who so often assault the moral sensibilities of the American people, is real and easily documented. I was happy to do everything in my power to end this funding.

The restrictions the Congress passed and the President signed were immediately challenged in the courts. These proceedings only further exposed the level of perversion that the NEA had previously funded as "art" and the uses unfettered funding would be put to in the future. It was appalling.

Let's be honest. We had been, and still are, being asked to fund sex acts on stage, countless homoerotic movies, photographs, and so-called "film festivals." From burning the American flag to desecrating their own (and one another's) bodies, the depravity of these self-proclaimed "artists" knew no bounds.

Their only religiously oriented "artworks" were scurrilous attacks on the Catholic Church and blasphemous insults on the deity of Jesus Christ. It was hard to decide what was more shameful, the "art" itself or the effrontery to ask those most offended by it to help pay for it.

In that crowd of decadent people there was a militant disdain for the moral and religious sensibilities of the majority of the American people. The artists, to quote a phrase, "laughed all the way to the bank"—with the taxpayers' money.

I received thousands of letters, telegrams, telephone calls, and petitions from citizens all over this country who were outraged that their tax money had been used to subsidize the poisoning of the very moral foundations of America. As the battle raged on in the Congress, the American people became sick of it. They deluged their Senators with letters demanding an end to the funding. They were not fooled by watered-down bills that provided no real relief.

Those good voices helped to drown out the hoots and jeers that my stand aroused from my critics. I heard from the "art lovers," too. One memorable letter came from a woman in San Francisco who let me know she hated me and everything I stood for. She said the mere sight of my picture in the paper or on the news made her throw up. I wrote back and said, "Dear lady, you may be on to something. The next time that happens, put a frame around it and send it to the NEA. They will probably send you $5,000."

One Senator on the other side of this issue was heard boasting on the Senate floor just two weeks before my election in 1990 that he had personally taken to North Carolina $1 million he had collected from artists in support of my opponent in that race.

The Senator also went back for the election-night victory party that November. But I had to tell him that I must have missed him, because I did not see him at *our* victory party. Apparently he went to the wrong place. Ironically, he managed to ignore the fact that his ability to raise that million proved that these particular "artists" didn't seem to be in need of a government grant. They had plenty of money to spare!

It was a long battle. Amendments got ground up in conference reports and misunderstandings of what the courts would support. I was determined to bring the issue up for as long as it took to make this situation right. I was confident that if we put it to a referendum of the American people, it would be about ninety to one *against* using their money for this purpose.

I told my colleagues the issue was simple. If they believed that the NEA should continue to fund works such as the Mapplethorpe photos they had seen (and I cannot even begin to describe those photos), then they should vote against my amendment. I reminded them that the photos were so bad that the very newspapers that were so critical of me, and others who stood up on this issue, did not dare publish even one.

Oh, they would publish Mapplethorpe's self-portrait, or they might publish a picture of a rose. But they did not publish a picture of that naked guy with a bullwhip protruding from his posterior, or the other Mapplethorpe trash the American people had been required to subsidize and reward. If they believed the NEA should continue to waste the taxpayers' money like that, then I encouraged the Senators to vote against the Helms legislation.

On the other hand, I suggested that those Senators who happened to believe that the National Endowment for the Arts should not be allowed to use the taxpayers' dollars to fund rotten material, such as works by Mapplethorpe and others "that depict or describe in a patently offensive way, sexual or excretory activities or organs," would want to vote *for* my amendment.

America was caught up in a struggle between those who supported values rooted in traditional morality and those who would discard those values in favor of radical moral "relativism."

For my part, I focused on the federal government's role in supporting the moral relativists to the detriment of the religious community. I confess that I was shocked and outraged, as the battle went on year after year, when I learned that, instead of heeding the public outcry, the federal government *had* funded an "artist" who had put a crucifix in a bottle of *his* urine, photographed it, and given it the mocking title *Piss Christ*.

The photographer obviously went out of his way to insult the Christian community, and that insult was compounded by the fact that Christian taxpayers had been forced, by their own government officials, to pay for it.

The controversy over Andres Serrano's so-called "art" had hardly begun when it was disclosed that the National Endowment for the Arts had also paid a Pennsylvania gallery to assemble an exhibition of Robert Mapplethorpe photographs that included photos of men engaged in sexual or excretory acts.

Another exhibit also included photos of nude children. A concerned borough president in New York City sent me a copy of an NEA-supported publication in New York, *Nueva Luz*, which featured photos of nude children in various poses with nude adults, men with young girls, and young boys with adult women.

All of those "works of art" were offensive to the *majority* of Americans (who are decent, moral people). Moreover, as any student of history knows, such gratuitous insults to the religious and moral sensibilities of fellow citizens lead to an erosion of civil comity and democratic tolerance within a society. Therefore, funding such insults with tax dollars surely was anathema to any pluralistic society.

There was no way I could let this matter drop—not in 1989, not in 1990, not in 1991, not in 1992.

One of the most stubborn defenders of the government's policy of mindless funding was Congressman Sidney Yates of Illinois. Mr. Yates was considered the NEA's best friend on Capitol Hill, and he wielded power as the Chairman of the House appropriations subcommittee responsible for NEA funding.

Congressman Yates got a lot of mileage out of his stonewalling. He could count on a standing ovation at any black-tie dinner with the arts crowd because he was their hero. He had defeated Helms, you see. Big deal. He did *not* defeat Helms. He defeated the vast majority of the American people, who were disgusted with giving their money to artists who promoted their unorthodox lifestyles insidiously and deliberately, who desecrated crucifixes by immersing them in urine, and others who engaged in whatever perversion it took to win acclaim as an artist on the "offending edge."

I sent a public message to the Congressman from the floor of the Senate. Old Helms had been beat before. But old Helms did not quit. If the Senate did not approve the amendment when it was before them the first or second or third time, or whatever number it rose to, the Senate would vote on it again and again, on bill after bill, month after month, year after year, until government subsidies for "artistic" perversion were prohibited once and for all.

No artist, no citizen, has a right to demand that the taxpayers subsidize his "artistic" endeavors. Period.

On June 25, 1998, the United States Supreme Court issued its decision in the matter of *NEA v. Finley.* In an eight-to-one decision, they ruled that the NEA could indeed follow Congressional directives that set standards of decency as a criteria for the federal funding of art. The plaintiff in the case, which took nearly a decade to wind its way through the courts, was Karen Finley, a performing artist who used her original NEA grant in the late 1980s to stage performances in which she covered herself with chocolate and chanted the phrase "God is death."

Following the original action of Congress to at least go on record against such funding, Ms. Finley applied for grants that she was certain would be rejected because of their obscene content. When they were rejected, she initiated her suit.

It might seem that I would feel vindicated by the Court's decision, but I was not. My vindication came from the people who mattered most—the citizens who thanked me for taking up their cause and going to battle against forces that seem intent on tearing down what millions of Americans and their parents and grandparents before them had worked so hard to strengthen and protect.

AIDS IN AFRICA

My concern about the worldwide AIDS epidemic began in the early days of my fifth and final term as a United States Senator. Until then, it had been my feeling that AIDS was a disease largely spread by reckless and voluntary sexual and drug-abusing behavior, and that it would probably be confined to those in high-risk populations. I was wrong.

There was a young man named Ryan White who contracted and died of AIDS as a result of having been administered tainted blood during a routine blood transfusion. That made clear the enormity of the problem, and it was a tragic case.

A bill approved in the United States Senate in 1990 called for a large appropriation designated for AIDS research. I voted against the proposal—not because I opposed AIDS research, but because I felt the sum allocated was out of proportion to money allocated for research on diabetes, cancer, heart disease, and other maladies that affected greater numbers of citizens.

Activists in the homosexual community, joined by Ryan White's mother, attacked me as being against the proposal because it would benefit homosexuals. The media joined in. Demonstrators came to my home in Arlington, Virginia, and draped a huge condom over the roof of my house in protest. My wife and I were out of town at the time, but neighbors and police took care of the problem.

Fortunately, in this country, contracting AIDS from tainted blood is no longer the threat it was.

By the end of the year 2003, one in five adults in southern Africa was living with HIV/AIDS. There were 3 million new infections in that region during that year and 2.3 million deaths. In South Africa alone, more than 5.3 million people were HIV positive in 2002. In Swaziland and Botswana an estimated 39 percent of each country's population was already infected.

Among these tragic statistics are the most helpless of victims, babies and children. In 2002 alone, more than half a million babies in the developing world contracted from their mothers the virus that causes AIDS, despite the fact that drugs and therapies exist that could have virtually eliminated mother-to-child transmission of the killer disease.

Contrast these statistics with the United States, where in 2001 the total number of new cases of HIV/AIDS in children was 175—and this number continues to drop each year with improved care and treatment options for pregnant women and children.

America first became aware of AIDS in the early 1980s, when the virus was isolated by researchers and was identified as the cause of illnesses and deaths that were centered in the gay communities of San Francisco and New York City. Additional cases contracted from blood transfusions and other causes, including the use of dirty needles by drug users, pushed the occurrence of the disease beyond the original population group.

Widespread publicity and legitimate concern fueled the public's attention to this illness, sometimes overcoming legitimate fact with emotion. Lost in the emotion was the clear fact that in the United States, growth in the spread of AIDS could be almost completely arrested by changes in behavior, "responsible" sexual behavior—even "responsible" drug use and care. Avoiding risky behaviors of many kinds would make a difference, and it did.

So, too, did the development of drug regimens that could reduce symptoms and prolong life. The numbers speak for themselves. Americans responded vigorously to the threat of AIDS, and the impact of changed behaviors, better health management, and new medications have made a difference, even while the search for a cure or a preventive vaccine goes on in our research labs, both publicly supported and privately funded.

Elsewhere in the world, unnoticed by most and too often unacknowledged or underreported by governments—particularly in the developing nations— the situation has been dramatically different. In these places, where people are least able to cope with medical challenges, AIDS has been allowed to rampage through entire villages and cross borders with the force of an invading army.

My own understanding of the issue and my now strong support of efforts to combat the epidemic were made possible by the concern of leaders who cared enough to see the scope of the problem and refused to rest until effective help could be given. Franklin Graham, a son of my close and dear friend Billy Graham and a close friend in his own right, is one of those people. The relief organization he heads, Samaritan's Purse, has worked in Africa for decades, providing food, shelter, and medical care to those displaced by wars and famines. Staff and volunteers saw for themselves the impact of AIDS and recognized its threat as no less dangerous than famine or war. Infants and children were being lost, as were their mothers and fathers.

Likewise, Bono, the lead singer of the well-known rock group U2, became deeply concerned about the rising death toll in Africa and began a public campaign to seek help. In 2001, I was asked if I would meet with Bono, and I agreed. I will never forget Bono's compassion.

We met for the first time in my office. I had never heard of him, but my younger staff members had. They quickly educated me. They lined up to have their pictures taken with Bono, and they were delighted to see the two of us together. Since that first meeting, Bono and my wife and I have become friends. We correspond from time to time. Dot and I were guests at two dinners hosted by Bono in Washington, D.C. To this day our grandchildren are very envious.

Bono—an enormously impressive gentleman—met with me formally on June 13, 2001. I was genuinely impressed by the sincerity and concern of this remarkable young man. It was clear that his interest in raising awareness of the needs he had seen in Africa came from his heart and not from any desire for self-promotion.

Along with fellow Senators Bill Frist, Barbara Boxer, Orrin Hatch, Rick Santorum, and Patrick Leahy, we had a long and meaningful conversation. Out of that meeting, and with our ongoing contacts, I was able to provide some assistance in arranging fact-finding trips for government officials.

In early 2002, Senator Frist led a trip, and in late 2002, then–Treasury Secretary Paul O'Neill led a ten-day four-nation tour in the sub-Sahara region. Both of those trips resulted in important policy changes and a greater understanding of the depth of the problems.

At a press conference after our first lunch, Bono joked to reporters that he and I meeting together was "bad for both of our images." Then he explained, as I did, that the need to help people who cannot help themselves transcends any perceived divide.

It was in that spirit that I happily accepted Bono's invitation to take my family to his U2 concert in Washington, D.C., that week. While I may not have been as "into" the music as my grandchildren were that evening, I *was* very much in sync with the band's desire to use their public platform on behalf of people in desperate need.

In March 2002, Senator Frist and I offered an amendment (to the Senate emergency supplemental appropriations bill) to add $500 million—contingent on dollar-for-dollar contributions from the private sector—to the U.S. Agency for International Development's programs to fight the HIV/AIDS pandemic. The goal of that new funding was to make treatment available for *every* HIV-positive pregnant woman. Based on all we had learned, Senator Frist and I believed there was no reason why we could not eliminate, or nearly eliminate, mother-to-child transmission of HIV/AIDS—just as polio was virtually eliminated forty years ago.

Drugs and therapies are already provided to some in Africa and other afflicted areas. Many more resources are needed to expand this most humanitarian of projects, at a time when the stakes could not be higher. In many African nations, an entire generation has already been lost to AIDS. Mother-to-child transmission of HIV could eliminate another.

Although reliable numbers are hard to come by, experts believe that more than two million pregnant women in sub-Saharan Africa already have HIV. Of these, nearly one-third will pass the virus on to their babies through labor, childbirth, or breast-feeding, making mother-to-child transmission of AIDS the number one world killer of children under ten. The number of deaths is tragic in both numbers and future consequences, as millions of children have become orphans.

There are obstacles to achieving universal availability of drugs and therapies. Many African nations lack the infrastructure and trained personnel to deliver health care on this scale. Moreover, some governments have not been cooperative.

The goal of our amendment was to provide the Bush administration with the flexibility to deliver the necessary assistance while addressing the obstacles. For instance, if the new Global Fund to Fight AIDS, Tuberculosis, and Malaria were deemed the most efficient way to deliver assistance, the President could then transfer money there. The United Nations has already set an ambitious goal of reducing the number of infants infected with HIV by 20 percent by 2005—and by 50 percent by 2010. We must accelerate these efforts, thereby saving hundreds of thousands of lives through a larger investment of public and private funds.

Private contributions, either financial or in-kind—such as GlaxoSmith-Kline's significant investments to open new HIV/AIDS clinics in Uganda, Malawi, South Africa, and Zambia and provide drugs at cost to these governments—are an essential part of a successful anti-AIDS strategy.

In addition, a national commitment is absolutely essential. The government of Uganda serves as an example of the impact that can be made. Through the leadership of that nation's first lady, Janet Museveni, Uganda has cut its HIV infection rate in half.

In February 2002, I said publicly that I was ashamed that I had not done more concerning the world's AIDS pandemic. I made this admission at a conference organized by Samaritan's Purse. This is the finest humanitarian organization imaginable. Indeed, it is their example of hope and caring for the world's most unfortunate that has inspired action by so many.

Samaritan's Purse was founded in 1970 by the late Dr. Bob Pierce. Dr. Pierce often described his mission this way: "Let my heart be broken with the things that break the heart of God." Today, I know of no more heartbreaking tragedy in the world than the loss of so many young people to a virus that could be stopped—if we simply provided more resources.

Some may say that, despite the urgent humanitarian nature of the AIDS pandemic, my involvement is not consistent with some of my earlier positions. I have indeed always been an advocate of a very limited government, particularly concerning overseas commitments.

Thomas Jefferson once wrote eloquently of a belief to which I have subscribed since I first read it: "I hope our wisdom will grow with our power, and teach us, that the less we use our power the greater it will be."

The United States has become, economically and militarily, the world's greatest power. I hope that we have also become the world's *wisest* power, and that our wisdom will show us how to use that power in the most judicious manner possible. We have a responsibility to those on this earth to exercise great restraint. But not all laws are *of* this earth. We have a higher calling; in the end our conscience is answerable to God.

Perhaps, in my eighties, I may be too mindful of my soon meeting Him, but I know that, like the Samaritan traveling from Jerusalem to Jericho, we *cannot* turn away when we see our fellow man in need.

I may have been late in seeing this need, but now that I have seen it, I feel committed to working as hard as I can to bring as many resources as possible to the resolution of the problem.

The amendment passed in 2002 was a start. The Bush plan presented in 2003 was indeed a step forward, as were the fund-raising efforts on the part of former President Bill Clinton and others. The ongoing work of agencies of the United Nations help, as do the ministries of international organizations like Samaritan's Purse and others.

The cooperation of national governments is indeed crucial, as is the involvement of business entities like the pharmaceutical companies. The influence of opinion-shapers like Bono and the comedian and actor Chris Tucker is invaluable.

But among all of these efforts, the ones that I believe will have the most impact are the ones that are least likely to be noticed—those that will finally turn the tide in this battle. One example of the kind of aid that will do far more than even the best of our other programs is the aid provided by a young church congregation in Charlotte, North Carolina, that has organized an HIV/AIDS ministry in the African community of Kapululwe in Zambia.

These people are working to sponsor five hundred AIDS orphans and other children struck by the disease. Working through World Vision, the congregation is organizing trips to Kapululwe where they work personally with the children and assist their "adopted" community by building a school and getting involved in other much-needed projects.

This is how we will stop the pandemic once and for all. Instead of being overcome by this evil, we can overcome it with good.

SCHOOL PRAYER

The late philosopher and theologian Francis Schaeffer spoke eloquently and wisely of the dangers of the "slippery slope" of morality. He would not have been the least bit surprised to read in 2003 about teachers in California who chose to rewrite one of the most popular patriotic songs of our time rather than risk having the children in their public school choir sing these words: "God Bless the USA."

It took an organized and public protest by the parents of these students to force the school to leave Lee Greenwood's words the way he wrote them—and sing the song expressing how they felt, even though it meant that God would be prominent in their musical performance.

Inane situations similar to that have turned up all over America in the years since simple oral prayer was shoved out of the schoolhouse. It was in an effort to keep an almost immeasurable minority from pretended discomfort that the Supreme Court made its own law. Their activism helped create a climate where obscenities are common in conversation, but the mention of God can lead to all sorts of problems ranging from failing grades on essays to the dismissal of dedicated teachers.

We are prompted to inquire which came first, the wholesale breakdown of moral values in our society or the collapse of these values in the schools?

What has been responsible for the explosion of behaviors that reject and denigrate the values and discipline and moral standards that the American people have respected and preserved throughout our history, honoring traditions and beliefs their families held for thousands of years?

Could the banishment of prayer and Bible reading from the public schools by order of the Supreme Court have had something to do with it? I think the answer is clear.

In 1962, the Court held in *Engel v. Vitale* that the constitutional prohibition against governmental establishment of religion was violated by the recital of a nondenominational prayer at the beginning of each public school day. This same prayer, we should note, was written by Americans trying to preserve the *right* to pray. They took great care in the wording, in order to meet the nonsectarian standards demanded by the representatives of the so-called American Civil Liberties Union.

So it wasn't the "official" prayer that this group and their partisans on the bench were opposing—it was prayer, *period*. Promptly after this decision came the proscriptions of Bible readings, the observance of Christmas as a religious holiday, and the singing of "God Bless America."

With that ruling, we forfeited by judicial fiat the rights of millions of American schoolchildren to invoke the blessing of God on their work. We took away from children a right that we celebrate with the opening of each session of both the U.S. Senate and the U.S. House. We took away from children a right that adults take for granted: the freedom to pray together.

A handful of determined atheists and agnostics, in collaboration with a handful of pharisees on the Supreme Court, succeeded in their great aim to use the power of the law to eradicate all mention of God and His Word in every public school classroom in America.

All this was accomplished in the name of civil liberties when a greater crime against our children could hardly be conceived. Can you imagine the injustice of forbidding a child to speak of—or to—their Creator, to ask a blessing over their meal, to wear a shirt with a Bible verse on it, or to be able to pray for comfort for the family of a fellow student dealing with a tragedy?

Not long ago, a young student in a South Carolina school died following a sudden illness. In his note to parents alerting them to the loss of their child's classmate, the principal could not even *ask* that these families pray *at home* for the distraught parents who had lost a child. Instead he suggested that they be "kept in their thoughts." This is the bitter fruit of the new civil right enunciated by our highest court: freedom from religion. We are raising children before whom we dare not model a dependence on the Almighty for fear that a law will be violated.

In this case, as in so many others, the Court forced from the Constitution exactly the opposite conclusion from what the Founding Fathers intended. It obviously escaped the Court's notice that this entire nation was colonized by individuals who were *seeking* free expression of their religious beliefs. The United States Constitution prohibited the establishment of a religion by the Congress so that the right of freedom of religion *could never be threatened*.

Anyone with good sense understands the great difference between freedom of religion, which is what our Founders intended, and the freedom *from* religion now impeding the legitimate right of an American to exercise his or her religion without governmental limits.

It is hardly coincidence that banishing the Lord from the public schools has resulted in the schools being taken over by a totally secularist philosophy. Christianity has been driven out. In its place has been enshrined a sort of permissiveness in which the drug culture has flourished, as have pornography, crime, and fornication—in short, everything but disciplined learning.

I think there is no more pressing duty facing the Congress than to restore the true spirit of the First Amendment. And that is why I began working, in 1979, to have a corrective law passed; that is why I worked until my retirement on behalf of legislation to permit the recitation of voluntary, nondenominational prayers in the public schools. That is why I continue to encourage the Congress to do the right thing. I am now retired, but as long as I can voice my feelings about it, this is an issue about which they can expect to hear from me!

Fortunately, our Constitution provides a solution to misguided judicial action under the system of checks and balances. In anticipation of judicial usurpations of power, the framers of our Constitution wisely gave the Congress the authority, by a simple majority of both Houses, to restrain the Supreme Court by means of regulation of its appellate jurisdiction. Section II of article III states, in clear and unequivocal language, that the appellate jurisdiction of the Court is subject to "such Exceptions, and under such Regulations as the Congress shall make."

A school prayer law that simply states that the federal courts shall not have jurisdiction to enter any judgment, decree, or order denying or restricting as unconstitutional voluntary prayer in any public school would restore children's rights.

Implicit in such a law would be the understanding that the American citizen will have recourse to a judicial settlement of his rights, but this settlement will be made in the state courts of this nation—not in the federal courts. It was in the state courts that our religious freedoms were carefully safeguarded for 173 years—until they were nationalized by the Supreme Court.

The limited and specific objective of the law I encourage would be to restore to the American people their fundamental right of voluntary prayer in the public schools. I stress the word *voluntary*. No individual should be forced to participate in a religious exercise that is contrary to his or her religious convictions, and the bill recognizes this important freedom. At the same time, we should promote the free exercise of religion by allowing those who wish to recite prayers (and they are the vast majority of our citizens) to do so, with or without the blessings of the government.

When I was in the United States Senate, there were countless occasions when I knew I could not rely on my own wisdom to decide how to proceed in a certain situation or how to cast a vote. I was free to slip away from the Senate floor and pray for the guidance I needed.

Every Senator has this freedom, and believe me, it is one on which all of them rely at some point. We know this freedom is precious, and yet we have allowed it to be taken from our children.

I think the conclusion is inescapable that in the *Engel* decision the Supreme Court in effect gave preference to a minuscule group of dissenters and, at the same time, violated the establishment clause of the First Amendment by in effect establishing a religion—the religion of secularism.

We must face up to the fact that public school children are a captive audience. They are compelled to attend school. Their right to the free exercise of religion should not be suspended while they are in attendance. The language of the First Amendment assumes that this basic freedom should be in force at all times and in all places.

Every year at election time the American people are subjected to a lot of pious talk about how government must be made responsive to the needs and wishes of the people. I myself have a small mountain of correspondence, along with reams of petitions, attesting that the American people *want* the restoration of voluntary prayer to the schools.

But to this day it remains an uphill battle to convince a majority of my former colleagues of their obligation to rectify the inequity perpetrated by the Supreme Court. I have been reminding them for years—and I intend to go on reminding them until the free exercise of religion is restored to its full constitutional status.

In 1999, following the tragedy at Columbine High School, the Senate passed, 85 to 13, an amendment to the juvenile justice bill that would have allowed the reading of Scripture and prayers, and the playing of religious music at memorial services held at public schools. It would also have allowed memorials that contained religious symbols to be erected at schools in honor of slain persons if that was the will of the students.

How tragic it is for all of us that it takes a shocking loss for us to recognize the rightful place of the Almighty in our schools and in our daily lives.

Over the years my focus on the issue of prayer in schools was described with harsh rhetoric as extreme, worthless, and insignificant. But I am convinced that we must not neglect the religious and spiritual values in America. We *must* be reminded of what our nation's first President acknowledged (and what so many in Congress have disregarded)—that America's material and spiritual wealth is bestowed by the Creator only when we seek His guidance in our nation's affairs. George Washington said, "The propitious smiles of heaven can never be expected on a nation that disregards the eternal rules of order and right which Heaven itself has ordained."

We have delayed too long in restoring the right of our children to seek the external rules of order and right.* I am not being flippant when I say it is my prayer that, one day soon, our children will again be allowed to turn their faces to their Maker and seek both guidance and comfort *whenever* they wish.

THE RIGHT TO LIFE

We hold these truths to be self-evident, that all men are created equal, that they are endowed by their Creator with certain unalienable Rights, that among these are Life, Liberty and the pursuit of Happiness.

For almost two hundred years our great nation held these words from our Declaration of Independence to be exactly what the Declaration proclaimed they were—*truths*. But in 1973 the Supreme Court, with its infamous *Roe v. Wade*

---

* In 1995, Dr. Norman Geisler, President of Southeastern Evangelical Seminary, wrote to *The Charlotte Observer* to provide "10 Reasons for Voluntary Prayer." They are worth remembering, and are included as Appendix 1.

case, declared that Americans were endowed with the right to life—only if it suited their mothers.

The Supreme Court's sweeping decision has often been compared to the foolish *Dred Scott* decision of earlier years that denied the right of freedom to people whose masters called them "property." As despicable as that decision was, the cost in lost human life did not compare to the loss we sustain right now—day after day and year after year.

In the thirty years since the U.S. Supreme Court legalized abortion, more than 40 million children have been denied their first breaths. They were denied *their rights*, both to liberty and to the pursuit of happiness, as surely as they lost their right to live. Who knows how many of these lost humans might have been research scientists or great artists? Which of them might have been educators or inventors? We will never know what greatness was lost.

We do know that the legalization of abortion inevitably led to the devaluation of human life, especially the lives of those who are not considered "productive."

In the late 1990s, one of America's most respected universities welcomed to its faculty an ethicist who believes that the disabled and the unwanted should be euthanized. This ethicist rationalizes that parents should be given a month to decide the worthiness of their newborns and have the freedom to discard those who do not meet their standards. This ethicist further argues that parents who choose infanticide for a "defective child" and then have a healthy child will have more happiness as a result of their choices, and therefore have somehow taken the moral path. Likewise, he sees *involuntary euthanasia* for those who have become a "burden to our society" as a similarly moral act.

When such patent nonsense is even given voice and therefore allowed to influence thought, the need to protect life is all the more urgent. That is precisely why, in session after session of the United States Senate, I introduced a bill to provide for the rights of unborn children. Critics often sneered that my bill had no possibility of passing, but I simply could not remain silent. I will never be silent about the death of those who cannot speak for themselves.*

If ever there was a time to remember the warning that those who cannot remember the past are condemned to repeat it, this is it. Sixty years ago, millions of European Jews and others died at the hands of Hitler's Nazis. Today many forget that horror—and the lesson that *all* human life is sacred.

---

* The provisions of the Unborn Children's Civil Rights Act can be found in Appendix 2.

I and others have been criticized for comparing the scourge of abortions with the Holocaust, but I reject such criticism because this is indeed another kind of holocaust, by another name. Killing unborn babies has become a tool of convenience in today's permissive society. At latest count, more than 40 million unborn children have been deliberately, intentionally destroyed. What word adequately defines the scope of such slaughter?

Roe v. Wade has no foundation whatsoever in the text or history of the Constitution. It was a callous invention. Mr. Justice White said it best in his dissent: Roe was "an exercise in raw judicial power."

Why has this Supreme Court exercise in "raw judicial power" been allowed to stand? More importantly, perhaps, why have *we* stood idly by for more than thirty years while thousands of unborn babies are disposed of every day as a result of "legalized" abortion?

The answer is simple. Even though *Roe v. Wade* was and is an unconstitutional decision, Congress has been unwilling to exercise its powers to check and balance a Supreme Court that ended the lives of the most defenseless and most innocent humanity imaginable.

In 1998, Karen Garver Santorum, wife of Senator Rick Santorum, published *Letters to Gabriel*, a moving book based on the journal she kept as she carried Gabriel Michael Santorum in her womb. In its pages, Karen recounts the family's joy in expecting Gabriel's arrival and their great sadness when a medical condition took his life before his birth. No one who reads this book could fail to understand the value of human life, born and unborn. A copy of this book was given to every member of the United States Senate, with the hope that as they read, their hearts would be softened.

As we launch out into a new century, *Roe v. Wade* still stands and the holocaust continues. It is *not* a failure of the Constitution. It is a failure of the Supreme Court—but, more importantly, it is the failure of Congress to do its duty, to overturn *Roe v. Wade*.

While legalized abortion remains a blot on our country's honor, there *are* small victories that will save some innocent lives. In 2003, Congress passed, and President Bush signed, the Partial Birth Abortion Ban Act. At the signing ceremony, the President said that protecting innocent new life from a sudden and violent end reflects the compassion and humanity of America. He said, and I agree, "The most basic duty of government is to defend the life of the innocent."

The latest advances in medicine are also working in favor of the unborn. We now know that "viability" begins much earlier in a pregnancy than previously thought, and 4-D imaging in ultrasound allows the mother to see the form, unique character, and even the movements of her unborn child. Nobody can see these intimate images of little ones sucking their thumbs or blinking their eyes and buy the lie that this child is less than human simply because it is inside the womb.

More important, women *are* speaking out. The woman at the very center of *Roe v. Wade*, Norma McCorvey, also known as "Jane Roe," whose protest of Texas's abortion ban led to the 1973 ruling, had a dramatic change of heart in the mid-1990s. She now leads a ministry where women in the situation she faced find positive alternatives to aborting their babies. In early 2005, she even filed a petition with the Supreme Court requesting that the case be heard again in light of evidence that the procedure may harm women.

This is a far cry from the actions of the liberal feminists who often confronted me in the 1970s and 1980s. I recall one such encounter in which a woman challenged me with the question "How can you support capital punishment when you are so pro-life?" To which I immediately replied, "I will wholeheartedly support capital punishment for any fetus who commits a capital crime!"

The rate of abortion is on a slight decline, but we cannot rest while any child, anywhere, is considered disposable. Just as the Congress, with the urging of Senator Santorum and others, persevered to pass the Partial Birth Abortion Ban Act, it must be alert and active to all assaults on the unborn. As the representatives of all the people, Congress must use every opportunity to assure that government money and government facilities are not used for the practice of abortion—or going to entities that promote it in any way. Individual Senators must act on their personal convictions about human rights—instead of giving in to anybody's party line.

The late Robert Casey, who was Governor of Pennsylvania and a vocal pro-life advocate despite the Democrats' attempts to keep him off their stage at their national conventions, took the long view of the battle for the rights of the unborn. Governor Casey said the real issue in deciding the fate of the unborn child is not when *life* begins but when *love* begins, and he added,

> I believe abortion is destined for the scrap heap of history. Abortion is being held aloft by the hot air of a small well-heeled elite. It's on the artificial life support system of foundation money, politically correct elite opinion, special interests, media bias and widespread ignorance of the

facts. . . . Legal abortion will never rest easy on this nation's conscience. It will continue to haunt the consciences of men and women everywhere.

The truth of these words—spoken more than a decade ago—is borne out in today's debate. There is *no* middle ground. As a nation, we came to an understanding that slavery was wrong, and we outlawed its practice. As a nation, we knew that we could not ignore the murderous philosophy of the Third Reich, and we went into battle.

And, as a nation, we know that every abortion ends the life of a human being—a child who became vulnerable and unprotected in what was once the safest place in all creation.

One day we will put an end to abortion and reclaim our role as a nation where the right to life, liberty, and the pursuit of happiness is not an empty slogan from an outdated document that far too many Americans have forgotten—or never knew in the first place.

CHAPTER 23

Race Relations

MUCH HAS BEEN WRITTEN over the years about things I supposedly have said or how I supposedly feel about race relations. The people who know me best know the truth about how I feel—and that has always been good enough for me. However, it would leave a gap in this book if I did not set the facts straight. It would be wrong for those who have deliberately or carelessly misrepresented me, including Bill Clinton in *his* memoir, to equate my previous refusal to dignify their remarks by refuting them as somehow giving credence to their inaccurate opinions.

Earlier, when I reminisced about my childhood, I recounted a story about the time, as a small boy, I had used the "N" word to refer to a playmate who had made me angry, and the immediate rebuke my father had given me for using that word. From that day to this one, I have never used the word again. My father left an indelible impression on me, teaching me that every one of God's children deserved my respect—and he was going to make sure I gave it!

That was the way he operated, and his influence in the community was as effective as it was at home. He did not support the rise of the KKK in our community, and he did not tolerate lawless activities like cross burnings or worse. Jesse A. Helms Sr. believed in fairness and in judging people by their character, not the color of their skin.

His example registered with me. I did not advocate segregation, and I did not advocate aggravation. By that I mean that I thought it was wrong for people who did not know, and who did not care, about the relationships between neighbors and friends to force their ideas about how communities should work on the people who had built those communities in the first place. I believed right would prevail as people followed their consciences.

When I was in a position to hire the staff at WRAL-TV in the early 1960s, the records will show that our organization had many women and minorities in responsible positions.* I have always counted many blacks among my friends and believe that friendship was returned. We did not always agree about matters like demonstrations and the heavy-handed involvement of the government in shaping social policy—because I believe those things slow true progress rather than help it. We did agree, however, that we are all people, made in the image of God and worthy of mutual respect.

During the turbulent times in the civil rights struggle, people from outside the South totally misunderstood the nature and intent of many Southerners. They thought opposition to the proposed laws meant hostility toward blacks. That simply was not true.

Many good people who supported the principle of progress for everyone could not agree to the destruction of one citizen's freedom in order to convey questionable "rights" to another. They believed forced social engineering was hazardous to the freedom we all deserve.

When a young South Carolinian by the name of Harvey Gantt entered Clemson University, I took note on the air at WRAL-TV of the dignified and positive way in which he handled his status as the first black American student on that campus. Mr. Gantt's dream was to become an architect, and he wanted to go to the best school in that field that he could find close to home. He didn't arrive with a throng of demonstrators, and he proved his point in the best way possible, by doing well then and in the years that followed. As he began his college years, neither of us could have imagined how our paths would converge decades later.

In the 1960s, a long campaign of ridicule and distortion was aimed at the Southern way of life. It ripped away at the customs and institutions people cared about. Black neighbors and white neighbors depended on each other, and the vast majority lived in harmony. But those stories seldom reached the news media because they didn't promote the image of oppression and misery the media chose to favor.

* See Appendix 3.

Were there problems in need of solution? Of course there were, but wicked behavior is color-blind, and neither race had a corner on its existence. Nor was such behavior as confined to the South as the news of the day would have liked us to think.

It was only after the laws enacted to force Southern schools to change were also applied to Northern systems that America saw the hypocrisy of pointing a self-righteous finger at the South.

It was one thing to work for the advancement of citizens throughout the nation; it was quite another to make of this a political issue and create difficult situations that fostered hatred and bigotry by polarizing the very people who most needed to work together for the good of their communities.

I felt that the citizens of my community, my state, and my region of the country were being battered by this new form of bigotry. I simply could not stay silent in the face of this assault—and I didn't.

It has always been my belief that people of goodwill on all sides of an issue can resolve their differences without the intervention of the government. We will never know how integration might have been achieved in neighborhoods across our land, because the opportunity was snatched away by outside agitators who had their own agendas to advance. We certainly do know the price paid by the stirring of hatred, the encouragement of violence, the suspicion and distrust. We do know that too many lives were lost, businesses were destroyed, millions of dollars were diverted from books and teachers to support the cost of buses and gasoline. We do know that turning our public schools into social laboratories almost destroyed them.

The billions being spent today to improve the quality of education for all of our children are our payment on a bill that we created decades ago when we diverted the local schools' priorities from their most important purpose.

The same might be said for economic progress. In the late sixties, a gentleman by the name of Reverend Leon Sullivan turned a job-training ministry at his church in Philadelphia into a national organization called OIC (Opportunities Industrialization Center), with branches in ninety cities, reaching more than thirty thousand individuals a year with training in formal education and the skills needed to get and keep jobs.

Estimates at the time indicated that the efforts of OIC in helping people to get off the welfare rolls and into the job force reduced welfare payments by more than $10 million per year. Even more embarrassing to those who demanded big-government programs to solve all of society's ills, the amount spent by OIC in job training was less than one-third, per trainee, of what the federal government was spending at the same time on its programs—and OIC showed far better results.

The Reverend Sullivan was an activist. He fought to uplift people, showing them that their path to a better life was tied to being a part of the "establishment," not in destroying it. Because of his great success in helping people improve their lives, Reverend Sullivan was named to the board of directors at General Motors, the first African-American named to the board of a major U.S. corporation. He brought to that board an important insight on racial understanding that opened untold opportunities for those he referred to as "his people."

It is an irrefutable truth about America that we always have a need for all the industrious, imaginative citizens we can produce—citizens who understand that a brighter tomorrow can be achieved by those who build, never by those who destroy.

Leon Sullivan's career was instructive in a number of ways, not the least of which was that a good many Americans need to get the chips off their shoulders and get to work. If they would merely take the time to look around them, they might just be amazed at the good faith and opportunity that abound everywhere. They need to stop knocking the system long enough to try it.

Unfortunately for America, the voices and examples of leaders like the Reverend Sullivan were muffled as others with much less productive goals pushed their way forward. Too many of these individuals had nothing to offer besides anger, violence, and disruption. Their rhetoric and action plans ruptured relationships. They ridiculed at best, and at worst vilified those who counseled against their radical approach.

Perhaps nothing in my thirty years in the Senate has been more twisted and misunderstood than my stand in opposition to the creation of a federal holiday to honor the Reverend Martin Luther King Jr. My decision was based on the facts, not on personality and certainly not on race.

Dr. King was a masterful orator. His initial commitment to nonviolence was laudable—but Dr. King was not always careful about his associates or his associations. Unfortunately, some of those associates were opposed to all that most Americans revere. When Dr. King was warned about these people and their records, he chose to let them remain in his circle of advisors.

Similarly, Dr. King was drawn into the Vietnam debate and went on record describing his own country as "the greatest purveyor of violence in the world today." At one point he likened this country to Nazi Germany. In an appearance in April 1967 at the Riverside Church in New York City, he delivered a speech that *Time* magazine described as "a demagogic slander that sounded like a script from Radio Hanoi." Columnist Carl Rowan, well known for his own advocacy for the progress of his people, warned that Dr. King "alienated many of the Negro's friends and armed the Negro's foes . . . by creating the impression that the Negro is disloyal."

The effort to squelch this part of Dr. King's history and many other disturbing facts was unprecedented. Steps were taken to seal his FBI files for fifty years. The bill to establish a Martin Luther King holiday was rushed through both houses of the Congress without any of the appropriate committee hearings.

Clearly, most politicians were concerned for *their* images. They did not want to be tarred with the charges of those who were determined to have their way. It was easier to bow to the pressure than to stand up for important principles.

And with all this, I simply could not go along. My remarks on the floor of the Senate on October 3, 1983, sum up why, to this day, I believe we were wrong in establishing this particular holiday.

It gave me no pleasure to state on the record the facts that could be told, nor to warn about the seriousness of the information that could not be released. But it *had* to be done because we were being asked to give our approval to this record through the honor we were being asked to bestow on this one individual. I felt this was wrong and I had to say so. Senator Sam J. Ervin, retired in his home in Morganton, called me at least three times every day to express his anger that such an action was under consideration. His calls meant a great deal when support for my position was in shorter and shorter supply.

Senator Edward Kennedy was among those who angrily brushed aside the record and rushed the vote. It should be noted that these facts were uncovered as the result of investigations ordered by and well known to his brother Robert, who was Attorney General at the time, and his brother John, who while President had counseled his friend Dr. King to separate himself from these agents of overthrow. It wasn't that the facts weren't there, it was that they simply didn't matter to *this* Kennedy.

I have never stated and do not believe that Dr. King was a Communist. I do regret his willingness to include among the advisors for his organization those whose records prove they were Communists. I do believe that those who wanted to advance the laudable goals that Dr. King articulated in his speeches about the future he envisioned for all the citizens of this country would have done well to expend their energies in providing more education, more job training, and more cooperation in building understanding instead of establishing a day off that costs the country many millions in lost productivity each year.

When the vote was taken on my motion to have the files opened and the King holiday bill follow the usual procedures of hearings and proper committee review, it was defeated 76 to 12. My colleagues were much more interested in having the issue go away than they were in making sure it was the right thing to do. More than a few holdout votes were changed when it was decided to have the King holiday fall on the Monday after Super Bowl Sunday, at that time the third Sunday of January—now the bill had something for everyone!

It was not until 1879, eighty years after his death, that George Washington was honored by Congress with a national holiday named in *his* honor—and now renamed Presidents' Day. It took just fifteen years and a massive media effort to shape Dr. King's image (as well as the sealing of records that would have shocked most Americans) to push through the Martin Luther King holiday!

What a shame that the supporters of this holiday were not willing to submit to a full examination of all the facts about Dr. King, so that the worthiness of this honor could have been examined without pressure or prejudice.

How much better it would have been for *all* Americans—especially for those whose ancestors came to this country against their will—to establish a day to honor the history of those generations of people who gave their all, as they worked, as they served in our military, as they built strong families and established communities, and as they embraced for themselves the miracle of America and encouraged their children to pursue their dreams.

In our emphasis on one man who emphasized discontent, we have overlooked the millions of people whose determination to look ahead instead of backward have done so much for us all. These are the people who deserve the parades and the holiday.

Not too long after her swearing-in, Senator Hillary Clinton and I happened to be on the same elevator in our Senate office building. Senator Clinton seemed quite surprised when the elevator operator and I fell into our usual conversation about him and his family.

The Senator, like many others of her political persuasion, still seems to have trouble imagining that people of goodwill can establish friendships out-side their races or creeds or nationalities simply based on what Dr. King called "the content of their character," without the artifice of a public program or a legal mandate.

Sadly, this "tunnel vision" makes it equally difficult for them to understand why the ranks of conservative blacks are growing, in spite of the ridicule heaped on them by the very people who claim to have championed their advancement. But America is a free society, and principled people will stand up for what they believe, no matter what names they may be called.

CHAPTER 24

The 1984 Campaign: Hunt v. Helms

B
Y 1983, THE LIBERALS WERE really eager to get rid of Jesse Helms. The state Democratic Party convinced Governor Jim Hunt to run against me because North Carolina constitutional law barred Governor Hunt from running for a third consecutive term as governor.

Jim Hunt had never lost an election, and it was assumed by all of the "experts" in these matters that he would swamp me if he challenged me for my Senate seat.

To hear the newspapers tell it, I was wasting my time even bothering to run; the polls had me down as a 17-point underdog. *The Washington Post* ran an article a year before the election declaring that "barring an act of God," Jesse Helms could not win—and that the '84 election was effectively all over but the shouting.

But in politics, like in football, you still have to show up and play the game before you can know for sure who the winner will be; so finally I "suited up" and hit the field.

It must be said, though, that I never was enthusiastic about any part of the campaign process when I was the candidate—and I probably grew a little less enthusiastic every time. Privately, after the 1978 campaign I had told my family that I did not intend to run a third time.

But when the time came to make that decision about the 1984 election, leaders in the conservative movement told me my presence in the Senate was essential to continued progress in changing government. I certainly didn't think I was essential—no one really is—but I understood their concern about losing a vocal conservative view in Senate deliberations.

I delayed both my decision and my announcement for as long as I could so that I could concentrate on doing the work, rather than running for the job. Finally, I let my campaign staff go to work and announced my candidacy. The polls indicated that I was well behind on day one!

For many years, the Hunt-Helms race held the record for being the most expensive Senatorial campaign ever run in the United States. That's not something I brag about, it's just a fact of political history, and I was happy to give up the "title" years later, when the record was finally broken by campaigns in California and New Jersey. Ours *was* a hard-fought campaign, that's for sure.

Both Governor Hunt and I were busy raising money all over the country, and I must confess that I, like most Senators, hated it. However, there was one fund-raiser that I am mighty glad I did attend. In late August 1983, I was scheduled to fly to South Korea to commemorate the thirty-year anniversary of our defense treaty.

However, I received a call from my friend Tom Landry, the football coach of the Dallas Cowboys, who said, "I know you have a tough race coming up. I'd like to get some friends together and raise some money for you here in Texas." I asked my schedulers if there was any way I could go to Korea by way of Texas. So instead of flying out of New York on KAL 007, I ended up going to Texas and then picking up its sister flight, which departed from Los Angeles.

Those were the days when you could not fly all the way to Asia nonstop, and both my plane and KAL 007 landed for refueling at Anchorage at the same time. So I got to spend time with my friend Congressman Larry MacDonald and others, who, unbeknownst to us then, would be murdered mere hours later, when the Soviets shot down KAL 007. I met one engaging young family in particular and played a little game with their children that I used to play with my grandchildren.

Needless to say, it was quite a shock to arrive in Seoul and learn of the Communists' treachery—but I was not surprised. The Communists had already killed millions of their own citizens—what did a few more innocents matter anyway? I returned to America more determined than ever to see the Soviets consigned to the dustbin of history. However, first I had a little campaign business with my friend the Governor to take care of.

For my part, after that race I decided that I would never again engage in campaign debates. While Jim Hunt and I had very different views on many issues, we had always been able to work together for the good of North Carolina.

The debates put a strain on our personal friendship, which I am happy to say we were able to repair in succeeding years, but I did not like the combativeness or the structure of the campaign debate format and resolved to avoid it from that point on — which I did.

What passes for debates in our media-driven races nowadays are more like badminton games with preplanned sound bites serving as the shuttlecocks. The core issues of the Hunt-Helms campaign boiled down to my conservative convictions and Governor Hunt's liberal inclinations. The cast and the details may have changed in the six years between my last campaign and this one, but the plot had not.

For my campaign staff's part, I should emphasize that we did all we could both to articulate where we stood *and* to point out the instances where the words and actions of the Governor didn't always match. The Governor's staff was not happy about those fact-checks!

The media set the stage for the campaign by describing it as an epic battle between political heavyweights. An editorial in a June 1983 issue of the *Durham Morning Herald*, titled "Political Gladiators Promise a Slugfest," wasn't even subtle:

> The all-but-certain opponents are U.S. Senator Jesse Helms, the Republican, and Governor Jim Hunt, the Democrat, two men whose political ambitions are insatiable, whose views are irreconcilable and whose strategies should treat us to a joust that will shock and provoke. . . . They are in their corners, teasing us with glares that promise a slugfest. . . . But you ain't seen nothing yet. This is just preliminary sparring to what may be one of the greatest political matches in North Carolina history. Indeed, it is likely to be a fight of national significance. Hurry, ring the bell.

By November 1984, the voters had seen and heard a record number of ads, watched or heard about our four long debates, and had the opportunity to hear from every political analyst in the country. Those we didn't manage to inform we simply wore out.

Our side had three big themes: First, we pointed out the Governor's record of sitting on the fence or appearing to take both sides on an issue so he wouldn't make anybody mad. The ad writers came up with a simple question: "Where do you stand, Jim?"

Next, because it was a Presidential election year, too, we also thought it was important for voters to know that the Governor strongly supported Democratic Presidential candidate Walter Mondale over Ronald Reagan.

Former Vice President Mondale and Governor Hunt agreed on every important issue. This was a major difference between the Governor and me because I could not support the liberal ideas of candidate Mondale—and I didn't believe most North Carolinians could, either. It wasn't as if Governor Hunt was "stuck" with his party's candidate—the Governor had helped him get the nomination.

Governor Hunt chaired the Democratic Presidential Rules Commission that wrote rules favorable to Mondale's candidacy. In December 1983, *The Wilmington Morning Star* declared, "The success of the Hunt Commission is evident in the grip Mondale has on the nomination at this point." The Governor had also been close to the Carter-Mondale administration. Our ads often reminded voters that "Jim Hunt could be considered . . . a Mondale liberal."

The Governor realized that this close association was costing him votes, and he tried to distance himself from the Democratic nominee. He even had the help of the state's liberal news media, which took offense at my saying that the Governor was a "Mondale liberal and ashamed of it; while I'm a Reagan conservative and proud of it." *The Charlotte Observer*'s editor, Richard Oppel, wrote a column saying: "I get tired of Helms saying *I'm a Reagan conservative, Hunt is a Mondale liberal. . . .*" Then this Charlotte editor declared, "Hunt certainly is to the left of Helms, but does anyone truly believe he is politically close to Mondale?" There were at least two people in the state who thought so. One was Joe Pell, a senior member of the Hunt campaign staff, who told the Raleigh *News & Observer* in February 1982 that "[Hunt] is closer to Mondale than any of the names I have seen mentioned about 1984."

The other was Jim Hunt himself. The same month that Joe Pell was positioning Mondale as Hunt's kind of leader, the Governor himself was lending his name and reputation to a fund-raising letter for the Mondale political action committee, saying, "[Mondale] has served us well during his many years in the United States Senate. . . . *You* know his potential for leadership in our nation in the future. . . . Walter Mondale believes as you and I do in the very best for the Democratic Party."

Over the years, there were lots of comments about the so-called "Jessecrats" in eastern North Carolina—and elsewhere in the state. I gained their support because their own political party leadership took so little heed of them when it embraced liberal candidates and liberal policies. I certainly welcomed the support of these disenfranchised Democrats in 1984.

The third major contrast between Jim Hunt and Jesse Helms was our approach to balancing the budget. In 1984, the National Governors Association passed a resolution calling for a tax increase of more than $200 billion to balance the budget. Jim Hunt had voted for the resolution. It was a matter of record. It was even on videotape!

There simply was no way that the state's newspapers could overlook the story. Clearly, Governor Hunt would *not* be heading to Washington in order to help taxpayers keep more of their money for their own use. He, in fact, was *looking* for a way to get a bigger share every payday rather than try to rein in federal spending and close the gap between income and outflow the old-fashioned way.

The Hunt campaign ran ads saying that Jesse Helms was too conservative, and that I was too involved in foreign policy to pay attention to my constituents, and, most outrageously, that somehow I had been responsible for deaths in El Salvador. None of the accusations stuck, because the voters knew me and knew the truth.

When at last Election Day came and went, the Greensboro *News & Record* put the race into proper perspective, saying,

> All too often in this election, the contest has been represented in cosmic proportions—that it was the battle of the century, a quest for the soul of North Carolina, the New South vs. the Old South, and so on. That's all applesauce. This race has always been between two different men—representing different points of view—and now one of them has won the race by a small percentage of the vote. . . . Far too much money was spent and far too much mud was slung. May such a campaign never again take place in this state.

When Jim Hunt once again took his place as Governor of North Carolina following his election in 1992, the two of us again focused on our areas of agreement, on the good of our state and its citizens. We renewed our friendship as well—and I was very pleased when Governor Hunt spoke at the groundbreaking of the Jesse Helms Center's new complex and helped turn the earth on that day. For both of us, it was a reminder that in this great country, and particularly our great state, political rivals can also be personal friends.

CHAPTER 25

George H. W. Bush

M Y FIRST ENCOUNTERS WITH George H. W. Bush were well before
he was Vice President or President. He had a long record of admirable
service as well as a well-deserved reputation as a war hero. I liked him personally, but as a conservative I had differences with his approach to some issues—
from foreign policy to economics. Because of those differences, I was not
supportive of his earliest campaigns for the Presidency or, to be very honest,
when Ron Reagan picked him as his running mate at the 1980 GOP convention. I was concerned, as were many other conservatives, that George Bush
would work at cross-purposes with Ronald Reagan or lessen his opportunity as
President to move forward on goals to put conservative principles into action.

Mr. Bush's well-known criticism of what he called Reagan's "voodoo eco-
nomics" was not easy to ignore—especially since the Democrats had turned it
into a part of their campaign against the Reagan-Bush ticket. There were other
questions on social issues that were important to conservatives, particularly
whether George Bush would support the party's right-to-life plank.

But Ronald Reagan had assured me privately that he thought George Bush
was the right man and that he would not turn out to be another Nelson Rockefeller. And I had a personal meeting of my own with Mr. Bush that gave me the
assurance I needed to get behind the Reagan-Bush ticket without reservation.

That was a decision I have never regretted. George Bush turned out to be
one of the most principled men we've ever had in government. We've had our
differences over individual policy matters and nominations, but by and large,
our alliance grew over the years along with our friendship.

As the Vice President, Mr. Bush could be counted on to keep the Democrats from abusing their majority status in the Senate. I particularly remember a time in February 1987 when Senator Robert Byrd instructed the new parliamentarian not to recognize Senator Phil Gramm or Senator Robert Dole when they asked to be heard. That maneuver was, of course, contrary to the rules, and Senator Byrd, of all people, must have known that. As President of the Senate, Vice President Bush was able to step in and override that instruction so the Republicans could get their business done.

(It gave me a lot of pleasure in May of that same year to discover an old Senate rule that was put into place in 1952, which we could use to prevent Senator Byrd from bringing up a defense authorization bill with an amendment that would have abrogated the Strategic Defense Initiative. Senator Byrd got a "taste of his own medicine," and our maneuver was completely legitimate! Vice President Bush was gentleman enough not to gloat over this GOP parliamentary win.)

During the 1988 Presidential primary season, our party united around George Herbert Walker Bush as our choice for the nomination. Even conservative voters discovered that they did not have much to criticize in the way George Bush had served his nation as Vice President. They were encouraged by the course he planned to follow, especially his commitment to build on the many successes of the Reagan years.

At the convention, any lingering doubts were quieted when the Vice President selected Senator Dan Quayle as his running mate. Those who knew Senator Quayle and his wife, Marilyn, knew they were no chameleons but genuine conservatives who had been supportive of other conservatives in government for many years. Senator Quayle was elected to the U.S. House of Representatives for the first time in 1976 and to the U.S. Senate for the first time in 1980. His record was one of which he and the GOP could be proud.

Because he represented Indiana and was only 41 when Bush selected him, Dan Quayle was not well known outside of the Congress. But among his colleagues, he was well known and admired for his legislative accomplishments. One of his most lasting accomplishments as Senator was the Job Training Partnership Act, which he coauthored with Senator Edward Kennedy.

Senator Quayle believed that putting tax money to work for the purpose of putting people to work made much more sense than fueling an ever-growing welfare system. He put in place a structure that other conservatives were able to build on a decade later when the country was finally ready for more reforms.

The polls showed the Bush-Quayle ticket behind by 15 points at the start of the campaign, but the only poll that counts—the election results—put thirty-eight states in their column. Even Dan Rather had to find the words to compliment Dan Quayle's contribution to the success of the evening.

I had a little surgical repair work done during the campaign season, and my doctor told me to take it easy, but I felt a responsibility to help keep the White House in the right hands, so I did what I could to help get out the vote wherever I was invited. I was always happy to talk about the importance of electing conservatives—to any job they were running for, from President to precinct captain!

Dot and I were delighted to have George and Barbara Bush in the White House. After eight years of such close association, including Barbara and Dot's involvement together in the Senate spouses chapter of the Red Cross, we knew they would serve us well, and they did.

While President Bush certainly had much to recommend him on his own merit, it was also clear that he was confident enough about his own skills to appropriate much of what had worked well in his predecessor's administration. At Ronald Reagan's state funeral in June 2004, President Bush said, "I learned more from Ronald Reagan than anyone I encountered in all my years of public life." That was clear in President Bush's willingness to stand firm on defense and on verifying that the progress we saw in the democratization of the former Soviet states was genuine.

This does not mean that I never had disagreements with President Bush's administration. I have seldom regretted failing to yield my position, but there were occasions when I regretted making the decision to yield for the sake of unity. One such case was the nomination of April Glaspie as Ambassador to Iraq.

April Glaspie was a career employee of the State Department. She began her service there in 1966 and held postings in Kuwait, Syria, and Egypt. She was part of a group inside the State Department known to be supportive of Syria, whose government at that time was not on good terms with Saddam Hussein, the leader of Iraq. This fact was well known to Saddam.

When Ms. Glaspie was nominated in 1989 by the Bush administration for the post of ambassador to Iraq, I made no secret of my disagreement with that choice. My objections were headed by the problem of her sympathy for Syria, but I had other significant objections as well, including her inappropriate experience for this responsibility in such a volatile part of the world and her refusal to call the Palestine Liberation Organization terrorists in spite of ample evidence that they were. Gender was the one issue to which I gave no thought. A man with the same views and lack of relevant experience would have been every bit as unacceptable.

I held up the nomination for as long as I could, hoping that wisdom would prevail and her name would be withdrawn. After six months I received a call saying that the State Department would not relent. I knew I did not have the votes to stop the nomination, so I stood aside. The public record is not entirely clear on the details of a meeting between Ambassador Glaspie and Saddam Hussein in late July 1990, but it would appear that the Ambassador's conversation did not make clear the United States' opposition to Iraq's troop buildup along its border with Kuwait or its threat to take action if Kuwait did not yield to its demands for control of Kuwaiti territory.

Whatever was specifically said in that conversation, the Iraqis came away from it with the impression that the United States would look the other way if they invaded Kuwait. We, of course, did not.

Ambassador Glaspie was quickly recalled from her post and finished out her career with the State Department in posts that were better suited to her, first at the United Nations, later in South Africa. She retired as consul general of Cape Town in 2002.

HAMPERED AS HE WAS by the unrestrained spending of a Democrat-controlled Congress, President Bush found himself boxed into a situation in which he felt he had no choice but to break a promise. I preferred confrontation, but he decided that the only way to pay for the Democrats' profligate habits was with a tax increase.

Instead of admitting their part in causing the problem—or thanking the President for his willingness to help avert a crisis they had created—the Democrats turned the "broken promise" into a major campaign issue in 1992. Their "twist" on the state of the economy, which as a matter of fact was headed for a robust recovery, helped deny George Bush a second term as President.

History will make all too plain what we lost as a nation as a result of that decision. Others will have their opinions about how George Bush, with his understanding of international issues and knowledge of the workings of the intelligence community, might have acted in the face of rising terrorist activities. Others may wonder what our own nation might have been like if we had continued to support uncompromising personal ethics as our standard for accept-able behavior in the most important residence in our nation.

Lesser people may have been bitter over the loss of a reelection that once seemed a certainty, but George and Barbara Bush have always made the choice to look ahead and embrace the new challenges. For President Bush, that has in-cluded skydiving—an interest I have no intention of taking up in my own re-tirement! But it has also included the generous donation of time and influence in encouraging countless good causes like tsunami relief—many of which were first identified as "points of light" during the Bush administration. And it has in-cluded support of the public-service careers of two sons who would make any family immensely proud—Governor Jeb Bush and President George W. Bush —as well as the support of their siblings who are not in the public eye.

Knowing how much I valued my own father's advice throughout my life, I can only imagine how much it must mean to these two current leaders to be able to call the forty-first President of the United States and begin the conversa-tion with "Hello, Dad . . ."

Dorothy Coble was the most beautiful bride I have ever seen.
I still marvel at my good fortune in having her at my side for
all these years and at her ability to become more beautiful
with each passing year.

The gentleman hosting this rare reunion for three local newsmen turned sailors is the legendary publisher of the Raleigh News & Observer *Josephus Daniels. I'm the seaman to the immediate right of Mr. Daniels. Shelley Rolfe is to his left and Ed Rankin is to my right.*

Willis Smith had indicated that he would bow out of a primary runoff against Senator Frank Porter Graham, but the crowd of supporters who came and stood in his yard to urge him to stay in the race finally convinced him to reconsider. I had no other role in the Smith campaign, but I'm proud to say I helped gather that crowd.

The most important service we provided the viewers of WRAL-TV was the
opportunity to learn about both sides of the issues we covered in the news.
We used our on-air editorials to discuss public issues and talk about viable solutions
that wouldn't depend on more taxes and more government intrusion in our lives.

Photos like this one of my parents; my brother, Wriston; my sister, Lib; me; and our
young families are rare indeed. Our lives took us many miles from our home, but, in
fact, we never really left it as long as we held on to the love we knew under that roof.

I was honored when President and Mrs. Nixon came to campaign with us in 1972. The President and I had gotten to know each other when I worked in Washington for Senator Smith.

It is hard to imagine an organization that is more valuable in developing character and leadership than the Boy Scouts of America. It was my privilege to introduce the Boy Scouts of America Equal Access Act to prevent unfair attacks or restrictions on this fine group and its historic values.

Before I visited the Panama Canal Zone for the first time, I was concerned about the prospect of renegotiating our treaty and giving up our control and management of this crucial shipping route. After I visited with other concerned Senators, including Strom Thurmond (right), Stuart Symington (second from left), and Dewey Bartlett (far left), I became convinced that this was and remains a foolish decision.

It was a genuine pleasure to greet Aleksandr Solzhenitsyn during his first visit to the United States Senate. Senator Scoop Jackson (left) hosted a reception in his honor. Senator Joe Biden (right) was an enthusiastic member of our unofficial welcome committee, too.

I made my first visit to Taiwan in 1974 in order to take part in a World Freedom Day rally in Taipei. The rally was sponsored by the World League for Freedom and Democracy, an organization with 120 national chapters worldwide.

Ruth and Billy Graham have been good friends of ours for many, many years.
Our times together, like this visit to the Grahams' home in Montreat, North Carolina,
have given us the opportunity to talk about everything from faith to family.

The best part of a political campaign is the day it's over, especially if you can
end the evening with a victory celebration, as we did here in 1984. We had five
of those celebrations, and every one came as a surprise to the major news outlets!

No matter how many times I've had the opportunity to fly aboard Air Force One, I've never lost my appreciation for what an honor it is to accompany the President of the United States in the performance of his official duties. Whenever I flew with President Reagan, he took the time to visit informally. (That's Mitch Daniels, now Indiana's Governor, in the picture with us.)

My friend Patches was a one-of-a-kind dog. He was happy wherever we were, and we made many a trip together going from Raleigh to Arlington and back again.

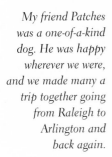

When Vice President Bush administered the oath of office to me in January 1985, my granddaughter Jennifer held the family Bible. In December 2004, I was there when Jennifer took her own oath of office to serve North Carolina as a district court judge.

In my thirty years as a Senator I met thousands of young people, and I never once tired of those meetings.

I have always been proud to serve the farmers of North Carolina, and I was delighted when Senators Elizabeth Dole and Richard Burr were able to win Congressional approval for a fair tobacco buyout program so our tobacco farmers can shift to other crops without risking financial ruin.

Why are these Senators smiling? The NFL has just announced that it has approved Jerry Richardson's league franchise application for the Carolina Panthers. From left: Senator Lauch Faircloth, Senator Bob Dole, me, and Senator Strom Thurmond. This Senator Dole is a Carolinian by marriage.

When His Holiness the Dalai Lama accepted my invitation to speak at my alma mater, Wingate University, the crowd overflowed into a second campus building. The scarf around my neck is a traditional Tibetan kata, a gift from the Dalai Lama.

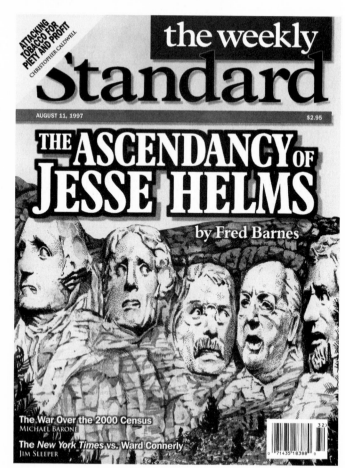

I made the cover of Time, too, but this illustration on the cover of The Weekly Standard still makes me laugh.

COURTESY OF THE WEEKLY STANDARD

Who would have imagined that someone from my humble beginnings would one day meet with Her Royal Highness Queen Elizabeth II?

Meetings like this one with General Hugh Shelton, the Chairman of the Joint Chiefs of Staff (far left), and Secretary of Defense William Cohen (far right) went well because of the presence and preparation of the man by my side, Bud Nance.

Hosni Mubarak, the President of Egypt, has been a reasonable and fearless leader in a region where those qualities have too often been in short supply.

Senator Joe Biden and I were able to accomplish much together because we knew we could trust each other's honesty and commitment to resolving differences.

Secretary of State Madeleine Albright gave me this shirt the day she came to speak at Wingate University. I'm wearing it for a softball game between members of my staff and members of the Secretary's staff. My team always played to win!

My speech to the United Nations Security Council in January 2000 marked what I hoped would be a new era in our relations and in the UN's commitment to reform in its operations and pursuit of its founding goals. Huge bureaucracies are not easily changed, so it is up to the United States, as a major contributor to the United Nations, to insist on real progress in cost-cutting and zero tolerance for the kind of corruption found in Iraq's Oil for Food program.

This photo was taken at the Pentagon right after the attack on 9/11. I've always made sure that the men and women in uniform knew they had a friend in me, but in the aftermath of this hateful attack, they needed to know that they had the support of all Americans.

Again and again President George W. Bush has shown himself to be the right leader for our times. This photo was taken following the President's State of the Union speech in January 2002. I wanted the President to know that he had my support in our war against terrorism. That war has proven to be every bit as hard as the President told us it would be, but we will win.

This picture of Dot and me with our three children, Charles, Jane, and Nancy, is a favorite of ours.

SAM GRAY/
CREATIVE
PHOTOGRAPHY,
INC.

Dot and I are surrounded here by all of our wonderful grandchildren. From right to left: Rob, Katie, Mike, Jennifer, Amelia, Julie, Ellen, and her husband, Will.

CHAPTER 26

Snapshots from the Senate:
Fellow Senators

T HE UNITED STATES SENATE, needless to say, is an interesting place to work. It is rich with tradition, but never quite the same place from session to session. I was not merely pleased—I was unfailingly delighted—to bring visitors onto the floor of the Senate, because they were always both honored and happy to be able to sense the history of that great chamber.

One day, as I neared the entrance to the Senate chamber, I paused to greet—and meet—a family with young children. The little girl was trembling with excitement. "I can't believe we're here. I can't believe we're here." I learned that their home was in the Midwest. This was obviously a trip the family had planned for a long time to enable their children to see the capital and learn more about their government.

I volunteered to escort this splendid family on an impromptu tour. It was such a pleasure to be in the company of a family with such an obvious devotion to their country. In fact, seeing those children taking turns sitting in my seat on the Senate floor was the most memorable part of that day. I hope that at least one of them returns one day to take his or her own seat as a U.S. Senator and thereby guide our country well.

For all our differences, the vast majority of United States Senators seek the office because of their genuine desire to serve the people whom they represent, along with the country they love.

Every student of modern U.S. history knows that North Carolina's legendary Senator Sam Ervin was precisely that kind of American. He was a Democrat of absolute principle and fairness. He never put his party above his principles. He unhesitatingly supported me, even after I had become a registered Republican. (That wasn't such a popular thing among Democrats, but Senator Sam didn't let it bother him at all.)

I got along fine with Senator Sam. In fact, I loved this old gentleman, which is why I decided it was best to leave the party issue alone. I wanted us to be able to work together. I needed his friendship, so I began at the outset to identify myself as the *liberal* Senator from North Carolina, or I'd identify myself as the *other* Senator from North Carolina. That stopped any animosity that otherwise would have to be endured. I praised Senator Sam whenever I had an opportunity. In fact, I've said in many speeches how proud I was of Sam Ervin and his record of service, especially in the difficult days of the Watergate hearings.

After his retirement, Senator Ervin called me at least once every day during the week, and sometimes even on the weekend, asking, "Jesse, have you read so and so?" When it first started, I'd say I had, but when I realized that he wanted me to hear his thoughts on a topic, I'd say that I had not. He would counsel me to get it and read it—and give me his view, in case I might draw a different conclusion. Senator Ervin was a good counselor. He made sense on whatever he was talking about. He was a *leading* Democrat—with a big D. He was a good Senator, a treasured longtime friend, and a truly fine man.

Senator Sam's seat has turned over many times since his retirement. The last junior Senator from North Carolina before my retirement was John Edwards. John was a personable fellow, and we had a sad and unusual tie in addition to our connections to Raleigh. John's teenage son, Wade, had been a visitor in my office shortly before his tragic death. The last picture ever taken of Wade was of the two of us together. Dot and I were so sorry to learn of his death, and we conveyed that message to his parents personally.

It is pure speculation on my part, but I have wondered many times over the last six years if Senator Edwards' involvement in politics is not, at least in part, a tribute to his son and to Wade's own interest in government. Certainly losing Wade had a profound role in shaping his family's life from that day on.

I watched Senator Edwards' run for his party's Presidential nomination, and then for the Vice Presidency, with more than passing interest. It is always nice to see a North Carolinian in the national limelight—like Clay Aiken and Fantasia Barrino's success on the *American Idol* television program, or the Carolina

Panthers reaching the Super Bowl in 2004—but watching a nice man with so little experience or familiarity with national and international issues try to project himself as an expert or refer to himself as the "senior Senator" from our state simply because he arrived in the Senate chamber shortly before the immensely qualified U.S. Senator Elizabeth Dole struck me as "overreaching." Even Senator Hillary Clinton had the good sense to promise the people of New York that she would make their business her priority for her first full term in office. Senator Edwards would have greatly benefited from the same attention to on-the-job training.

When I was first a junior Senator, I had a very special mentor: Senator James B. Allen of Alabama was a master of the Senate's rules, and a sort of instructor to me regarding those rules. On the day of my swearing-in, Jim Allen was the first person from across the aisle to greet me. He told me that I was the only candidate for the Senate he called, and the only freshman Senator to whom he had made a $1,000 contribution. Then Senator Allen quietly mentioned, "I consider that this is going to be as great a day for me as for you. I am glad to see you, and I want to do anything I can to help you."

I said, "Well, thank you, Senator Allen."

He chuckled. "It's Jim," he said.

"Well, Jim," I said, "I want you to teach me the rules," to which he said, "Well, what little I know about them." I told the Senator that anybody could be an accomplished Senator if he or she ever came close to learning the rules like Senator Jim Allen had.

Senator Allen's offices were on the sixth floor of the Dirksen Building, on the corner. The suite of rooms that I was assigned were on the third floor, and I'd go up to the sixth floor regularly, two times a week.

Jim Allen was an excellent teacher. He'd begin each of our visits together with a procedural problem for me to solve. For example, he would say, "Now, the Senate is in this posture with respect to moving ahead. What can you do with the rules to help it *not* move ahead?" The first day, I said I didn't have the vaguest idea. Senator Allen said, "All right, I've got three situations here I'm going to give you. You study the rule book, and you come and tell me what you've learned." Well, I looked it up, and looked it up, and I guessed a little bit; so the next time I met with him, I wrote out exactly what I thought we ought to do in such situations. He said, "Exactly," and then he said, "You know that they are going to call on freshman Senators to preside over the Senate."

I remember thinking, "Gee, I would like to preside over the greatest delib-

erative legislative body in the world." Jim Allen was right: All freshman Senators, including me, presided. After about the third or fourth week, it got to be a
little bit on the drudgery side. And then, after about the fifth or sixth week, I was
doing my best to learn the rules.

I'm bound to be honest: I took every possible minute I could spare from
what I was supposed to be doing and I sat in that chair and I figured out what
the various rulings by the chair ought to be. Finally, I told the Parliamentarian
(who was sitting right below me), "Don't tell me what to rule unless I am screw-
ing up."

It wasn't too long before he told me, "Senator, you sound like a guy who has
been here for years." I told this nice gent that he was pulling my leg—but you'd
better believe that I studied the rule book and listened to Senator Allen's wisdom, and it sure did help. It *really* helped!

When Nelson Rockefeller was appointed to the Vice Presidency by Gerald
Ford, he chafed under many of that position's traditional expectations, once
saying that he felt he was on standby for funerals and earthquakes. He decided
he would be an activist as presiding officer of the U.S. Senate. Vice President
Rockefeller developed an imperious approach to control of the Senate's rules
and injected himself into the issue of how the Senate might vote to end fili-
busters. At one point in this process, the Vice President informed the Senate
Parliamentarian that he was going to make a ruling on his own in spite of the
Parliamentarian's advice to the contrary. On another, Vice President Rockefeller obstinately refused to acknowledge Senator Allen or Senator Brock of
Tennessee as they called for the right to speak. Instead, the Vice President ordered a roll-call vote over their loud objections and in a break with the traditions of Senate procedure.

The Vice President later apologized to the Senate for his discourtesy. He
belatedly learned what the Senators already knew—that my friend Jim Allen
was a master of the way the U.S. Senate was supposed to work. Jim passed away
suddenly in 1978. No one has yet been his match for knowing those rules and
how to use them.

Understanding the rules was *essential* if you were going to challenge somebody like Senator Jacob Javits of New York. I'll put it this way: They told me that
Jacob Javits was the kind of fellow whom I didn't want to challenge unless I had
learned the rules—or unless I wanted to have my hat handed to me in front of
everybody in the chamber, as well as those watching on national television.

Senator Javits was a gentleman about whom you would say, "This is the sort of guy I wish was on our side." At least, that's the way I felt about it. So I went to the Senator and I complimented him. I asked him how he'd learned—and he said, "By getting my ass kicked." That's it: If you are going to be a Senator who votes right down the middle, and you don't want to do anything difficult or to be challenged, you don't need to know the rules all that well. But if you are willing to take on some responsibilities with important implications, you *must* know the rules. I tried to do that.

Nobody is thrilled when the rules are working against him. One time we were locked in a real battle over gasoline taxes, and I had kept the Senate in session until four o'clock in the morning. (They wanted to go home because it was nearing the Christmas holiday.) I said, "Well, either you're going to vote this down or you're going to vote it up before we go." The Senators would take their turns to get up and debate it and condemn it and so forth and so on, hour after hour. (This is the way our democracy works. We talk through issues and abide by the majority vote.) But Senator Alan Simpson of Wyoming, who sat right behind me in the Senate chamber, became really angry at our inability to settle and replied, "You son of a bitch." I said I was sorry he felt that way about the situation, and I sat down, but I felt I was obliged to do what I thought was right. I knew he was tired, and I said so. I added that I was, too.

Several minutes later, I went into the cloakroom to get a glass of water, and Alan was sitting over to one side. He had what appeared to be a tear in his eye. He asked if I had a minute, and I said, "Sure." He said, "*I'm* the son of a bitch. Can you forgive me?" I told him I hadn't convicted him of anything, and I told him he had a right to be upset with me because I was indeed delaying the Senate. We never let that incident mar our close personal friendship. (But Alan was the only Senator who ever, to my face, called me that name.)

Senator Bill Frist is one of the hardest-working Senators I ever saw. He has applied the intellect he used to become an excellent physician to the task of being Majority Leader, and he's very popular among his colleagues because they recognize his competence and his skills as a leader, including his ability to persuade people to reach an agreement whenever possible.

I am so glad Bill was willing to work with me in putting together a bill to provide resources to battle AIDS in Africa. I knew that Bill would keep on pressing the issue after my retirement, and he has. The AIDS epidemic on that continent must hold the attention of the Congress while the need remains.

Of course, you can't agree on everything or with everyone, but you can make it your business to get along. When the junior Senator from New York, Hillary Clinton, was elected in 2000, I was concerned that we might have some problems, but I was determined to do my part—and it was soon clear that she was determined to be collegial as well.

Senator Clinton took time to learn her way around the Senate. From time to time, she would call on me for help with a rules question or something of that sort. Once or twice, she jokingly introduced me to some friends as her boyfriend. Since I'm so much older than she is, everybody knew that she was kidding about that! While we certainly were on opposite sides on most votes, we were cordial, and I appreciated her genuine concern when I returned to the Senate floor after my heart surgery.

I suppose I should not have been surprised by that relationship, based on the genuine friendship that Senator Paul Wellstone and I enjoyed by the time of my retirement. As I mentioned earlier, Senator Wellstone used his opposition to me as a campaign issue in his first run for the U.S. Senate in 1990. The papers in Minnesota salivated at the prospect of Paul's "progressive express" slamming full speed into those of us at the other end of political philosophy, especially me. He was once quoted as having said, "I don't have anything in common with Jesse Helms at all. I think he represents an awful politics. So of course we'll be on opposite sides. Doesn't mean you hate anybody. But I'm a teacher, and I just don't like what he stands for."

Not long after the Wellstones arrived in Washington, Dot had an opportunity to do a favor for Paul's wife, Sheila. Anyone who has ever known Dot Helms will not be surprised to find out that Sheila developed an entirely positive opinion of what a gracious woman Dot is. They liked each other at once. For my part, when I met Paul, I told him how close I had been with Senator Hubert Humphrey, and that I knew Paul honored Humphrey's work and memory. Then I just left Paul alone.

One day, after Paul had been in the Senate for several months, he came up to me and said, "I know you aren't going to help me, but I need some support for my position, which I know is the same as yours on this bill." I asked him to come to my office so we could see what we had, and we spent an hour or so putting together what he needed. That meeting broke the ice between us.

Paul Wellstone was a thoughtful and caring person. When my dear friend Bud Nance, the chief of staff for the Senate Foreign Relations Committee, was in the hospital near the end of his life, Paul took the time to go and visit with him. To my knowledge, no other Senator did that, and I appreciated that visit as much as Bud did.

At my retirement, Paul was more than gracious, talking about the things we both knew were most important, like being appreciative of the support staff in the Senate, from pages to elevator operators. Paul was earning his own reputation for kindness.

Dot and I were deeply saddened by Paul's and Sheila's tragic deaths, and the loss of their daughter, in a plane crash in 2002. Despite the marked contrast between Paul's views and mine on matters of government and politics, he was my friend and I was his. He unfailingly represented his views eloquently and emphatically. Paul Wellstone was a courageous defender of what he believed.

Years before, when news of Hubert Humphrey's death reached me, I wept. Shortly before his death, Senator Humphrey visited the Senate chamber for the last time. He knew it was the last time, and so did we. Hubert's frail body was racked with cancer, his steps were halting, his voice feeble. But as he walked down the aisle, Hubert saw me standing at my desk. He walked over to me, arms outstretched. Tears welled up in my eyes as Hubert hugged me, saying softly, "I love you." I loved Hubert Humphrey, too, and I told him so.

Hubert and I disagreed on almost all policy matters, large and small, but we worked well together and frequently found ourselves hammering out the details of the final versions of legislation. Often Hubert got the better of me in debates. A few times I did it to him. But we agreed on what mattered most—duty, honor, patriotism, faith, and justice, the very essence of America. How we missed his wisdom during the dark days of the impeachment proceedings in 1998.

Agreeing or disagreeing didn't always have anything to do with party affiliations. Dick Lugar and I haven't always seen eye to eye, but I have always admired him. We served together on both the Agriculture and Foreign Relations committees, and we both chaired each of those committees at different times. It was that overlap that created some competition between us when I opted to become Chairman of the Foreign Relations Committee instead of the Agriculture Committee. Senator Lugar had served in that capacity in an earlier Congress, when I had taken the Chairmanship of the Agriculture Committee in response to the urging of North Carolina farmers. Senator Lugar wanted to be Chairman again and contested my bid, even though I was the ranking committee member.

The decision as to which one of us should chair was put in the hands of the

Republican caucus. The caucus decided that the long-standing practice of giving the Chairmanship of committees to the ranking member of the committee had served Senators well throughout the history of the Senate and that they ought not to change it. Senator Lugar was elected to the Senate in 1976, so I had four years' seniority, and my selection prevailed.

Senator Lugar put aside any disappointment and remained a key member of the Foreign Relations Committee. While he does some things differently from the way I would have done them and holds some views with which I disagree, Senator Lugar has acquitted himself well in his role as Chairman since my retirement.

I was once asked whom I might identify as the most effective member of the U.S. Senate, and I immediately thought of Senator Robert C. Byrd. Senator Byrd is a great student of history, often turning the Senate floor into a classroom to teach today's Senate about the great personalities and debates of the past. Senator Byrd was born in western North Carolina, and his family moved to West Virginia when he was a boy. By the time I reached the Senate, Senator Byrd had already been there more than a dozen years. Before that he had served three terms in the House of Representatives.

The Senator and I found many issues on which we could work together. He was always a man of his word, and I knew he would never tell me anything but the truth about how he might be planning to vote or why. When we disagreed—and there were times when we certainly did—we limited the disagreements to the topics at hand and never let political differences infect our personal relationship.

Painting is Senator Byrd's hobby, and I think he has a real talent for it. He told me that he worked in a shipyard during World War II. One Saturday morning, he said, he put on his Sunday clothes and was about to go out the door when his wife, Erma, said, "Robert, where are you going?" He said, "I'm going downtown." She said, "What for?" He said, "I'm going to buy some canvas and an easel and some brushes and some paint." She said, "Robert, you can't paint." And he said, "Well, I can try." Dot and I were so pleased when he made us a gift of one of his first paintings, beautifully framed and inscribed on the back. We proudly hung that painting in our home, and I never look at it without being thankful for the friendship it represents and the artist who created it.

The ranking Democrat on the Senate Foreign Relations Committee, Senator Joe Biden, is a man for whom I hold nothing but affection and respect. We are good friends. Elsewhere in this book I will talk about the United Nations and the agreements we were able to broker there, but this is the place for me to talk simply about the man from Delaware.

We entered the Senate at the very same time. He had won an upset, just as I had, but that was where the similarities stopped. Joe was only twenty-nine years old on Election Day. He had turned thirty between Election Day and the start of 1973, and he had suffered a staggering loss: His wife and infant daughter were killed in a December auto accident that also left his sons seriously injured. Joe's grief was enormous, and had it not been for the gentle counsel of Senator Mike Mansfield, he may never have taken his seat. But Senator Mansfield reminded Joe of his commitment to service and how much his wife had wanted him to make a difference in the Senate. Joe was sworn in at his sons' hospital bedside, and he became a commuter Senator, taking the Metroliner from Wilmington, Delaware, to Washington, D.C., each day so he could be with his two young sons as they recovered. Senator Mansfield met with Joe each week to help and encourage him, just as Senator Allen had done with me.

Senator Biden tells a story about a day when he was very discouraged about the progress of a bill he supported and particularly upset about one of the Senators who opposed the bill. After he ran out of steam, Senator Mansfield told him a story about Harry Truman that he never forgot: One of Harry Truman's first letters back home to his wife, Bess, was full of enthusiasm about being in the Senate and being with all those great men. But not long after, he wrote another letter home and said he couldn't understand how that bunch of guys had gotten there.

Then Senator Mansfield told Joe that every single person he would ever work with as a fellow Senator has something very special that his or her constituency sees—and that his job was to look for that quality. Joe took that lesson to heart, surprising himself with unlikely friendships, from his affection for Senator Strom Thurmond, who was forty years his senior, to our own close relationship, which continues to this day.

Joe and I knew we could trust each other and that we shared the same goals, even when we had differences about how to achieve them. Dot and I were so pleased when Joe met and married Jill. Their daughter is a lovely young woman now, and Joe's sons have made him a grandfather. It's their interests he has in mind as he uses his leadership position in the Senate. Senator Mansfield, who went on to serve his country as Ambassador to Japan from 1977 to 1988, must have been very proud of Joe and all he has accomplished so far.

In 1984, when Jim Hunt and I were in opposition to each other, one of the nicest things that happened to me was having my friends Bob Dole and Howard Baker fly down from Washington so they could be part of the audience at one of the debates.

Senator Baker's family ties to the Senate are unique. He is the son of a former U.S. Senator, Howard Baker Sr.; the stepson of a U.S. Representative, Irene Bailey Baker; the son-in-law of the revered Senator Everett Dirksen; and, since 1996, the husband of Nancy Landon Kassebaum, who served with us as a U.S. Senator from 1978 through 1997. (Nancy's father was never a Senator, but he was Governor of Kansas and the GOP candidate for President in 1936.) It was my honor to chair the hearing when Senator Baker was nominated by George H. W. Bush to become our Ambassador to Japan.

Bob Dole had been in the Senate for just three years when I got there. We had a good relationship from the beginning. Anyone who knows Bob Dole knows him to be sharp and focused and articulate. Of course, I enjoyed his wit, too. He often used it to cut through the oratory and get to the issues.

I think history will show him to be one of the most effective Majority Leaders ever to manage the Senate. I was sorry that he felt he had to resign from the Senate in order to run for the Presidency in 1996. We lost one of our best people then. Fortunately, Bob didn't let his loss to Bill Clinton stop his service to this country. He's headed up the effort for the long-overdue World War II Memorial in Washington, and he and former President Clinton joined together after 9/11 to raise $100 million for the Families of Freedom Scholarship Fund.

Our best tie to Bob Dole is Elizabeth Dole. Her decision to run for the Senate after I announced my retirement pleased Dot and me more than some people understood. When I was first thinking about making my own run for the Senate, a dear lady in Salisbury, North Carolina, became one of my most encouraging supporters. Her name was Mary Hanford, and she was a vigorous seventy years old. She wore a cute hat and sat in the front row at many of the events we had around Rowan County.

Not too long after I came to the Senate, Bob approached me on the Senate floor and asked if I could do him a favor. He told me that his relationship with Elizabeth Hanford was getting serious and that he would be going down to Salisbury that weekend to meet her mom. Elizabeth had told Bob that her mom and I were good friends, so he asked if I would give Mrs. Hanford a call to vouch for his character. Of course, I said I would be happy to.

When I got Mrs. Hanford on the phone and told her what a fine gentleman Bob is, she posed the following: "Well, Jesse, does he drink hard liquor?" I hon-

SNAPSHOTS FROM THE SENATE: FELLOW SENATORS | 185

estly answered, "No, not to my experience or knowledge." This seemed to satisfy her, and Bob and Elizabeth married shortly thereafter.

Elizabeth's career took her to Washington, but she was always a North Carolinian, and I was glad the voters saw that when they elected her. With her solid experience in other government posts (and as President of the American Red Cross), plus the fact that she has instant access to an expert on just about any issue sitting at her kitchen table at breakfast, it didn't take long for Elizabeth to start putting her campaign promises into action.

One of those promises, to require a unique identification on fabrics that puts a stop to the import of illegal goods, is vital to protecting the textile industry. The bill Elizabeth sponsored was passed and signed into law before her first year was up. That was a good omen for the kind of success U.S. Senator Elizabeth Dole has had since, and will have in the years ahead.

Elizabeth knew from the first day of her candidacy that she would have my support and access to my counsel if and whenever she thought she needed it. We talk often, and I am happy to say that when people call my office in Raleigh, I am always comfortable referring them to Senator Dole's office. Senator Dole has made constituent service a priority. As one of her constituents, I find that very reassuring!

IT WOULD BE DISINGENUOUS to leave the impression that every relationship with every Senator was marked by camaraderie. Three relationships have gotten a lot of publicity, and I'd like to say a little about them.

Former Senator Carol Moseley Braun got a lot of mileage out of her version of an encounter we had following a vote in the Senate. That encounter has taken on urban-legend status, and the facts as I recall them should be on the record somewhere.

In 1993, I offered what could be considered only a courtesy amendment to renew, once again, the patent that the United States Senate had routinely renewed for the official insignia of the United Daughters of the Confederacy every fourteen years since 1898. The UDC is an organization of older women who have an interest in their regional history, a desire to honor the memory of loved ones lost in the War Between the States, and a desire to recognize the part played during the war and reconstruction by the women of the South, who endured great hardships in those years.

The flag that is a part of the UDC insignia is the First National Flag of the

Confederacy. It is not the Battle Flag or the "Southern Cross" that is much more commonly seen. Before the Senate voted, Senator Braun entered her objection to the vote, along with her disdain for anything that she considered supportive of the War Between the States. Recognizing the vote for what it was—routine and harmless, *not* any kind of endorsement of the long-gone Confederacy—the Senate passed the amendment 52 to 48.

Senator Braun, who had been a member of the Senate for just six months, decided that since she had failed to block this amendment in committee and now on the floor, she would simply bring proceedings of the Senate to a halt until she had her way. She railed against the insignia and slavery and anyone who might dare to think that good people had been on the Confederate side of the war because they believed in states' rights or simply did not want to see their towns and farms invaded and burned by invaders of any kind.

Seeing an opportunity to look "politically correct," several Senators changed their vote, and the amendment failed. Aside from insulting a harmless group of older women, the tempest changed nothing. The insignia was then, and is now, protected by a completely legal trademark.

During a break following that vote, Senator Braun and I found ourselves in the same elevator car, along with Senator Orrin Hatch and some other folks. Noting Senator Braun's success on the floor, I jokingly told her I was going to sing "Dixie" until she cried. Entering into the good-natured banter, she slapped me on the back and told me to hush. She said my singing was so bad that she would cry no matter what I tried to sing. We all laughed, and that should have been the end of the story.

Somewhere between the elevator and her office, Senator Braun forgot about her end of our conversation and began to repeat endlessly a story that made it sound like I had taunted her and she had to beg me to stop. That was not reality, and I would be surprised to learn that *anyone* else who was in that elevator remembers it that way.

Several years later, when Mrs. Braun appeared before the Senate Foreign Relations Committee as part of a confirmation hearing for an Ambassadorship, I asked if she would like the opportunity to reconsider her intemperate remarks about the women of the UDC. She declined.

Senator John Kerry was a member of the Senate Foreign Relations Committee during my tenure as Chairman and while I was ranking minority member. We were often on opposite sides of issues, most disappointingly during the time of the Clinton administration, when a more unified committee would have sent the White House the clear message that the reorganization of the State Department could no longer, in good conscience, be delayed. Senator Kerry tried every tactic in committee and later on the floor of the Senate to prevent the critically needed changes.

There was, however, an issue that arose during the Senator's freshman year in the Senate on which we stood side by side. Our collaboration is now better known because of Senator Kerry's decision to run for the Presidency, but it was also widely covered at the time it happened.

Our mutual concern was a part of the Iran-Contra matter that was a cause célèbre in Ronald Reagan's second term. Senator Kerry had taken the time to make some independent inquiries into the exact circumstances concerning the whole guns-for-hostages matter. He came to me and shared what he had learned, including the troubling fact that some Contra officers were taking U.S. money and investing it in drug smuggling. Those drugs were coming to this country!

As far as I was concerned, any plan of action that was supporting drug lords and ruining lives in our own cities and towns, no matter how high-minded it might have seemed to someone else, was just plain wrong. When Senator Kerry made his presentation in a closed-door hearing before our committee and called for us to open a formal investigation into the Contras and the Contra-drug connection, I supported him.

My action at first surprised members of the committee. They knew how much I wanted to see an end to the corrupt Sandinista government then in power in Nicaragua. But I told them that I would never knowingly support drug trafficking or drug traffickers. The committee voted to begin its formal investigation.

I did not win any popularity awards from the Reagan White House for siding with Senator Kerry in opening this investigation. But they knew what Senator Kerry knew, and I was more interested in doing what I believed was right than what might have been "correct."

This collaboration does not mean that Senator Kerry and I were particularly close. On a personal level, I found him to be a bit arrogant and overbearing, always looking for a television camera to preen in front of. Dot and I have known Teresa Heinz for many years and always found her a most interesting and dynamic woman. We were shocked and saddened when her husband, Senator John Heinz, was lost in a plane crash and Teresa was left to care for her family without their father. So both Dot and I were pleased when she and John Kerry began to see each other. Their marriage seems to bring her genuine happiness.

I never picked a fight with Senator Edward Kennedy. I never had to. We just woke up every morning on the opposite side of every debate.

Of course, in reality, things were not nearly that contentious, and our staffs worked hard to keep legislation flowing when we could find agreement. We even cosponsored a bill to assure that insurance plans would cover tests for colon cancer for every policyholder whenever a doctor recommended that testing. The Kennedy-Helms bill wasn't signed into law before my retirement, but the very fact that there was such broad support for this change in coverage encouraged many insurers to take action voluntarily to include this benefit. It would have been ironic, however, if our bill had been passed, for we certainly have been a pain in the rear to each other, as well as to a few other folks, over the years.

With this rare "life and death" health care exception, the differences between Senator Kennedy and myself are core deep. Philosophically, Teddy is a "textbook" liberal who believes in big government and sees conservative approaches to things like welfare and education and medical care as patently unacceptable. It was because of liberal politicians like Teddy that I ran for the Senate, and if Teddy thought I was there to oppose him and his allies, he was right. We were very different people, and I tried to keep my attention on the political and not on the gossip. But I must confess that in one rather well-known floor debate in 1993, I did not.

The Senator from Massachusetts had delivered a blustery speech in favor of his bill to allow for the unrestricted immigration of all individuals who tested positive for HIV. When he had finished, I took the floor to explain my opposition, and I started my speech by saying, "Let me adjust my hearing aid. It could not accommodate the decibels of the Senator from Massachusetts. I can't match him in decibels or Jezebels, or anything else, apparently."

As different as we were, we had in common the fact that we were lightning rods for our respective oppositions. Senator Kennedy played to win, and that made us work harder and dig deeper for every victory we gained. Without his opposition, we conservatives very likely would not have done so well in the past thirty years.

CHAPTER 27

Reelection 1990

I F THE 1984 CAMPAIGN WAS among the most expensive, then surely the 1990 campaign has been among the most discussed.

This was my fourth campaign. While I was no more excited about the prospect of campaigning for myself than I had been the other three times, I understood that there was a great deal of work yet to be done in Washington, and I was willing to keep my job if the voters were willing to keep me in it.

Early in the campaign cycle, it was assumed by many that Jim Hunt would want to run against me once again. He remained the state's most popular Democrat, and the nomination would have been his without much of a fight if he had wanted it. But in August 1989, Governor Hunt announced that he would not oppose me. That was fine with me, not because I feared losing, but because I did not want to further damage a friendship that I valued.

Not too long after the Governor signaled that the field was open, two Democrats, Bo Thomas and Mike Easley (who later ran for Governor himself and was elected in 2000—to succeed Jim Hunt), announced their candidacies for the U.S. Senate nomination.

I formally announced my decision to run again at a rally on January 14, 1990. We had a big barbecue in Raleigh and eighteen hundred people came to enjoy the meal and give me their support. That felt good because I knew I sure wouldn't be reading or hearing much to encourage me from the big North Carolina newspapers or the major TV stations in the next eleven months.

At the end of January, the Democratic candidates got a surprise. A third contender entered their race. Harvey Gantt, an architect and former Mayor of Charlotte, announced that he would run, too. Mr. Gantt was active in state Democratic leadership, but his decision to run for the Senate came as a surprise to many. He was hardly known beyond Charlotte and had lost his last bid to be reelected as Mayor.

The Democrats tried to settle the issue with their primary, but when Mr. Gantt posted less than 38 percent of the vote, his closest competitor, Mike Easley (who had 30 percent), called for a runoff. Mr. Gantt took that second contest with 57 percent of the vote. The Gantt campaign was confident that Mr. Gantt's liberal views had helped him beat Mr. Easley (who was more moderate in some positions). This confidence shaped their strategy in campaigning against me.

The Gantt camp was convinced by their primary win and by outside advisors that the voters in North Carolina no longer wanted a Senator who supported conservative principles. Their ads—and rhetoric—highlighted decisions that I had not kept secret but that Gantt's camp tried to portray as ill-advised and ill-informed.

For our part, while our opponent had an inconsequential voting and policy record from his brief time as Charlotte's Mayor, he did have a significant public record—including a curious business deal that had earned him a handsome profit. Mr. Gantt had taken advantage of a minority preference to gain an available television broadcast license. Less than six months after he and his associates received the license, they resold it to the highest bidder—apparently without worrying about the fact that the new broadcaster was not minority-owned.

While not illegal, the quick transaction was clearly not in the spirit of the Federal Communication Commission's intent, and it exemplified the kind of self-enrichment at public expense that most Americans find ethically offensive. Our ad exposing this transaction was the truly fatal blow of the Gantt campaign.

Of course, the liberal pundits who have discussed this campaign ad nauseam would have you believe something very different. Just a few weeks before the election, the Senate failed, by one vote, to override President Bush's veto of legislation that would have required employers to hire and promote a percentage of their employees based on their minority status. The override was defeated because the legislation was correctly identified as a "quota" bill by numerous individuals and groups, including the United States Chamber of Commerce.

As written, the bill would have forced employers into a morass of record keeping to appease regulators who, under this law, would have assumed employers were guilty of breaking the law until the employers could prove—every time a bureaucrat asked—that they were innocent. Aside from being grossly unfair to employers and a perversion of the American ideal that people, even businessmen, are innocent until they are proven guilty, there was also every reason to believe that implementing quotas, racial or otherwise, is unconstitutional. Subsequent court decisions on similar laws have confirmed that to be the case. I opposed the bill the first time the Senate considered it, and I certainly supported President Bush's wise veto.

So of course I voted to uphold the President's veto.

In a speech he gave shortly after that vote, Mr. Gantt stated that he strongly supported the legislation and that had he been in the Senate, it would have become law. He might have been right about that, because the vote to sustain the veto was very close.

To help voters understand the practical reality of the law Gantt favored, my campaign staff created an ad to explain how it would have worked: People who were fully qualified for jobs could be passed over so that jobs could be filled by an individual who satisfied other criteria having nothing to do with the requirements of the job. The point was that Mr. Gantt was comfortable with government policies requiring employers to hire and promote for the purpose of filling quotas instead of recognizing individual abilities, and Gantt was not bothered by the law's unfairness to those who had been passed over, or by the constitutional questions it raised about equality under the law.

By the time the ad made it to television, there were less than two weeks left to the campaign. There were accusations that this was a planned last-minute attack, but of course that was simply not true, since the vote and Mr. Gantt's comments had happened just a few days earlier. There were even some charges that the ad was intended as "racist," but that was untrue as well—minority classifications were not limited to race, and we had no more interest in a race-based vote than we did in race-based jobs. This campaign was never about Mr. Gantt being black; it was always and only about him being a liberal.

We wanted our support to be based on the job I had been doing and nothing more. So many stories about this ad have been written since the campaign that it has begun to seem like this was the only ad we ran, and that we jolly well made sure it was run over and over. In fact, it ran only a very few times, and at such a late point in the campaign that it could not have accounted for many votes.

Without a doubt, that ad pointed out an important difference between Mr. Gantt and Jesse Helms. I believe every person is entitled to go as far as he or she can by making the most of every talent and every opportunity. I believe every person should know the satisfaction of personal success, while Mr. Gantt has less confidence in the ability of individual citizens to handle challenges without excess government involvement.

On Election Day, the voters sent me back to Washington for my fourth six-year term. I was honored that more than one million North Carolinians had honored me with their support.

CHAPTER 28

Bill Clinton

I DON'T SUPPOSE IT SHOULD have been a surprise to any of us who listened to the notoriously long speech Governor Bill Clinton gave to introduce Mike Dukakis at the 1988 Democratic National Convention in Atlanta that the former President's memoirs should top 950 pages. In my experience, the gentleman has rarely been at a loss for words, with that notable well-known exception—when he had trouble explaining under oath what "is" is.

President Clinton and I were on the opposite sides of just about every major issue that came up during his administration, but we managed to hammer out accommodations on some important issues, including the reorganization of the State Department and new policies with respect to our financial arrangement with the United Nations. Those two things alone are proof that if two sides are determined to find agreement, some agreement can be found. Mr. Clinton even signed the Helms-Burton Act, when he couldn't figure out a way to ignore aggressive Cuban behavior that his own UN Ambassador had called on all of the civilized nations of the world to condemn.

Because of my position as Chairman of the Senate Foreign Relations Committee, I was frequently invited to meetings and events at the White House. On each of these "social" occasions, the President and his family were gracious and thoughtful, both to Dorothy and to me. He and I were both a part of the official delegations for the funerals of former President Richard Nixon, who had quietly provided insights on international affairs to each of his successors, and Israeli Prime Minister Yitzhak Rabin, who had met with each of us separately on his visit to Washington just weeks before his life was taken.

The business meetings I had with Mr. Clinton were cordial and productive, especially after the arrival of Erskine Bowles as White House Chief of Staff.

Erskine is the son of my close childhood friend, the late Skipper Bowles. Skipper died much too early of amyotrophic lateral sclerosis, but he left behind a family of whom he could be proud. Erskine was a successful businessman who had also served as head of the Small Business Administration. When he was asked to take on the challenge of managing the White House operation, he put aside his own career. Erskine's private-sector experience was invaluable in trying to shape a White House staff of very young and mostly inexperienced people into a productive office team. I certainly felt better about working with him.

MADELEINE ALBRIGHT IS another member of the Clinton administration with whom I collaborated effectively. The Ambassador and I worked together closely during the years she served at the United Nations. Following the reelection of Mr. Clinton in 1996 and my becoming Chairman of the Senate Foreign Relations Committee, I immediately began receiving feelers about a possible successor to Warren Christopher as Secretary of State.

For years I had hoped that a competent and qualified woman would be tapped for that responsibility. In fact, several years earlier I had done my best to promote Ambassador Jeane Kirkpatrick for Secretary of State—but I was not then Chairman of the Foreign Relations Committee, so my opinion was not quite as important.

In any event, this time my favorite among the possible candidates for the post was selected. Mr. Clinton promptly sent Mrs. Albright's nomination up to the Senate, and it was referred to the Foreign Relations Committee. A public hearing was called immediately, and we pulled out all the stops to expedite her confirmation. Madeleine Albright was the first Clinton nominee to be confirmed by the Senate of the new 105th Congress.

Secretary Albright accepted my invitation to present one of the Jesse Helms Center lectures early in 1997. The event was a huge success, much to the annoyance of many members of the media assigned to cover the Secretary of State. They could not fathom why she would choose a place *they* weren't familiar with as the location for a major address. Nor could they grasp the idea that Secretary Albright and I might have met each other, much less might have known each other well, long before the day she was introduced at her confirmation hearing before the Foreign Relations Committee.

On the day that Secretary Albright spoke at Wingate University, we held a joint news conference where I announced that I would hold hearings on the chemical weapons treaty, which I did not favor. It was suggested by some in the media that I relented and agreed to hearings as a payback for the Secretary's visit. Horsefeathers! I simply agreed to hearings on this flawed treaty because I did not have the votes to stop it. My goal was to force some modifications while the bill was in committee or on the floor, which we did.

Of course, Secretary Albright and I did not agree on very many issues while she held her office. However, we decided early on that we would always treat each other as friends and find those places where we could work together.

IN SPITE OF HIS MANY ATTEMPTS to "talk the talk," Bill Clinton never could morph himself into another Ronald Reagan, or even a political moderate. There would always be lots of nice phrases in each year's State of the Union speech about bringing down government spending and encouraging private-sector investment, or about protecting American industries. Then the reality would arrive on Capitol Hill, in the form of proposals for new government entitlements and regulations, and a sheaf of poorly crafted international agreements. The Clinton administration might also be known in history for its unapologetic nominations of some of the most unsuitable people in America to make and carry out government policies. Actions really do speak louder than words.

Questioning Presidential appointments was nothing new to me, and I was as hard on the nominees of Republican Presidents as I was Democrats, especially if their records raised serious questions about their fitness to serve. I would rather have somebody, even the President of the United States, mad at me than have the wrong person in a position where harm could be done—to our Constitution, our country, or our citizens. This had never made me "Senator of the Month" at 1600 Pennsylvania Avenue, but a new adversarial tone set in with the Clinton folks that too often blinded them to the real problems.

I was, for example, adamant about the quality of judicial appointments. In my view, and in the view of many legal scholars and legal historians, judges who reinterpret the law to match popular culture, or who ignore proper enforcement of laws they don't like, are a threat to the foundation of our nation. I believe a court is better off with fewer judges than with liberal judges who attempt to make new law with their decisions. The Fourth Circuit Court includes North Carolina, so I was able to hold off an onslaught of liberals by using prerogatives of the office of U.S. Senator.

It never seems to occur to liberals that someone might find their activist philosophy or their public record so troubling that they do not want them to have a larger sphere of influence or government authority. Inevitably, if the liberal whose nomination I was opposing happened to also be black, I would be called a racist. If the person happened to be gay, I would be labeled a homophobe.

Even Mr. Clinton, who certainly should have known better, claimed that my opposition to his nominees for the Fourth Circuit was because they were black, when he knew my only objection was that they were liberals—a category, not a color.

Ironically, when the Honorable Claude Allen, President Bush's chief domestic policy aide (and a former member of my own staff), was nominated to the federal judiciary by George W. Bush, no one dared to say that the opposition mounted against Claude was due to the color of his skin. Should Senator Charles Schumer be called a racist because he has opposed this outstanding public servant, who has an enviable record of service and a conservative philosophy toward the role of the judiciary, and happens to be black? I assume he's doing the same thing I did, making a decision based on his view of the man's history without regard for his ethnicity.

Mr. Clinton had a similar problem in separating the facts from the stereotype when it came to conservatives. Frankly, the idea that there could ever be a "vast right-wing conspiracy" for any purpose—or even a teeny right-wing conspiracy that had a shelf life of more than a few days—makes me laugh. Conservatives value independence and encourage independent thought and action. They are as apt to disagree with each other as they are to disagree with liberals. Even when conservatives agree about core ideas, they differ dramatically in their approach to promoting those ideas. Conspiracies are just not a part of our skill set.

And it made me laugh (before it made me mad) to think that three old friends from North Carolina (Lauch Faircloth, David Sentelle, and I) having lunch together, catching up on the news, telling stories, and swapping medical advice were assumed to be plotting the ouster of the President of the United States. As the saying goes these days, "Please!"

There is, of course, no proof that there was a plot or conspiracy because, of course, there was not one. Unfortunately, because I couldn't imagine that anyone would ever care, I didn't think to jot down notes on our unremarkable lunch conversation—or even the punch lines to Lauch's usual collection of good jokes. All people have to do is choose whether to trust in the word of one highly respected federal judge and two United States Senators, or the opinion of theorists like James Carville and company.

Whenever I hear this baseless conspiracy charge or see it written about as if it were fact, I remember an old proverb: "The wicked flee when no man pursueth."

IT WOULD BE DISINGENUOUS to write about Bill Clinton without discussing the impeachment proceedings. For those of us who were in the U.S. Senate in 1974, the prospect of an impeachment was particularly painful. No one with the best interests of the United States at heart would ever want to put the country through the pain of such a proceeding if it could be avoided.

Much had changed since those difficult days in the early seventies, particularly in the way elected officials chose to make decisions that would yield good poll numbers in the next day's news. In 1974, President Nixon acknowledged his wrongdoing and resigned before he was impeached. President Clinton decided to take his chances on the trial. Even though there was no doubt that wrong had been done, in some places doing what was right in response to that wrong was not popular.

My comments to my colleagues in our closed-door discussions on impeachment sum up my thinking on this sad chapter in our country's history. What I said that day still holds true today.*

Under the Constitution, two-thirds of the Senate must be in favor in order to remove a President from office. The final votes were 45 guilty and 55 not guilty on the perjury charge, and an evenly split 50-50 tie on the obstruction of justice charge. Of course no one, not even the President, disputed that he had lied under oath or that he had attempted to keep his lie secret. They just didn't think

---

* Those comments can be found in Appendix 4.

it was "bad enough" to remove him from the one office in America that Americans used to hold in the utmost respect.

As hard as this may seem for some people to understand, my adamant stand in favor of President Clinton leaving his post was not personal. I certainly understand the fallibility of every human, and the power of Grace. I absolutely wished for him, as I did for my friend Richard Nixon, a life where there would be new challenges and new opportunities to do good for the country. But just as I could not have voted in favor of Mr. Nixon remaining in office once I knew the truth of what he had done, I could not pretend that the Constitution allows for gradients of wrongdoing on the part of those who are sworn to uphold its laws.

Following the impeachment, the President and I resumed our efforts to find areas on which we could agree, including how to handle UN funding and move forward on State Department reorganization. We sparred on more nominations and over international agreements. Neither of us underestimated the other.

In his "retirement" Mr. Clinton has risen to the challenge of doing something more for his country and has sought to relieve the problems he saw in the world's poorest nations. While I applaud his efforts to help with tsunami relief and other humanitarian causes, I hope he resists the urge to take up the role of heading up a large multinational agency. His record in support of more and more international control of decisions that should be made only by individual countries makes him the wrong choice for any organization that is intent on imposing its will over that of a sovereign nation. And while, as a conservative, I cannot hope that he will one day be the nation's "First Gentleman," I can wish him well.

CHAPTER 29

The Republican Revolution

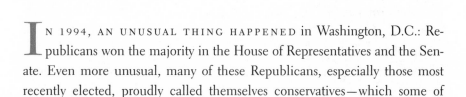

I N 1994, AN UNUSUAL THING HAPPENED in Washington, D.C.: Republicans won the majority in the House of Representatives and the Senate. Even more unusual, many of these Republicans, especially those most recently elected, proudly called themselves conservatives—which some of them were!

It was an amazing moment for me. When I went to Washington as a U.S. Senator, all of the conservatives on Capitol Hill could have comfortably toured the city in a minivan.

While this majority shift is often referred to as a "revolution," it was, in my view, the anticipated result of a steady evolution. Years before, most notably after the 1976 Republican convention, conservatives had gained an understanding of the importance of "grassroots" politics. They got active in their precincts and in campaigns for local government posts from school boards to soil and water commissioner.

This activism led conservatives to work for leadership positions within county and state parties. As people gained experience, they also gained support and moved up the organizational and elective ranks, eventually challenging more liberal incumbents in party primaries and finally winning general elections. Those successful campaigns included contests for Congressional seats.

The process was steady and consistent, with each candidate running his or her own race. There was no master plan or single leader to jockey people into position for a unified "takeover." There was a lot of encouragement from an assortment of national organizations and political figures, but when it came down to it, every candidate had to run his or her own race and be elected on his or her own merit.

I had watched the tide come up and welcomed every conservative we could get, especially as some of the staunchest veterans left the chambers through retirement or death. The bright young people who were first inspired to get into politics because of their admiration for Ronald Reagan arrived in Washington with their energy and their idealism fully intact. For some, however, the reality of seeing government from the inside was a rude surprise.

While the U.S. Senate is the deliberative body, designed by the Founders to take its time in reaching decisions, the U.S. House of Representatives is also a web of committees and "clogged arteries" that can turn the short and simple into the long and complex. For those who were impatient for change, the pace was a daily source of frustration.

Others discovered the reality of competing goods—and the difficulty of making decisions that are reasonable and equitable. They also learned that no decision made in government stands on its own. There are obvious and sometimes unexpected ramifications to everything. A well-informed legislator must know how a proposed law will impact *everything* else in order to know whether the proposal is good or bad.

The pressures on the decision-making process may also be shocking. People talk about a "flood of constituent mail," but until you are on the receiving end of endless bags of mail and hundreds of e-mails and a nonstop stream of calls from constituents who insist that you stand on *their* side of an issue, you cannot imagine the push-pull conflict some in Congress feel—especially if they are concerned for their popularity.

Washington life can also overwhelm. Invitations to receptions and galas and dinners and all kinds of other special events can easily overcrowd schedules and distract lawmakers from the job they are elected to do. Members of Congress who get caught up in their celebrity status can all too quickly get an inflated idea of their personal importance—when in fact it's their *status* that is being courted by the party-givers.

And sometimes the glamour overrides common sense. Family life moves to second place behind career-building, and the values on which a Congressman may have publicly campaigned are the very ones he tramples privately.

For all of these reasons, as well as the usual one—when voters decide they'd rather have the other guy—there has been a fair amount of turnover among members of that 1994 batch of new Congressmen. At the same time, other conservatives have been elected since then, including my good friend Robin Hayes, who represents my hometown. Robin works closely with Representative Sue Myrick, whose district is right next to his.

Sue was a part of the 1994 wave of new conservatives, and until 2005 she was the Chairman of the Republican Study Committee in the House. That committee recently handed out a "Conservative Check Card" to all of their colleagues. It lists six principles that should be bedrock to conservative lawmakers anywhere in the United States. They should be for: less government, lower taxes, personal responsibility, individual freedom, stronger families, domestic tranquillity, and national defense. They should be asking themselves if the proposed laws before them promote or weaken these principles—and vote accordingly.

In this new phase of our political culture, a check card has become necessary because the term "conservative" has been used too loosely to describe anyone who is not obviously liberal. Some have assigned categories like "fiscal conservative," "political conservative," "practical conservative," "social conservative," "neoconservative," and "paleoconservative." To put it in the plainest terms, people who need to qualify their brand of conservatism may not be conservatives at all.

So, as nice as it is to have Republican majorities, it is naive in the extreme to assume that this means conservative principles are the standard for lawmaking. The electorate can never give up its responsibility to hold its representatives accountable to follow through on what they promised. Officials who will not stand for something (in this case, the something is what they *said* they would do if elected) will fall for anything—especially the lure of making the "popular" decision to support legislation that in fact violates their avowed principles.

When the electorate makes it clear that they have no interest in vacillating, pragmatic chameleons or representatives without sound character, they will be rewarded with more elected leaders who are willing to do what is right, no matter what the polls or the pundits might say.

Imagine, if you will, a United States Congress where the focus is on less government bureaucracy and less government spending, so there could be lower taxes. Picture legislation that enables people to manage their own lives and ensures their freedom to pursue *their* goals. Consider a country where the Congress does not equivocate on the defense of marriage or the protection of traditional family values. Think of the strength we would have as a nation if *all* of our legislators held as a primary value the maintenance of a strong national defense and domestic tranquillity procured without compromising civil liberties.

That might qualify as revolutionary!

CHAPTER 30

The Senate Foreign Relations Committee

THE CONSTITUTION OF THE UNITED STATES,
  Article 2, Section 2

CLAUSE 1: The President shall be Commander in Chief of the Army and Navy of the United States, and of the Militia of the several States, when called into the actual Service of the United States; he may require the Opinion, in writing, of the principal Officer in each of the executive Departments, upon any Subject relating to the Duties of their respective Offices, and he shall have Power to grant Reprieves and Pardons for Offences against the United States, except in Cases of Impeachment.

CLAUSE 2: He shall have Power, by and with the Advice and Consent of the Senate, to make Treaties, provided two thirds of the Senators present concur; and he shall nominate, and by and with the Advice and Consent of the Senate, shall appoint Ambassadors, other public Ministers and Consuls, Judges of the supreme Court, and all other Officers of the United States, whose Appointments are not herein otherwise provided for, and which shall be established by Law: but the Congress may by Law vest the Appointment of such inferior Officers, as they think proper, in the President alone, in the Courts of Law, or in the Heads of Departments.

CLAUSE 3: The President shall have Power to fill up all Vacancies that may happen during the Recess of the Senate, by granting Commissions which shall expire at the End of their next Session.

With their prudence fully intact, the founders of this great nation vested power in three coequal branches of government, thereby providing the checks and balances so often discussed among our leaders. This sharing of equal but different powers has yielded the enormous benefit of collective wisdom in guiding our country.

Clause two of article two, section two of our unique road map for democracy declares clearly that the President shall engage in the most serious matters of foreign policy with the "advice and consent" of the Senate. Throughout our history, the exercise of this responsibility has prevented our country's making mistakes—and has demonstrated our national unity in times of testing. This responsibility is *never* to be taken lightly or ceded to other branches of government.

The first North Carolinian ever to serve as Chairman of the Senate Foreign Relations Committee was Senator Nathaniel Macon, who first assumed the post in 1817.

By all accounts, Senator Macon didn't have much interest in being a yes-man. Vice President John Calhoun said he had "a narrowness of mind which education cannot enlarge," adding that Macon was "covered by an encrustation of prejudices which experience cannot remove."

A colleague of Macon's in Congress, Charles Ingersoll, said, "Negation was his ward and arm. . . . No ten members gave so many negative votes." In other words, Senator Macon knew his constitutional responsibility pretty well, and I was proud to succeed him more than one hundred and fifty years later as North Carolina's *second* Senator to chair the Senate Foreign Relations Committee.

When I arrived in 1973, I found that the Senate had surrendered, de facto, any serious involvement in foreign policy decisions. The Senate was content to let the "professionals"—the career diplomats in the State Department—shape and guide our international relationships. Even the Secretaries of State were viewed as not much more than figurehead political appointees who came and went without having made any real impact on the actual direction of what was happening in "Foggy Bottom."

If ever there has been a more apt description of a government department,

I have not heard of it. Foggy Bottom is one of Washington, D.C.'s oldest neigh-borhoods. In addition to being the home of George Washington University (lo-cated on the *exact site* that George Washington himself is said to have selected as the place for "his" university), the neighborhood is also home to—guess what!—the U.S. State Department.

At first "Foggy Bottom" referred only to the neighborhood, which had been built on a swamp, but it wasn't long before it was in common usage as a nick-name for the State Department. Perhaps the name stuck because people real-ized how succinctly it also described the environment in those offices.

Even today, in the mist and murkiness of the State Department, plain speech can become diplomatic discourse in which *no one* knows exactly what, if anything, has been said—or if any agreements have been reached. What to others would appear to be useless conversations at a cocktail party are called at Foggy Bottom "exercises in diplomacy." Just as they created their own dress code with striped pants and cutaway coats, the folks at Foggy Bottom created their own code of conduct as well, where innumerable meetings (at which nothing was accomplished) could be *called* successful because no challenges were issued—and no voices were raised. If you were looking for people to or-ganize your next reception or cotillion, Foggy Bottom was the place to go. But if you wanted actual movement toward the settlement of issues vital to U.S. in-terests, you were going to leave disappointed.

When I got to Washington, Senator J. William Fulbright was in his four-teenth year as Chairman of the Senate Foreign Relations Committee. Senator Fulbright was a professor and the former president of the University of Arkan-sas. His lifelong belief was in the power of education to resolve human conflict. He said: "If large numbers of people can learn to know and understand people from nations other than their own, they might develop a capacity for empathy, a distaste for killing other men, and an inclination for peace." This philosophy colored Fulbright's advice on foreign policy, even leading him in the 1960s to counsel that the United States should understand that

> Communists are present in all Latin American countries, and they are
> going to inject themselves into almost any Latin American revolution
> and try to seize control of it. If any group or any movement with which
> the Communists associate themselves is going to be automatically con-
> demned in the eyes of the United States, then we have indeed given up

all hope of guiding or influencing even to a marginal degree the revolutionary movements and the demands for social change which are sweeping Latin America.

Fulbright went on to say,

In the eyes of educated, energetic, and patriotic young Latin Americans—which is to say, the generation that will make or break the Alliance for Progress—the United States committed a worse offense in the Dominican Republic than just intervention; it intervened against social revolution. . . .

In other words, according to *that* former Chairman of the Foreign Relations Committee, the United States shouldn't be concerned about the rise of Communism in our own hemisphere—as long as the intelligentsia in the countries where it holds sway think it's okay.

Of course, those who believe in appeasement don't ever know when to stop. By the mid-1970s, I had an "up close and personal" view of the most amazing paradoxes in behavior by the very people who were supposed to be supplying wisdom to the government in the handling of its relations with other nations.

The Senate was carelessly handling issues that were, in a very real way, crucial to the survival of the liberties of the American people. Month after month, week after week, day after day, often far into the night, the Senate debated legislation relating to such matters as foreign aid, arms control, national defense, and all manner of other vital issues, and made proposals with no apparent understanding of their impact.

At one point a colleague of mine told me, "Sometimes when I listen to those fellows out there, I feel like I'm in the midst of a nightmare." I wanted to shout *Amen!* It was no wonder we felt that way. The Senate could not find the will to shut off foreign aid to Idi Amin, one of the most brutal dictators in all of history. There was a push to legalize marijuana—but ban saccharin. Some Senators devised a scheme to hike their own pay through automatic raises (and passed the legislation in a way that shielded them from letting the folks back home know how they had voted).

They were fine with blanket amnesty for deserters and draft dodgers, and clamored for what they called "normalization of relations" with the Marxist tyrant of Cuba, Fidel Castro—and with the brutal Communists of North Vietnam. There was talk of sending billions of U.S. tax dollars to *both* countries as a part of this "normalization."

I did not believe then, and I do not believe now, that people who advocate appeasement ever realize the utter *immorality* of what they propose! How could—and why should—the American people ever "write off" the slaughter of countless thousands of innocent people as if it were no more than a bad debt?

Do those who advocate such abandonment of principle not realize that the American people are bound to become a part of what they are led to condone?

Had these people learned nothing from history? The record does not show aggressors becoming disabused from their greed for land or wealth or domination by becoming literate. The record *does* show that when the forces of freedom reduce their vigilance, aggressors take the time to do their homework so that they can have greater success in achieving their evil goals. We must never forget that the only sure defense against an enemy that would destroy us is an offense that prevents their insurgency—under *any* guise.

Instead of pursuing a "normalization of relations" with the likes of Fidel Castro, we should demand that Castro and every *other* Communist regime stop exporting their terror and revolution across the world.

Even today we are reaping the whirlwind of our lack of vigilance. It was a Soviet adventure in Afghanistan (with the goal of spreading Communism) that birthed Al Qaeda, and it was Soviet support for his government (in Iraq) that allowed Saddam Hussein to thrive—long after his original Soviet patrons had lost their power.

The stakes of freedom are far too high for anything less than the Senate's *full* engagement in matters of foreign policy. I made it my business to do what I could to encourage the Senate to embrace its constitutional responsibility, even when—no, especially when—the occupant of the White House or the staff at the State Department wished we would occupy ourselves with other issues.

Because of my conviction that foreign policy is a rightful and vital concern of the Senate, I involved myself from the very beginning of my Senate career. As I noted earlier, the day *before* I was officially sworn in for my first term, the first official visitor to my office was the Ambassador to the U.S. from the Republic of South Vietnam.

His was the first of many such meetings with representatives of governments, leaders of anti-Communist groups, freedom fighters, and citizens of other nations, including refugees who had fled for their lives, who needed the help of our government in the cause of freedom.

From the beginning, I was an "outsider" on the Senate Foreign Relations Committee because I wanted to be sure we were getting all of the facts and not just the facts the State Department or other government agencies wanted to share. I was particularly concerned about the aggressive encroachment of Communism in the Western Hemisphere, and took my place on the Western Hemisphere subcommittee immediately after I joined the committee itself.

As far as I was concerned, Senator Fulbright and others who thought it was just fine for Communists to be involved in the governments of countries close to our borders were just plain wrong.

In order to prove my point, I had to have facts. The most reliable way to get those facts was to get them from trustworthy outside sources. Members of my personal staff, most notably Deborah DeMoss, established solid contacts throughout the region that enabled us to help prevent Communists from taking over Latin America.

Even when I was Chairman of the Senate Agriculture Committee, I continued to keep my involvement in the Senate Foreign Relations Committee as a top priority. In fact, in November 1985, when Ukrainian seaman Myroslav Medvid jumped from a Soviet grain ship in New Orleans and sought political asylum, I used my prerogative as Chairman of the Agriculture Committee to attempt to serve a subpoena on the seaman that would have kept him in this country for the hearing where I had planned to tell his story. We had to smuggle that subpoena onto the ship inside a carton of cigarettes.

My staff members were refused access to Medvid, and the Reagan administration, in order to avoid an upset to improving relations with the Soviet Union, allowed the ship to leave port with him aboard. (They were less concerned about relations with me, or with the many Americans who flooded the phone lines into my office with words of support for our attempt to help this young man — including twenty-five lawyers who volunteered their services on his behalf, or the nurses in the Russian prison where he was detained who protected him by delivering drugs intended to incapacitate him into the mattress instead of the seaman.)

When the ship sailed, Medvid was in the captain's custody, so we did not know what would become of him. But in the spring of 2000, the Reverend Myroslav Medvid, now a priest at a small orthodox church in the city of Chervonohrad, applied for a visa to come to the United States from his native

Ukraine so that he could mark the fifteenth anniversary of his jump for freedom from the deck of a Soviet ship into the Gulf of Mexico. Astonishingly, once again the American government turned him away—this time claiming that he was probably dishonest about his intent to simply visit our country before returning to his church and his congregation in the Ukraine.

At this point, my staff became involved, and a visa was secured. It was a wonderful day on January 30, 2001, when the Reverend Medvid finally met with me and other members of the Senate Foreign Relations Committee and of Congress to relate personally how those brief moments of freedom in New Orleans and the outpouring of concern about his welfare had changed his life and led him to his faith in God.

It is because of incidents of this kind that every Presidential administration needs to be reminded from time to time that our first priority in foreign policy is to preserve and extend freedom—and to lead through strength. Therefore, I decided following the 1994 election that as the ranking Republican on the Foreign Relations Committee, I would take up the responsibilities of Chairman. From that post I would have "higher visibility" in helping to shape U.S. policy in the world.

When the Republicans were in the majority in the 1980s—and there was a Republican in the White House—I was comfortable with the option of chairing the Agriculture Committee, and the farmers in North Carolina were pleased by my decision.

But in 1994 things were different, and those same farmers were much more interested in seeing me do what I could to protect our nation's international standing. They understood that I could do more for them and their families in my role as Chairman of the Senate Foreign Relations Committee.

As I explained earlier in this book, there was a brief challenge by Senator Lugar to my taking up the Chairmanship, but it was quickly settled under the seniority rules by which Republican Senators have always operated when choosing committee chairs—as well as the post of ranking minority member. This system has the particular advantage of keeping the post of committee Chairman from ever becoming a popularity contest, and it makes sure that there is a wealth of experience to draw on in committee deliberations.

Over the years I was often portrayed as a minority of one on the Senate Foreign Relations Committee, but in truth, as Senators saw the facts about the issues I had brought to them, they lent their support—either within the committee or in the Senate itself.

Because I knew that facts make persuasive arguments, I made sure that the data I presented were the best that could be gathered. Everything was checked and double-checked. Much to the dismay of the State Department, we *knew* what we were talking about when we said they were in error in their reporting or their conclusions about the potential impact of U.S. policies.

When I arrived in Washington in 1973, I was concerned that the U.S. Senate had allowed itself to become irrelevant in matters of foreign policy. If there is one thing that I would claim as an accomplishment upon my retirement, it is that the Senate now takes its responsibility to "advise and consent" *very* seriously. I only wish that had been the case in the 1970s, when the Carter administration painted a rosy picture of how good it would be for the U.S. to give up the Panama Canal or walk away from its agreements with Taiwan in order to please the Communists in charge in China.

I am delighted that the U.S. Senate has wisely voted down foolishly conceived treaty agreements and refused to send unsuitable people to represent the United States in posts around the world. Sometimes, simply knowing that their plans must be enacted by the U.S. Senate is enough to make people think twice.

I pray that the U.S. Senate will never again let itself be a spectator in world affairs. While it is true that America must speak to other nations with one voice, we must *never* speak with a voice that has been filtered through a "professional" bureaucracy that is not accountable to the people.

NO DISCUSSION OF MY TIME as Chairman of the Senate Foreign Relations Committee could be complete or accurate without talking about the role of Bud Nance as staff director. Bud Nance was everything his country could have wanted him to be: courageous, resourceful, determined, and intellectually brilliant. He received many justified decorations for a military career that included service as Deputy Chief of Staff to the Supreme Allied Commander, Assistant Vice Chief of Naval Operations in Washington, and Director of Naval Administration, before becoming skipper of the aircraft carrier USS *Forrestal*.

Following his retirement, Bud served as Assistant National Security Advisor in the Reagan administration. His advice to me proved invaluable.

In 1991, I asked Bud to join the Senate Foreign Relations Committee as Republican staff director. Saying the government already had done plenty for him, Bud accepted the job on the condition that he would work for free. But, as it turned out, laboring without a salary was not an option under Senate rules. He was therefore paid Congress's then minimum wage of $2.96 a week. Later, two cost-of-living pay increases bumped Bud's weekly salary to $4.53.

Bud was an expert in foreign affairs and in dealing with people. His work earned the admiration of Senators on both sides of the aisle and the respect of all with whom he worked, from the Secretary General of the United Nations and the United States Secretary of State to the career staffers whose contributions seldom get acknowledged.

At my request, Bud had stepped into a difficult situation and quickly reorganized operations so that the office became a model of productivity. When Republicans assumed majority status, Bud Nance led the entire committee staff.

He worked behind the scenes on our most difficult challenges, including the impasse over payments to the United Nations. He was tireless in making our position clear to the United Nations.

If Bud Nance had been less warmly human and delightfully approachable, I might have stood in petrified awe of him and his knowledge and intelligence. But, though both of us had long ago ceased to be boys, when we got together it was as though we were still two skinny kids walking barefoot in the woods back home in Monroe, North Carolina, circa 1935. Even if we had been brothers we could not have been closer. Bud had my complete trust, just as he had the absolute loyalty of those who worked with him, because he had no agenda, no favorites, no personal goals other than doing what was best for America.

When Bud died in May 1999, it was said that there were more Democrats than Republicans in attendance at his funeral. There were Senators and sailors, the Secretary of State and student interns, united in the knowledge that they had suffered a great loss. Bud is at rest now at Arlington, that hallowed place where heroes are forever honored. I miss him every day.

One of my most vivid memories of Bud during this time may be the most publicly dramatic moment of my time as Chairman of the Senate Foreign Relations Committee. It was a bit of political theater that opened in Boston and closed in Washington.

In July 1997, President Clinton announced that he was nominating Massachusetts Governor William Weld as his choice for U.S. Ambassador to Mexico. Mr. Weld is a Republican, so it was wrongly assumed that his would be an easy confirmation that pleased both sides of the aisle.

I and others in Senate leadership had reservations. Our staff research indicated that Governor Weld's record was not as strong as it could be on the use of marijuana and, by extension, drug prosecutions and the problem of drug trafficking. Mexico, as our neighbor along an all-too-porous border, has for a long time been a part of the U.S. drug problem.

We had made genuine progress in pressing our case with the Mexican government, so it made no sense to me to post as Ambassador someone whose record could be interpreted as "soft" on the issue of drug production, drug use, or drug smuggling into U.S. towns and cities.

Our border with Mexico was then the epicenter for the import of illegal drugs into this country. My own state of North Carolina had just been identified as a major hub in this trafficking, with millions of dollars of drugs arriving by truck from Mexico and being repackaged for transshipment to the rest of the country. The only hope of cutting off the supply of this poison was with the proactive cooperation of the Mexican government.

It was clear to me that an Ambassador who was known to be comparatively liberal about drug use would not be taken seriously on the life-and-death issue of drug control.

When I first conveyed my opposition to the possibility of this nomination to the administration, I also made clear that I *would* be able to support Governor Weld if he were to be nominated for a different post, namely as Ambassador to India. I believe the Governor would have done well there, and he would have been aided by his wife, Susan, who was an East Asia scholar at Governor Weld's alma mater, Harvard. Apparently, the Governor was not interested in the India option. He resolved to give his full attention to securing confirmation to the post in Mexico.

To that end, the Governor resigned the position to which the people of Massachusetts had elected him and took up a public-relations war centered on attacking me—as if no one had done that before.

I made my position clear. As long as I was Chairman of the Senate Foreign Relations Committee, I was not going to insult that committee by wasting its time in discussions about a nominee who was clearly unsuited for the job. The administration had ignored my advice—and I had no intention of giving my consent.

It was summer, and apparently there wasn't a lot of other news to engage the media during this time, because the standoff got coverage far beyond what I would have given it when I was running a news operation. I wonder what else they might have talked about that August without us.

Seeing a chance to promote what they saw as an intramural squabble, a number of Democrats approached Senator Lugar and convinced him to sign a letter that, under the rules, would force a meeting of the committee over my objections.

Bud and I decided that if we were going to follow the rules, we would follow *all* of the rules. The "showdown" meeting that Senator Lugar had used his prerogative as a member of the Foreign Relations Committee to call was set for Friday, September 12. We used our prerogatives to manage the meeting itself.

Mr. Weld was invited to the meeting, but he said, through the State Department Legislative Affairs Bureau, that he would not attend. We assumed (correctly, as it turned out) that the lure of the expected media coverage would be more than he could resist. Mr. Weld's supporters also assumed that he would attend and that he would find a seat at the witness table, right where the TV cameras could get both the Governor and me in the same shot. But their assumptions ran headlong into Bud's arrangement! It was only a meeting, not a tactical naval maneuver, but Bud handled it with the same kind of precision. Since the meeting definitely would not be a hearing, he had the unnecessary witness table moved into the hall. Then he made sure that the rows closest to the front of the room were available to the staff and interns of my Senatorial office, who rarely had an opportunity to attend SFRC meetings. They were joined by many others who wanted to attend the meeting. Well before the meeting time of 11:30 a.m., the audience was standing room only and spilled out the doors. We had attracted quite a crowd!

Under the rules of the Senate, committee meetings may not run beyond the first two hours of that day's session without unanimous consent of the full Senate for their extension. The Senate had been called to order that day at 10 a.m., and an objection to extending meetings had been filed by several Senators. Therefore, under the rules, our committee meeting had to end no later than noon.

I gaveled the meeting to order promptly at 11:30 a.m. Just before then, Mr. Weld and the State Department staffers in charge of his nomination came through an anteroom door. With no witness table to sit at, and no seats available, Mr. Weld and his entourage had to walk through the crowd to find a place where they could stand in the back of the room. They may not have been as comfortable as they had expected, but I am certain they were able to see and hear without any problem.

Since we had to have this meeting, it seemed like a good time to provide a brief review of the recent history of the nomination process in the United States Senate and a clarification of the situation.

I began my remarks by explaining that rule three authorized Senator Lugar and his supporters to request a meeting, but rule three did not provide that they could place any further restrictions on the agenda or the meeting or the procedures to be followed at the meeting. Therefore, I was using the forum to set the record straight.

Both Senator Biden and Senator Wellstone made attempts to interrupt as the meeting progressed, but I ignored them and continued with my remarks. I said,

> I'll tell you, I've never seen such a barrage of misstatement of fact or such a collection of idle speculation, mostly erroneous but published as fact. For example, the suggestion by editors and reporters who saw no point in their going to the trouble of checking the facts produced the allegation that my declining to schedule a hearing on the Weld nomination is unprecedented and that it is a rare departure from common Senate practice and procedure. Well, of course, anybody who knows anything about the Senate knows that nothing could be further from the truth. I feel I should present the facts in some detail for the record.
>
> And I will do that. . . . You called this hearing, which is not a hearing; it's a meeting. Now, I insist that you exercise some decorum. There have been many contrived reports to the effect that my decision that there will be no hearing on the Weld nomination is somehow a radical departure from Senate procedures. Some have resorted to unfortunate name-calling, for example, that I was "dictatorial." And I have been lectured regarding what the Constitution says about hearings. And it says nothing. And about the traditions of the United States Senate and about democracy in general, Mr. Weld himself joined once again in a parade of misstatement of fact when he appeared briefly on ABC's *This Week* program without the foggiest notion of what he was talking about.
>
> Mr. Weld declared during that appearance, "You would be very hard pressed if you looked back in the precedence of the United States Senate to find a case where a Presidential nominee for Ambassador was denied a hearing."
>
> Well, we'll see about that.

Then I told the meeting that I had asked the Congressional Research Service to provide a list of every Presidential nominee in the past ten years who had been denied a confirmation hearing before the relevant committee. I said, "The Congressional Research Service reported to me that during the past ten years alone there have been 154 failed nominees who never received a hearing. Unprecedented? You make up your own mind about that."

I took the trouble to point out which among those 154 failed nominations had been blocked by either Senator Biden as Chairman of the Judiciary Committee or Senator Lugar as Chairman of the Agriculture Committee.

Then, as the time mandated by the Senate for our meeting was about to expire, I concluded the meeting with these words:

> Let me simply say that while Mr. Weld was deciding whether to launch, as he put it, a ground war or an air war, Jesse Helms was working behind the scenes with the White House to see if an acceptable compromise might be possible.
>
> On August 1, the first day of the Congressional recess, I sent to the White House a four-page letter that I wrote personally, setting out my objections to Mr. Weld for the Mexico post. In that letter I made an expanded offer to the President of the United States.
>
> That offer was that I would—immediately—convene hearings on the Weld nomination to any other country in the world that the President chose, provided it was one where drug trafficking is not the principal U.S. foreign policy interest.
>
> For his part, Mr. Weld appeared to threaten that unless his nomination to Mexico was moved, he would begin a war within the Republican Party. I said, "Let him try." I have been tempted to say—but haven't— that I, Mr. Weld, do not yield to ideological extortion.

From start to finish, the meeting was political theater at its finest. The director was none other than Bud Nance, who had planned it down to the last detail, from how to arrange the room to how best to display the facts we had gathered on previously blocked nomination hearings to quietly passing me notes helping me manage the carefully allotted time—even inviting the Senate Parliamentarian to attend in case someone questioned the rules in play.

Of course, the television audience for the meeting included President Clinton himself. He was asked to comment on what I had said by a reporter who asked, "What do you make of Senator Helms' implied threat that this could have fallout in your relationship with him on other foreign policy matters?"

The President replied, "Oh, I don't think it was implied. I thought it was explicit. See, I like that about Senator Helms. He always tells you where he is and what he's doing. This is just a—you know, we've had a very cordial relationship, partly because we've been very candid and honest with each other. And this is just an area where we have a disagreement."

Finally, even Governor Weld got the message that his nomination was not going through, and withdrew his name the Monday morning following the meeting, saying he "had enough of Washington for the next little while."

Jeffrey Davidow, an experienced Foreign Service careerist with particular expertise in Latin American affairs, was then appointed by President Clinton as U.S. Ambassador to Mexico, and quickly confirmed. At the request of President George W. Bush, Ambassador Davidow remained in his post, serving his country well until 2002, when he retired.

The Weld nomination episode is not so important in itself, but it is vital as a lesson in the importance of knowing the rules of the U.S. Senate and being willing to use them in the best interests of the nation.

If there is any satisfaction in coming out on top in struggles of this sort, it is found in the encouragement of the citizens we're supposed to be serving.

The day after that nationally televised meeting, the telephones in my offices in Washington and Raleigh "rang off the hook" all afternoon. More than a thousand ordinary citizens took the time to call and say they were happy with the way I had handled the proceedings. Their opinions counted for much more with me than those of the editorial writers at *The Boston Globe*.

CHAPTER 31

Foreign Relations Experiences

REORGANIZING THE STATE DEPARTMENT

THIS MAY BE A LEGEND, but to be honest, I hope it's true. A member of my staff once claimed to have seen a big framed picture of me sitting on the desk of a career officer at the State Department. Curious—and surprised to have found a fan of mine anywhere in *that* building—my staff member stopped by the gentleman's desk to ask why he had a photo of me on display. The State Department officer said he kept my picture around to remind him that the enemy is always watching!

If I had thought it would have done any good as a way to change "business as usual" at that department, I would have personally autographed an eight-by-ten glossy for every State Department career employee—in every post around the world.

Battles with the State Department were nothing new. For years we had made it our business to check fully the credentials of every nominee for every post under the State Department's authority, from Ambassadors on down. And we did stop a significant number of these nominations when we found the nominee's record to be incompatible with the responsibility to represent the United States well.

Concern about the factual accuracy, or the slanting of information, we received in State Department briefings had led us to do our own committee fact-checking and to develop our own resources for information, particularly in

Central and South America. (Too often, the facts *we* uncovered were at odds with State Department claims, sometimes even with the CIA.) But based on our rules for fact-gathering and fact-checking, I was always willing to challenge the claims when they were at odds with what we had learned through our sources—or had seen for ourselves.

At first, the State Department professionals were annoyed by our questions and our refusal to accept what they told us about who were the "good guys" and who were the "bad guys." Then they were angry when we challenged their conclusions or their decisions to provide support to one group or another in a civil conflict.

Later, they were infuriated when our data proved to be correct and their agenda was exposed. And, finally, they were chagrined when gaffes like failing to pay attention to exactly whom our tax dollars were supporting through their largesse were exposed.

One comparatively small example from 1994 illustrates the problem. The State Department did nothing when the UN Economic and Social Council, of which we were a part, granted consultative status to the Brussels-based International Lesbian and Gay Association.

One of the members of that association is the notorious North American Man/Boy Love Association, or NAMBLA, a group founded in Boston in 1978 to promote consensual relations between men and boys.

I went to the Senate floor to get this incredible wrong corrected. I told my colleagues that I had never fathomed that the day would come when the United Nations would officially condone the sexual molestation of children. However, the United States had joined more than twenty other nations in voting to give consultative status to the International Lesbian and Gay Association.

Four nations voted against it and seventeen abstained. The United States' excuse? Our State Department was *not aware* that the North American Man/Boy Love Association was a member of the ILGA. The department claimed they were horribly embarrassed about this episode, as they should have been.

This competition between the "do as we please" bureaucrats and the Senate watchdogs could have gone on forever, but the real solution to putting an end to the de facto autonomy of the State Department lay in a major reorganization that would rein in the autonomy of their agencies. As with every government bureaucracy, these agencies had started small, with clearly defined roles, but they had ballooned into independent operations that were creating and following their own foreign policies—too often working against our own Presidents and the goals of our government.

To me, this was clearly a violation of the constitutional authority of the President to set foreign policy with the advice and consent of the U.S. Senate, and it had to stop.

I took my concerns directly to President Clinton in a meeting at the White House that included my aides Admiral Bud Nance, Steve Biegun, and Steve Berry.

The President had invited the Vice President to join the meeting, along with other senior advisors.

The President listened very carefully as we emphasized the point that the making of foreign policy and the instructions for how it will be implemented can come *only* from the President and be managed, under his supervision, by people under his authority in the State Department.

He then asked to see our recommendations for change, and my staff members laid out a plan for State Department reorganization that merged the United States Information Agency and the Arms Control and Disarmament Agency with the State Department and brought the Agency for International Development under the State Department's control.

The President agreed to take a serious look at our proposal, and he made good on that agreement.

On April 18, 1997, *The Washington Post* ran an article by John F. Harris and Thomas W. Lippman that gave the full story:

> President Clinton Thursday approved a broad reorganization of the State Department and three other foreign affairs agencies, a move that administration officials said was spurred in part by the need to accommodate congressional Republicans and keep them from thwarting Clinton's foreign policy agenda. . . . The reorganization, which officials said would be announced soon, is a longstanding priority of Senate Foreign Relations Chairman Jesse Helms, R-N.C. . . .
>
> In principle, the administration plan sounds much like what Helms wants. . . . White House officials made clear their view that there are sound policy reasons for the reorganization regardless of Helms' views. Gore and his staff shepherded the reorganization as part of the "Reinventing Government" program he has championed, aimed at stream-

lining and modernizing the way federal agencies work. As a practical matter, however, the plan Gore ultimately unveiled strongly resembled one offered by Helms two years ago.

Conservatives like Helms are broadly skeptical of both international development and disarmament, and both AID and the arms control agency have been favorite targets for years. The administration fought Helms tooth and nail over his proposal throughout 1995.

In describing our reaction to this news, the reporters said, "A Helms aide sounded triumphant." You bet he did; we *all* did. Reshaping the State Department to be an arm of the U.S. government and not a government of its own was a significant achievement. We were proud to see our years of work pay off so well.

On October 21, 1998, the Foreign Affairs Reform and Restructuring Act of 1998 was signed into law. At long last the United States Information Agency and the Arms Control and Disarmament Agency were brought under the control of the State Department and the President of the United States.

To the bitter end, Senator John Kerry and a few other liberal Senators fought the reorganization in committee hearings and on the floor of the Senate.

Fortunately, the majority of the Senate understood, as the President did, how urgent reorganization had become, and they rejected appeals to continue to allow independent agencies to run their own uncontrolled little foreign policy factories.

It was almost four full years from the day we first brought the issue of State Department reorganization to the Senate Foreign Relations Committee to the day the authorization bill was signed by the President and the changes authorized. As tough as this battle was, it was worth every bit of the effort it took to win it!

TREATIES

As far as I could see, President Bill Clinton never saw a treaty he didn't want to get in on—no matter how bad a deal it would have been for our country.

In April 2000, when it looked like President Clinton would attempt, in his final months in office, to strike a major arms-control deal with Russia including an anti-ballistic missile (ABM) treaty that would have limited the United States' ability to defend itself against ballistic missile attack, I took my concerns to my colleagues.

White House officials had openly stated their concern that Mr. Clinton faced the prospect of leaving office without a major arms-control agreement to his credit—the first President in memory to do so. It appeared that Mr. Clinton or members of his staff wanted an agreement, a signing ceremony, a final photo-op picture of the President shaking hands with the Russian President, broad smiles on their faces, large, ornately bound treaties under their arms, as the cameras clicked for perhaps the last time—a final curtain call of sorts.

I observed that if the price of that final curtain call was a resurrection of the U.S.-Soviet ABM treaty that would prevent the United States from protecting itself against missile attack, then that price was far too high. With all due respect, I did not intend to allow this President to establish his "legacy" by binding the *next* generation of Americans to a future without a viable national missile defense.

For nearly eight years, while North Korea and Iran raced forward with their nuclear programs and while China literally stole the most advanced nuclear secrets of the United States, *and* while Iraq escaped international inspections, President Clinton did everything in his power to stand in the way of deploying a national missile defense.

Want some facts? Let's state some for the record: In 1993, just months after taking office, President Clinton ordered that *all* proposals for missile defense interceptor projects be returned, unopened, to the contractors who had submitted them. In December of that same year, he withdrew the Bush administration's proposals for fundamentally altering the ABM treaty to permit deployment of national missile defenses (at a time when Russia was inclined to strike a deal).

By 1996, three years after taking office, Mr. Clinton had completely gutted the national missile defense program, slashing the national missile defense budget by more than 80 percent. In 1997, Mr. Clinton signed two agreements to revive and expand the U.S.-Soviet ABM treaty, including one that would expand ABM restrictions not just to prevent national missile defense for the American people, but to constrain theater missile defenses to protect our troops in the field as well.

Then, for the next three years, the President, heeding some of his advisors, refused to submit those agreements to the U.S. Senate (despite having made a legally binding commitment to do so) for fear that the Senate would reject them in order to clear the way for rapid deployment of missile defenses. In December 1995, Mr. Clinton vetoed legislation that would have required the deployment by 2001 of a national missile defense with an initial operational capability.

Three years later, in 1998, he again killed missile-defense legislation—the American Missile Protection Act, which called for the deployment of national missile defense as soon as the technology was ready—by threatening a veto and rallying Democratic Senators to filibuster the legislation.

Only in 1999 did he, at long last, sign missile-defense legislation into law—but only after it passed both houses of Congress by a veto-proof majority, and only after the independent Rumsfeld Commission had issued a stinging bipartisan report declaring that the Clinton administration had dramatically underestimated the ballistic missile threat to the United States.

But while Mr. Clinton was doing all this, at a cost to America of almost eight years in a race against time to deploy missile defenses, our adversaries were forging ahead with their missile systems. At the same time that Mr. Clinton was dragging his feet, foreign ballistic missile threats to the U.S. grew in terms of both range and sophistication.

Today, several third-world nations possess or are developing ballistic missiles capable of delivering chemical, biological, or nuclear warheads to targets in the United States. So if Mr. Clinton was in search of a legacy, he already had one: our nation's continued and inexcusable vulnerability to ballistic missile attack. Eight years of negligence equals eight years of lost time.

In the twilight of his Presidency, Mr. Clinton wanted to strike an ill-considered deal with Russia to purchase Russian consent to an inadequate U.S. missile defense—one single site in Alaska, to be deployed (but not until 2005) in exchange for a new, revitalized ABM treaty that would permanently ban any truly national missile defense.

The President attempted to lock the United States into a system that could not defend the American people against even the limited threats we faced at the very beginning of the twenty-first century. The President tried to resurrect the U.S.-Soviet ABM treaty to make impossible any future enhancements to national missile defense.

After dragging his feet on missile defense for nearly eight years, Mr. Clinton would have, in his final months in office, tied the hands of the next President. I insisted that we not allow him to constrain the next administration from pursuing a real national missile defense.

I did not want anyone to misunderstand my position. As long as I was the Chairman, any modified ABM treaty negotiated by the Clinton administration was dead on arrival at the Senate Foreign Relations Committee. Their failed security policies had burdened our nation long enough, and a new President deserved to have the freedom and flexibility to establish his own security policies. It should have been clear that the United States was no longer legally bound by the U.S.-Soviet ABM treaty, because it expired when the Soviet Union—our treaty partner—ceased to exist.

I did not want to waste the committee's time looking at the equivalent of "going out of business" deals put together for expedience instead of the benefit of our country. I believed we could wait a few more months for a new President, committed to doing it and doing it right, to protect the American people. Fortunately, I was right, and in George W. Bush we did get a President who understood the critical importance of a strong defense.

It has been suggested that I should concede that the opponents of a missile-defense shield may have creditable arguments for their view. I cannot concede any such thing, based on what I have learned in thirty years of consideration of effective options to protect U.S. citizens. It is our delays and diversions of resources that have made this program so expensive. Instead of acting when we should have, we have left ourselves unprotected while we wasted money on other things. We must not think for a minute that our defense can be assured by someone else's promises. We must move ahead on our missile-defense system.

Critics have accused me over the years of being an obstructionist or isolationist because of my refusal to hop on every treaty bandwagon lined up in the liberal parade. I *have* been selective, but it has been my pleasure to be part of significant decisions that have been good for freedom-loving countries around the world, and good for us.

That was certainly the case when it came to the expansion of the North Atlantic Treaty Organization in 1988. I was pleased to encourage my fellow Senators to vote in favor of changes in those agreements that would allow Poland, Hungary, and the Czech Republic into the NATO alliance and recognize their status as stable, democratic countries. After a thorough debate and careful fact-gathering, the Senate reached a broad consensus on the wisdom of NATO expansion.

That work stretched out over almost a year and included many discussions with leaders within the Clinton administration to amend their approach to NATO expansion. The Senate Foreign Relations Committee and the Senate

NATO Observer Group made concerted efforts to address the contentious issues early on, to ensure that the major problems with NATO expansion were addressed by the time the issue reached the Senate floor.

When we began the Foreign Relations Committee's extensive hearings on NATO expansion, I gave the administration a clear warning, emphasizing that there was a right way and a wrong way to expand NATO and that in my view, and in the view of many Senators, the administration was doing it the *wrong* way.

When Secretary Albright first came to testify before the Foreign Relations Committee, I told her that while I wanted to be helpful to her in achieving Senate ratification of NATO expansion, it was essential that we work together to fix what was wrong with the administration's approach — and make sure it was done the *right* way. During the ensuing months, that is exactly what we did.

We held eight separate hearings in the Senate Foreign Relations Committee to discuss and debate all aspects of the administration's plan for NATO expansion. We heard from thirty-eight different witnesses and produced a hearing transcript that was 532 pages long. Concurrently, the Foreign Relations Committee worked with Secretary Albright to make the necessary course corrections in the administration's approach to expansion. When we finally voted on the Senate's resolution of ratification, we were not voting just to expand NATO; we were voting to expand NATO the *right* way.

Some have suggested that we take steps to curtail NATO's ability to act "out of area" (i.e., outside the North Atlantic area). That would be a serious mistake. The threats to the NATO alliance are changing and evolving. The day may not be far off when the principal threat to the territory of NATO members will be not a resurgent Russia but a missile strike or terrorist attack launched by a rogue state from another and different region of the globe. In fact, that day may have already arrived with NATO's takeover of peacekeeping in Afghanistan in August 2003.

Would we really want to constrain NATO's ability to respond out of area with disproportionate force against a regime that dared to use chemical or biological weapons on the territory of a NATO member? Would we want to bar NATO's ability to strike "out of area" to prevent such an attack? Of course not! With the end of the Cold War, NATO's ability to act out of area will be more important, as threats to the territory of NATO members change and evolve.

Some have said that NATO expansion would be unnecessarily provocative to Russia. That view has proven to be just plain wrong. NATO expansion in no way threatened Russian democracy, nor did it do anything to preclude building friendly relations with Russia.

As Dr. Henry Kissinger pointed out, NATO expansion encouraged Russian leaders to "break with the fateful rhythm of Russian history . . . and discourage Russia's historic policy of creating a security belt of important and, if possible, politically dependent states around its borders." In other words, Russia no longer has the option, should the temptation ever arise, of seeking to restore its hegemony in Central Europe. With that avenue shut off, Russia is more likely to seek constructive options in its relations with the West.

Some others suggested that the Senate require Poland, Hungary, and the Czech Republic to first gain admission to the European Union before they would be admitted into NATO. With all due respect to our friends in Europe, the European Union could not fight its way out of a wet paper bag. Giving the EU a veto over who does and who does not get into NATO would be nothing less than the abdication of American leadership in Europe.

The fact is, admitting Poland, Hungary, and the Czech Republic to NATO was in America's security interests. These nations are among the most reliable, pro-American NATO allies we could hope for. Indeed, I'd go so far as to say that not only do these countries need NATO, America needs these countries in NATO.

While many of our current NATO allies stuck their heads in the sand over the threatening menace of Saddam Hussein, it was Poland, Hungary, and the Czech Republic that immediately, and without hesitation, said they would send their troops in alongside American forces if a military response was necessary in Iraq. They were indeed among the "coalition of the willing" who stood with us in 2003.

Further, while many of our friends in Europe pursue mercantilist policies in Cuba and China, these countries stand with us in working to promote human rights and democracy in those last bastions of Communism.

I remain convinced that Poland, Hungary, and the Czech Republic will always be among the first to stand with us in times of crisis, and will support America as we work to ensure that NATO remains what it is today—the most effective military alliance in human history.

I consider it one of my proudest moments as Chairman of the Senate Foreign Relations Committee to have helped usher in those three nations' admission to NATO and thus help them secure their rightful place in the community of Western democracies.

But still we face the moral challenge of working to right the wrongs perpetrated in the last century at Yalta, when the West abandoned the nations of Central and Eastern Europe to Stalin and a life of servitude behind the Iron Curtain. We have not yet fully erased those scars. I was one of a group of Senators who defended the independence of what came to be known as the "Captive Nations," the Baltic states of Lithuania, Latvia, and Estonia—and who worked to make sure that the United States never recognized their illegal annexation by the Soviet Union.

With the collapse of Communism, those nations finally achieved their rightful independence from Russian occupation and domination. Yet Russia still looms menacingly over these countries. In looking at the current Russian government, one gets the distinct impression that the Russian leadership still considers Baltic independence to be a temporary phenomenon. That is an impression the Russians cannot be allowed to long entertain.

Just as we never recognized the Soviet annexation of the Baltic states, we must not today repeat the mistakes of the 1940s by acknowledging a Russian sphere of influence in what Russian leaders ominously call the "near abroad." These nations' independence will never be fully secure until they are safe from the threat of Russian domination and are fully integrated into the community of Western democracies.

I believe it is right for the Baltic states to join their neighbors—Poland, Hungary, and the Czech Republic—as members of the NATO alliance, along with Slovenia, Slovakia, Romania, and Bulgaria. This is vital not only for their security but for ours as well.

Among the treaties wandering the world with U.S. signatures and no logical hope of ratification as long as one-third of the U.S. Senate is in control of its senses are pacts based on spurious science or "political correctness." These treaties, the Ottawa Land Mine Convention and the Chemical Weapons Convention, are objectionable on many levels, but none of them are as genuinely dangerous and un-American as the International Criminal Court.

In the opinions of most legal experts who have studied the issue, it was outrageous and unconscionable for the Clinton administration to sign the Rome treaty in January of 2001 establishing the International Criminal Court. The President himself said at the time he agreed to sign: "In signing, however, we are not abandoning our concerns about significant flaws in the treaty. In particular, we are concerned that when the court comes into existence, it will not only exercise authority over personnel of states that have ratified the treaty, but also claim jurisdiction over personnel of states that have not."

The court still claims today to hold the power to indict, try, and imprison American citizens—even if the American people refuse to join the court. This brazen assault on the sovereignty of the American people is without precedent in the annals of international treaty law.

In 2002, President George W. Bush signed into law the American Service-members Protection Act. This legislation, which Senator John Warner and I introduced along with a number of our House and Senate colleagues, protects U.S. citizens from the jurisdiction of the International Criminal Court. By law, we reject any claim of jurisdiction by the ICC over American citizens. Period.

In treaties, as in all of government, the price of freedom is eternal vigilance. There is nothing inherently wrong with entering into treaties. The risk and the wrong are directly tied to our diligence in carefully considering what the agreements will mean to us and to generations who will be bound by our decisions.

We must remember that only America has America's best interests at heart, and that we have a sacred responsibility never to commit our country to an agreement that does us harm—today or one hundred years from now.

TAIWAN

In the late nineteenth century, the Chinese ceded Taiwan to the Japanese. Following World War II it was returned to the Chinese. In 1949 Taiwan became the refuge of freedom for two million Chinese nationalists who fled for their lives after the Communists took over their government on the mainland. These Chinese nationalists established a government that was based on the democratic constitution accepted for all of China in 1947. In the decades since then, the people of Taiwan, both native born and citizens by choice, have forged a society that is a model of what can be done when the principles of personal freedom and free enterprise are protected. One can only look at Taiwan and wonder what the people of China could have accomplished in those same decades if theirs had been a democratic government and they had been allowed to live as free men and women.

The brave and able people of Taiwan have always been close to my heart. I admire their record as the Republic of China, both for their past history and their present achievements. I admire the fact that the Chinese people in Tai-

wan are staunchly anti-Communist. I admire the fact that they are hardworking. I admire the fact that they cherish their culture and their history. The
people of Taiwan knew that they could count on me to speak up on their behalf
whenever I could.

In my experience, few matters bother the American people more than the
fact that the cause of freedom, the cause of justice, the cause of personal dignity
and development, have too often been trampled by the forces of socialism and
Communism and exclusionary religious fundamentalism throughout the world.

The American people are opposed to this sort of repression. They realize
that all of these "isms" have at their roots a philosophy in direct opposition to
our own deeply entrenched views of liberty, law, and the Supreme Being. In
the end, there can be no compromise. Either freedom will triumph or the
forces of repression will.

The American people feel this way, and it follows that our foreign policy
should reflect the view of the people. We should be working to undermine
the economic power, the social stability, and the military strength of every anti-
freedom regime in the world. We should be working to encourage those governments that adopt free enterprise principles and a constitutional system, and
that support the traditional values of our civilization. But the American people
know that this has not been a policy we have followed very consistently.

There was a time when the American people were told that Mao Zedong
was "an agrarian reformer" working for noble goals. There was a steady drum-
beat of propaganda. "Experts" argued that America should support the Communist forces in China. And, as many scholars have demonstrated—and as
many hearings in the Senate later conclusively revealed—there were those in
the State Department who worked quietly to implement a pro-Communist policy in China. The public campaign in the media was matched by those in the
State Department who sought to undercut the anti-Communists and to, as they
say, "normalize" relations with the Communists without regard for abhorrent
policies on the human rights of their own citizens. President Jimmy Carter took
it on himself during his administration to abrogate a treaty we had signed with
Taiwan after World War II pledging our mutual defense. Mr. Carter's audacity
in ignoring the role of the U.S. Senate in making, modifying, or ending treaty
agreements was an exhibit of the disrepair of our foreign policy apparatus.

In 1979, following Jimmy Carter's unexpected and unreasonable decision
to transfer diplomatic recognition from Taipei to Beijing, the Congress passed

the Taiwan Relations Act to preserve our relationship with this courageous nation. We believed that it was vital for our allies and for those who were not our allies to know that the United States would not abandon its friends. We wanted to make clear our continued opposition to Communism and our support of Taiwan's right to pursue the path of democracy.

The quarter century since the passage of the Taiwan Relations Act has been historic. Much has changed in that region of the world, but instead of shrinking under the pressure of the Communist government in Beijing, Taiwan has become the best possible example of what is possible when a nation has the advantages of an open society, a democratic government, and an economy based on the miracle of the free-enterprise system.

At one point, in 1985, my good friends in the State Department nominated Morton Abramowitz to be Assistant Secretary of State for Intelligence and Research. While I did not have all the facts on his background, I knew that he had held many positions in the State Department, in the Department of Defense, and in the diplomatic corps relating to the Far East. When his hearing came up, the sellout of Taiwan was particularly on my mind. I asked him if he thought that Taiwan should be pressured into making an accommodation with the Communist government in Beijing.

The candidate refused to answer my question. To his credit, he didn't give a mealymouthed answer. He simply said that he did not have to answer questions on policy. In other words, he felt that the State Department should not be accountable to the people of the United States. He seemed to think that the Constitution should be set aside in his case, since he was so much more important than a mere U.S. Senator.

While he was reticent to speak up at my request, a number of his former colleagues made themselves helpful, particularly in making me aware of the nominee's previously published work laying out a plan for the U.S. to abandon its allegiance to Taiwan in favor of the People's Republic.

He recommended all of the following:

1. That the United States should not fight too hard to keep Taiwan in the United Nations.

2. That we should convince Beijing that we are serious about the Taiwan issue by adopting the policy that there is but one China and Taiwan is its province.

3. That we should not allow Taiwan to become militarily independent.

4. That we should move step by step toward the abrogation of the
mutual defense treaty.

5. That we should always allow our policy toward Beijing to be
guided by the goal of convincing Taiwan that it is in its best interest
to accept autonomy or some other arrangement under Beijing's sovereignty.

If you recognize this list, you recognize an outline of the steps that became
the Kissinger foreign policy, which was continued by President Carter and by
succeeding administrations. But in 1970, none of these events had yet happened.
The American people and the U.S. Congress were strongly opposed to the betrayal of the freedom and independence of the Republic of China. That is why I
have called these actions a secret campaign against the American people.

Here is the most important reason for insisting that we must always be informed about what is happening in our government. We must be constantly on
guard against backroom policy makers who are promoting concessions to those
who work against our express interests. America is a great country and it has
great leaders. But even great leaders make mistakes when they are misinformed
about the facts.

The Taiwan Relations Act proved its value again and again by prohibiting
the implementation of ill-advised policy. It did not matter what undersecre-
taries and their colleagues thought. It did not matter that the success of Taiwan
was an annoyance and an embarrassment to Beijing. The promises of the
United States would be kept. Through the administration of five different U.S.
Presidents, the Taiwan Relations Act has remained unchanged. Its provisions
have assured that our policies toward China and its neighbors have been sound
no matter who was elected or appointed to implement them.

In the summer of 1999 we called a Congressional hearing to review Taiwan's self-defense capabilities and advocate for bolstering U.S. defense sales to
Taiwan in light of the threat posed by the People's Republic of China.

I believed the need to enhance our defense relationship with Taiwan was
obvious. The reunification of Hong Kong with China and the upcoming return
of Macau slated for December 1999 made reunification with Taiwan an increasingly high-agitation issue for Beijing. Our own Pentagon report had concluded that China was engaged in a massive missile buildup opposite Taiwan,

and undergoing a multifaceted military expansion that included increased emphasis on Taiwan.

All this activity was accompanied by ugly, threatening rhetoric aimed at Taiwan by the highest levels of the Chinese government. It was clear to me, and to anyone else who fairly considered the evidence, that Taiwan faced a very real threat. Taiwan's military has operated in virtual isolation for decades. It does not conduct joint exercises with our troops and it is not even able to observe many of our exercises. No U.S. officers above the rank of colonel or Navy captain can go to Taiwan, and those who do are limited in the things they can say and do. Past and present U.S. administrations had bent to Chinese pressure to limit or cease arms sales to Taiwan. I believed these restrictions on joint U.S.-Taiwan military cooperation had a corrosive effect on Taiwan's military preparedness, at exactly the time Taiwan faced a growing military threat from China.

Senator Bob Torricelli and I offered the Taiwan Security Enhancement Act to the Senate. The goal of this legislation was to ensure that Taiwan would have essential self-defense capabilities through the purchase of needed equipment and assistance to achieve and maintain an adequate military readiness.

A part of Beijing's strategy includes pressure on the U.S. to limit or cease arms sales to Taiwan. This has had an effect at various times on successive U.S. administrations. Of course, it was the Reagan administration that signed the regrettable 1982 communiqué that set a ceiling on arms sales to Taiwan and promised China that we would gradually reduce these sales.

Over the years, the United States has refused to sell Taiwan needed defense items, such as submarines and advanced medium-range air-to-air missiles (AMRAAMs), solely to assuage China. The Clinton administration withheld several arms-sale notifications from Congress and considered further measures in an obvious attempt to curry favor with Beijing and punish Taiwan for President Lee Teng-hui's remarks on Taiwan's status.

The United States' strategic interests, law, and moral values dictate that we help our longtime friends in Taiwan to meet these challenges. Sadly, an interest in economic gain has trumped our concern for those principles.

In 2000 I sent a letter to President Clinton before he went overseas to meet with the President of China, Jiang Zemin. In that letter I detailed my misgivings about our relations with China and their negative impact on Taiwan.*

Before President George W. Bush made a trip to China in 2002, I offered

---

*The letter appears as Appendix 5.

him some guidance, too. I wanted him to know that when he arrived in China, three issues would be pleading for his attention: (1) religious freedom for the Chinese people; (2) the People's Liberation Army's intimidation of Taiwan; and (3) China's cooperation with what the President has accurately called the "axis of evil."

It has become a custom for the Chinese leaders, just prior to an American President's visit, to take long-overdue actions—and in 2002, they did it again: The Beijing government released Hong Kong businessman Li Guangqiang after having jailed him for "smuggling" Bibles into China. This fakery—pretending that Communist China might, at long last, be relenting on its religious persecution—did lead a few critics to hope the Beijing regime was at last getting set to adopt a more permissive approach.

Such hopes were, of course, false. It was merely fantasyland all over again. Indeed, several explosive documents came forth detailing the Chinese government's strategy to crush religion in China. A document dated October 2001 blew the cover off the highest levels of the Chinese government. Another document exposed tactics such as monitoring, infiltration, outright force, and coercion of church members by spies planted in the congregations.

This issue is close to President Bush's heart but has fallen into a favorite trap of U.S. diplomats: the sad routine of having a "dialogue" with the Chinese government. I believe that President Bush simply must speak directly to the Chinese people about religious liberty and its benefits to humanity. Business as usual with the Chinese government should be unthinkable unless and until Beijing allows true religious freedom, for example by allowing Vatican-approved Catholic churches, bishops, and priests in China to hold services.

Beijing's double-talk about religious freedom is highly instructive when one contemplates China's phony charm regarding Taiwan. U.S. editorial writers promptly gushed approval of China's softer, new line on Taiwan. It is, of course, obvious that Beijing's first-ever offer to meet with officials from Taiwan's ruling party (provided the Taiwanese accept the one-China policy) is the same old bait and switch.

Clearly, mere tactical political maneuvers must not mislead—let alone interest—the United States. What is of interest must be Beijing's strategic intentions regarding Taiwan. Every effort should be made to prevent Beijing's achieving them.

The record of China's failed promises to the people of Hong Kong cannot be ignored when they offer their solutions to the "Taiwan issue." The one country/two systems option held out to the citizens of Hong Kong has proven to be a worthless and malicious promise. Each passing month has seen new examples of repression that expose the unwillingness of a Communist regime to risk even the smallest pocket of freedom. The "democratic reforms" that the citizens of Hong Kong were promised have been delayed and diminished over and over—in violation of their own laws.

If one city cannot be allowed to have local democratic rule, how could anyone expect that Taiwan would be allowed to continue to live in freedom as a part of the Chinese Republic? Clearly, the fate of a democracy can never be put in the hands of a totalitarian regime.

Until democracy comes to the mainland, we must continue to do our part to maintain the safety of Taiwan. We must continue to press for Beijing to renounce the use of force against Taiwan. We must insist that Beijing reverse the military buildup that is so clearly aimed at Taiwan.

Until and unless the threat is removed, the United States must remain steadfast about our intent to defend Taiwan. We cannot assume that the threat will diminish simply because so many years have passed without overt attack.

Our vigilance and refusal to negotiate away the right of the citizens of any nation to live in freedom must be matched by a forceful military posture. In this case, the joint U.S.-Taiwan commitment to mutual security has alone created deterrence in the Taiwan Strait, while maintaining the U.S. "relationship" with the Communists in Beijing has had little effect.

President Bush must challenge China's rampant distribution of dangerous weapons to the "axis of evil." In his State of the Union address of 2002, President Bush properly linked terrorism and proliferation, warning, "States like these, and their terrorist allies, constitute an axis of evil, arming to threaten the peace of the world." Thus the "axis of evil" included not just Iran, Iraq, and North Korea, but also unspecified other countries that support such regimes.

All three of the regimes identified by President Bush were major recipients of China's deadly exports. As long as there is evidence that Chinese shipments of dangerous materials to the axis (or any terrorist regime, for that matter) continue, then how can China itself be considered anything but part of the axis? One can only hope, as some have speculated, that September 11 forced the Chinese regime to rethink its priorities and align itself with the United States. Based on our long experience with the Chinese, we can only hope they will finally understand that while they might win battles and may bend the will of the weak, their narrow and fear-driven rule can never triumph over freedom.

And we can pray that our own character as a nation will remain strong, and that we will never again give in to the lure of putting commerce ahead of common decency—or our commitment to stand with those who love freedom as much as we do, like our friends who live in Taiwan. As long as the defense and preservation of democracy is our national goal, our investments in freedom will pay valuable dividends of the sort we have seen in Taiwan.

ISRAEL

In 1984, people who were working against my reelection spread a rumor among my friends indicating that I was not supportive of Israel.

Of course, nothing could have been further from the truth, but until that time I had never had the opportunity to meet with pro-Israeli leaders in the United States. My friend and colleague U.S. Senator Chic Hecht of Nevada decided that the best way to put the rumors to rest was to introduce me to the people who had been told the lies with the hope that they would repeat those lies to others who would respect their opinion. Chic thought the truth would be obvious once people heard me speak for myself on the issues that concerned them.

Chic arranged a breakfast in New York City so that these leaders, who knew him well and would trust his opinion, could get to know me and ask me directly about any concerns that they had. Chic invited thirty-nine people to a 7 a.m. breakfast just a month before Election Day. Every one of them showed up!

They all wanted to see this monster they had heard about. At first, they were polite but not cordial. I said, "Let's talk a little about the things that you know we agree on." I went down the list. I commended them on their family values. I explained my idea about aid to Israel.

Then they relaxed, and we began a very animated discussion. The breakfast wound up with my talking about moral principles. I never will forget it. They all came up to speak with me personally, and it was just like old home week in eastern North Carolina. One lady in particular had tears streaming down her cheeks. She said, "I want to apologize to you." I said, "Well, for goodness' sake, why?" and she said, "Well, before today I just have actively disliked you—and I was unfair to you. I'm on Jim Hunt's advisory committee, and I'm going to call him as soon as I get to my office and tell him to take my name off his stationery." I never again had any more such trouble.

Chic thought it was important for Dot and me to see Israel for ourselves and to get to know the leaders in government and in education, along with some ordinary citizens. I was willing to make the trip but not at the taxpayers' expense, so Chic arranged for a private trip in August 1985.

We spent seven packed days meeting with members of the Israeli Foreign Ministry; the chancellor of Hebrew University; Prime Minister Shimon Peres; Ariel Sharon (then minister of industry and trade); the foreign minister, Yitzhak Shamir; the mayor of Hebron; and as many Israeli citizens as we could during our time in the Golan Heights, Tel Aviv, Jerusalem, Judea, and Haifa. Our week included many moving moments, such as visits to schools and medical facilities that the Hecht family had made possible through their personal generosity. It was my honor to be a witness to the dedication of the Hecht Synagogue, built on the campus of Hebrew University on Mount Scopus to honor Chic's father, who turned ninety-six that year.

Chic was right. By going to Israel without any "agenda," I was able to ask many questions and see for myself the challenges facing Israelis in their maintaining a hold on their ancient homeland. Beyond that, I established lines of communication that proved invaluable as I attempted to get to the facts about issues related to Israel in coming years.

Our trip was not a big media event, but it did get some publicity that turned out to be a portent of things to come. In September 1985, CBS ran a negative story on the evening news about "Congressional junketeering" and showed clips from our trip to Israel as their example. The only problem was that CBS hadn't bothered to check the facts. If CBS had made even so much as one call to either Senator Hecht or to me, they would have learned that our trip didn't cost taxpayers a dime. The reporter would have been told, as if it wasn't already well known, that I was not a fan of nonessential trips either. But, of course, CBS didn't call—and they didn't check—and a few nights after their "hard-hitting report" aired, anchor Dan Rather made a public, on-air apology for the errors in that report. (In September 2004, when CBS proudly paraded false National Guard documents as real—documents that in fact wrongly smeared President Bush—Mr. Rather and his team once again skipped the most basic rule of fair reporting: Get the facts straight.)

AS OUR TRIP TO ISRAEL revealed, there are many reasons why the United States should be a good friend to Israel, but none is more important than the right of Israeli citizens to live with freedom from fear of their neighbors. Indeed, this is a right the innocent citizens of every country should enjoy.

For all of his talk when it was to his advantage, Yassir Arafat was an agent of terrorism. He supported in every way the attacks on innocent children, families at worship, and civilians going about the routines of their day on buses, in markets, and even in the presumed safety of their own homes.

Israel, of course, has an ancient and moral right to exist, repeatedly affirmed by the civilized nations of the world. But from the first day of its existence as a modern, independent, democratic nation, it has faced the hostility of nations, groups, and individuals who have made it their goal to see Israel obliterated.

Until his death in 2004, this hostility was primarily orchestrated and engineered by Yassir Arafat, who began his personal war against Israel as an arms smuggler in the late 1940s. In the 1950s he organized the terrorist organization Al Fatah. In 1968, following the Arab-Israeli war, he was made head of the Palestine Liberation Organization. For the next two decades the PLO specialized in acts of terrorism against the people and interests of Israel.

In 1988, Arafat changed public tactics and claimed that he would be willing to accept the existence of Israel. In 1993, he began secret peace talks that resulted in the Oslo Accords. Arafat shared the 1994 Nobel Peace Prize with Yitzhak Rabin and Shimon Peres. In 1996, Arafat was elected the first President of the Palestinian Council.

None of the new titles were matched by a genuine change in his support for terrorism. When he grew too old to do his own gun-running, Arafat was only too happy to cheer on new generations of fighters, even those who would kill themselves in pursuit of the death of their enemies.

It is beyond rational understanding to imagine anything less noble than a leader who deliberately encourages the death of his followers. Yet there is proof that the families of young men and women—even children—who blew themselves up with the bombs they carried on buses or into wedding halls, or into shopping areas or schools, received cash payments from organizations and individuals allied with Arafat.

But as faithless a leader as Arafat was, he cannot be given all of the credit for the situation in the one part of the world that should be most protected by all of the people who respect the history of their religion—whether Muslim, Jew, or Christian. Over the years the Middle East has become the flash point for worldwide rivalries. The relationships of "client states" have shifted as the fortunes of other governments, most notably the Soviet Union, have ebbed, but Israel has always been the target.

Among the nations with interests in the Middle East, only the United States has remained steadfast in support of Israel, and even that support is tempered by our concerns that the Israeli government not provoke hostility or embroil their allies in conflict.

We have used every channel to promote peace, from secret meetings to public negotiations, none more visible than the meeting between Egyptian president Anwar Sadat and Israeli Prime Minister Menachem Begin hosted at Camp David in 1978 by President Jimmy Carter.

While the negotiations themselves were secret, the agreement was signed with a great public flourish in the Rose Garden, where Israel and Egypt agreed on the location of their border and an end to hostilities. They mutually invited the United Nations to make sure the agreements were kept, and invited the United States to participate in future talks about how the accords might be implemented.

We've been talking ever since. To their great credit, the governments of Egypt and Israel have labored to maintain communications and model peaceful coexistence. But progress in the region is hard to discern. We are often asked to imagine how bad it would be if we were to lessen our involvement. That is a terrible way to try to find a hint of success.

As a consequence, we have become, if not the peacemakers between Israel and her neighbors, at least the peace*keepers*, by balancing weapons sales and using our influence with reasonable government leaders on all sides to restrain those who would overrun Israel. We have sought to be fair, to be the friend of all who want to pursue an end to hostilities.

We have used reams of paper to draft successive agreements, like the Oslo Accords, only to see them broken, often before the negotiators were able to get back to their homes. And yet we must not give up.

I believe peace in the Middle East must be a cornerstone of U.S. foreign policy. The Arab-Israeli conflict has for too long been an excuse for the Arab world to avoid democratization, economic liberalization, and political and civil reform. All the people of the Middle East deserve to live within safe and secure borders. However, I will never support a peace between Israel and any of its neighbors that is not a real peace, made without inducements or threats. A peace that is made under the thumb of any third party cannot be genuine or lasting.

Nor can any real peace be purchased. While we might be expected, as a nation whose generosity is unparalleled, to continue to respond to human need wherever it occurs, we must never give in to the blackmail of those who would barter peace for payments. That is not aid, it is blackmail, and it is certain to bring nothing but new hostilities and new demands.

It is one of the sad ironies of our time in history that the very land and even the very sites where the one we call the Prince of Peace spent His time on earth know so little respite from disputes and danger. We must do better, no matter how many years it takes. Surely the God of Abraham and *all* of Abraham's descendants will give us the wisdom to find a way.

THE POWER OF SANCTIONS

In December 2003, the government of Libya shocked the world by announcing that at long last it was willing to conform to all the requirements that had been set for their country as conditions for lifting the sanctions that had been placed against it. This dramatic change in a country that had flaunted its defiance of the international community and aligned itself with outlaw nations and terrorists was "facilitated" by sanctions. Sanctions have proven their value time and again as an effective means of persuasion. The change they brought about in Libya made that country keenly aware of the risk it ran if it continued its defiant behavior.

For years Saddam Hussein, another head of state who knew the sting of U.S. sanctions, had subjected the people of Iraq to deprivation rather than renounce his imperialism. When his mischief could no longer be tolerated, a coalition of countries removed him from power and offered the hope of liberation to all of Iraq's citizens. I am convinced Saddam could have been pulled from power much sooner if other governments had not allowed holes to form in the wall that sanctions were intended to erect. Those contacts fueled Saddam's continued cruelty.

Muammar Qaddafi must have seen his own reflection in photos of Saddam being rousted from the spider hole he called home, after the liberating troops had turned his Baghdad palaces into their own billets.

Sanctions have much to recommend them, including their proven effectiveness, but they do not work instantly. Congress has always been cautious and circumspect in its consideration of economic sanctions, passing just a handful of carefully targeted sanctions laws in recent years. Between 1993 and 1996,

Congress passed, and the President signed, five new sanctions laws: the Nuclear Proliferation Prevention Act of 1994; the Cuban Liberty and Democratic Solidarity Act of 1996; the Antiterrorism and Effective Death Penalty Act of 1996; the Iran-Libya Sanctions Act of 1996; and the Free Burma Act (included in the 1996 foreign operations appropriations bill). During the same period, the executive branch took four actions imposing new sanctions: declaring Sudan a terrorist state; banning imports of munitions and ammunition from China (announced simultaneously with the decision to renew China's most-favored-nation status); tightening travel-related restrictions, cash remittance levels, and gift parcels to Cuba (restrictions which have since been lifted); and imposing a ban on new contractual agreements or investments in Iran.

Economic sanctions are as American as apple pie and have been a vital tool in our nation's foreign policy arsenal since before the Republic itself. The first American economic sanctions were imposed by the American colonies in response to two separate pieces of unjust British legislation—first in response to the passage of the Stamp Act, and then again in response to passage of the Townshend Acts—in both cases forcing their repeal.

Both Thomas Jefferson and James Madison were passionate advocates of economic sanctions. They believed not only that sanctions were legitimate tools, but also that commercial weapons should be America's primary diplomatic tools.

In an 1805 letter to Jefferson, Madison argued: "The efficacy of an embargo ... cannot be denied. Indeed, if a commercial weapon can be properly crafted for the Executive hand, it is more and more apparent to me that it can force nations ... to respect our rights." Jefferson, for his part, contended that in foreign affairs, "three alternatives alone are to be chosen from. 1. Embargo. 2. War. 3. Submission and tribute."

Jefferson raises a good point. There are, in fact, only three tools in foreign policy: diplomacy, sanctions, and war. Take away sanctions and what would our options be when dealing with terrorists, proliferators, and genocidal dictators? Empty talk or sending in the Marines. That is not only unwise; it is a recipe for a retreat into isolationism. Without sanctions, we would be virtually powerless to influence events in any circumstance where the American people were not willing to spill the blood of U.S. soldiers.

Unilateral sanctions have been the linchpin of our nonproliferation policy. According to a now-public analysis by the Arms Control and Disarmament

Agency, "the history of U.S.-China relations shows that China has made specific non-proliferation commitments only under the threat or imposition of sanctions." Unless the United States intends to go to war with China, sanctions are the principal leverage we have to secure nonproliferation concessions. Sanctions have also played a crucial role in securing important trade concessions. The threat of unilateral U.S. sanctions on China over issues such as intellectual property rights and unfair trade barriers have several times in this last decade forced China to yield at the bargaining table after diplomatic negotiations failed.

Unilateral U.S. sanctions helped bring down the Soviet Union, as the Reagan administration skillfully employed economic weapons to cripple the Soviet economy. And certainly the hard-hitting U.S. sanctions imposed on Communist Poland after its martial law crackdown in 1981 played a pivotal role in forcing that regime to release political prisoners, including Lech Walesa, and to legalize the Solidarity movement—sparking the collapse of Communism in Poland and across the entire Eastern Bloc.

Simply "decertifying" Colombia for drug corruption without actually imposing any sanctions (in fact, U.S. aid to the Colombian police was increased) contributed to the Colombian people's repudiation of former President Ernesto Samper's narcodemocracy and his defeat in a bid for reelection.

When sanctions don't work, it's often because the target governments doubt our resolve to impose them and keep them imposed. When an administration treats sanctions not as a foreign policy tool but as a PR opportunity, or when the President signs a sanctions law with great fanfare in order to earn plaudits from domestic constituencies but then never follows through, that administration gains a well-deserved reputation for bluffing and grandstanding. No one yields to such toothless posturing.

Consider: In an elaborate White House ceremony, President Clinton signed the Iran-Libya Sanctions Act live on CNN. But once the camera lights dimmed and it came time to implement the sanctions, he lost his nerve. The message this sent to Iran (and other rogue states) was that the United States talks a tough game, but that under adequate pressure the administration will cave.

Iran is not an isolated case. After the Castro regime murdered four innocent people (including three American citizens) by shooting down two unarmed civilian planes flying over international waters, the President talked tough for the cameras and signed the Helms-Burton Act. But then he did everything in his power to avoid imposing the very sanctions he signed into law.

A 1996 *Wall Street Journal*/NBC News poll showed that only 30 percent of Americans agreed with the statement "We should maintain good trade relations with China, despite disagreements we might have with its human rights policies." Twice as many—60 percent—felt "We should demand that China improve its human rights policies if China wants to continue to enjoy its current trade status with the United States." Since 1996, that sentiment has grown even stronger.

This may shock pro-business lobbyists, but it was no surprise to me. Unlike some of our European brethren, Americans don't feel the need to sell our souls—or our national security—to create jobs and economic prosperity. Americans don't need to create jobs by selling thumbscrews to the world's tyrants.

I believe we must continue to support our policies isolating terrorist regimes. I believe we must oppose U.S. aid to countries and governments that support terrorism, commit genocide, harbor war-crimes suspects, or transship illegal drugs that poison our children. I believe all Americans should support banning the sale of lethal weapons to violent regimes. We should also continue to support seizing the assets of drug traffickers, banning imports from companies that use prison slave labor, and denying government-procurement contracts to foreign companies that sell dangerous missile technology to terrorist states. We must continue sanctions against companies and governments that spread nuclear, chemical, and biological weapons of mass destruction. We can do no less than support sanctions on countries that murder their own citizens and pile them into mass graves. We must never raise our pursuit of profits and comforts above our commitment to helping others have the opportunity to keep profits or have the comforts of freedom that we Americans enjoy.

THE UNITED NATIONS

The official history of the United Nations says that the name "United Nations" was first used by President Franklin D. Roosevelt in World War II when he issued a "Declaration by United Nations" on New Year's Day 1942. Representatives of twenty-six nations gave their assurance that day that their governments would fight together against the Axis powers who had gone to war against them.

After the Allies won the war, representatives of fifty nations met together in

San Francisco in 1945 at the United Nations Conference on International Organizations. The delegates at this conference considered proposals approved earlier by representatives of the United States, the Soviet Union, the United Kingdom, and China during a meeting at Dumbarton Oaks in Washington, D.C.

The conference began its work on April 25, 1945, just two weeks after the death of Franklin Roosevelt, who had first laid out the plans for the United Nations when he met at Yalta with Stalin and Churchill. It concluded nine weeks later when the United Nations Charter was signed on June 26, 1945, by all fifty of the nations represented.

The charter was twenty-six pages long, *double* the size of the proposals with which the representatives had begun. That should have been our first clue as to what lay ahead.

The cornerstone for the UN headquarters building was laid in New York City in 1949, a year after the first UN observer mission had been deployed to Palestine, and months before the Security Council called on "member states" to come to the aid of the South Koreans, who were being invaded by the North. The armistice to this conflict was signed in July of 1953, but more than fifty years later no peace agreement had been completed.

Before the first desk was moved into headquarters, it was clear that the United Nations was going to be bigger and more involved in both the internal and the external affairs of nations than anyone could have imagined.

An organization chart of the United Nations system provided by its Department of Public of Information in 2003 identifies the six principal organs that were established under the original charter, plus thirteen programs and funds, five "entities," nine functional commissions, eight regional commissions, five related organizations, fourteen specialized agencies, eighteen departments and offices of the Secretariat, seven major committees operated by the Security Council, and an indeterminate number of committees of the General Assembly, known as "main committees," "other sessional committees," "standing committees and ad hoc bodies," and "other subsidiary organs."

The annual budget for the United Nations in 2004 was $3.16 billion. The budget director who announced the budget noted that 75 to 80 percent of the $3.16 billion will go to payroll. This "no growth" budget is actually $270 million higher than the previous year's—an amount chalked up to "currency and inflation adjustments."

With this history of seemingly unstoppable expansion—obvious on any page of any report or press release from the United Nations—and the growing philosophy inside the organization (and in other quarters) that the UN should assume powers for itself that rightly belong to sovereign nations, America said enough is enough. In fact, it was well *past* time for the United States to make its displeasure known when we took a stand by means of the only process that would get the UN's attention: withholding money.

The United States Senate insisted that U.S. taxpayer money not be used to fund programs in opposition of U.S. policies, or billed as unfair assessment amounts, or without appropriate fiscal management of their budget.

As the amount by which the U.S. was "in arrears" climbed in the late 1990s, so did a willingness to listen to our concerns and a willingness to make changes that would improve the operation of the United Nations. Even if it could no longer be hoped that the UN could be kept from an unending proliferation of committees and agencies, perhaps, we thought, a tightened budget might encourage it to shut down some unnecessary operations before it opened more.

The first sign of a willingness to work together came when Kofi Annan was selected to succeed Boutros Boutros-Ghali as Secretary-General. Boutros-Ghali was a proponent of empowerment for the UN, seeking more and more ways in which it might assert itself in areas that were rightfully the province of individual member states. His expansionist priorities had driven the costs of operation beyond defensible levels, and the General Assembly's wisest members knew that to be fact.

As soon as Kofi Annan was chosen as Secretary-General, I sent him a letter of congratulations and an invitation to come to Washington. We could then meet and see how we might work together to resolve the differences between the United States and the UN over the by now $1 billion being held in arrears over the UN's failure to make reforms the Congress believed essential.

Following our meeting, I announced that I would personally introduce legislation to begin payment of the funds held in arrears as soon as benchmark reforms mandated by Congress were implemented. The Secretary-General agreed to my proposal and we spent the next year on the details that would make our hope for cooperation a reality.

In June 1999, the United States Senate passed the Helms-Biden bill. This legislation reflected the goodwill effort of Senator Biden and myself, UN Ambassador Holbrooke, Secretary Albright, and the White House to negotiate legislation that addressed (1) the need for the United Nations to rein in its spending, (2) the need for other nations to take on their fair share of UN expenses instead of enjoying a "free ride" paid for by the U.S., and (3) the responsibility of the United States to honor its legitimate agreements.

Once again we were able to demonstrate that standing firm for what is right inevitably would yield a good outcome.

In January 2000, I was given a historic invitation to be the first member of a legislative body to make a formal address to the United Nations Security Council. I was honored by this opportunity to talk frankly to this body about the issues that concerned and challenged us.* Our trip to New York along with other members of the Senate Foreign Relations Committee and our excellent staff opened new avenues of communication with both representatives of other governments and the leadership of the Security Council and the General Assembly.

Perhaps because I have never gotten the hang of talking like a diplomat, my speech made news because, as one thoughtful reporter put it, "it was straightforward and to the point." Apparently that provided quite a shock in a place where fluency in nuance and oblique references is a job requirement. If I had to give that speech again tomorrow, I wouldn't change a sentence.

It would be wonderful if I could point with pride to permanent changes under way at the United Nations because of our efforts, but that is not the reality. I am convinced there will never be real change in the United Nations without constant watchfulness.

Those who thought the outrageous notion of worldwide taxation promoted by former UN Secretary-General Boutros Boutros-Ghali had been put to rest now realize that it is again being discussed not just by representatives of the United Nations, but by some heads of government! We must make it clear in every possible way that the United States of America will never be a party to any such notion.

We must also make it clear that we will not countenance the thievery and greed that led to abuses in the Oil for Food program, intended to help the people of Iraq but turned instead into a source of revenue for Saddam and for the very UN administrators who were supposed to be assisting his oppressed citizens.

It is never popular with crooks to point out their crookedness, and it may

---

* The text of this speech is in Appendix 6.

not be popular with the folks who care more about increasing the power of the United Nations than they do about honoring the original limited and laudable purposes of the organization, but we ignore the day-to-day operation of the United Nations at our own peril.

When Secretary-General Kofi Annan dared to suggest that the action of the United States of America to depose a growing threat to our security in the nation of Iraq was "illegal," he exposed the flawed thinking of those who would turn the United Nations into some supragovernment. Those who responded to the Secretary-General's remarks by softly reminding him that he himself had previously made the legality of our country's actions clear, missed the point—nobody but the United States of America makes decisions for the United States of America. We saw a danger; we acted to protect our security. No one, especially not the Secretary-General, who knew for an absolute fact how many extra miles we had traveled to avoid conflict in the face of rising provocations, should dare to call that "illegal."

WHAT SHOULD WE DO in the face of unwarranted criticisms of our actions? What should we do in light of the flow of new revelations of corruption by poorly behaved peacekeepers in the Congo and more revelations of scandal in the Oil for Food program? What should we do as we learn more about the breadth of individual bureaucratic misadventures, from outright theft to favoritism? Should the United States finally throw up its hands and renounce its UN membership? I believe we should not. For all its flaws, the fact is that we would want to create a cooperative organization like the United Nations if it did not already exist.

That statement may shock those who have always equated my criticism of the United Nations with a desire to see it abolished, or at least to see the United States withdraw its membership.

Quite the contrary. I believe that the United States must be the strongest and most persistent voice for reform. I believe we must be the leader in keeping the United Nations true to its founding principles. I believe that instead of wasting time and resources on projects that are outside its mandate, the United Nations should focus its attention on the areas of common good around which all decent nations can unite.

Because we are the largest contributor to the work of the United Nations, we have the most to lose if the UN should collapse. Conversely, we have the most to gain if the UN should take on its rightful role as a champion of principled government and protector of those who are least able to help themselves.

The collective membership of the United Nations makes it almost a certain multiplier of power to promote freedom and stability around the world. A rogue nation or a rogue tyrant may ignore the concerns of an individual nation or even several nations, but when many nations band together to bring pressure on the rogue, the potential for a positive response is enhanced by their unity and determination.

This is exactly why corruption or mismanagement of any sort cannot be tolerated in the United Nations, why it must stand as an example of the best intentions of fair and honest governments and not as a practitioner of the actions and conditions it was intended to help eradicate.

In the years ahead, the United Nations must face the realities of the crimes against the world's most helpless citizens and act to eliminate trafficking in persons. The U.N. must pursue a universal ban on *all forms* of human cloning. It must address the problem of cyber-crime and theft of intellectual property. It must promote the rights of women and children, including women's suffrage in those countries where women still do not have the right to vote. It must be an agile responder when natural disasters demand emergency aid that is beyond the capability of the affected nation. It must model fairness and respect in its own treatment of its members and manage its affairs in a manner that is consistent with the trust those members have placed in its leaders.

In pursuing these goals, the United Nations can return to its original mission. It can fulfill the dreams of those who hope for an organization that will maintain international peace and security, develop friendly relations among nations, achieve international cooperation in order to solve international problems, and be a center to harmonize the actions of nations in the achievement of common ends.

No one could ask for a clearer mandate or a more noble purpose.

AMERICA'S PLACE IN THE WORLD

In the Sermon on the Mount, Jesus challenges His listeners with these words: "From everyone who has been given much, much will be demanded: and from the one who has been entrusted with much, much more will be asked" (Luke 12:48).

If it is right—and expected—for individuals to be generous with their blessings, how much more must it be true of a great nation? In all of human history, no country has ever had all the resources that we enjoy as Americans. Along with our riches, we have been given the wisdom to embrace the responsibilities that come with all we enjoy.

We are the most powerful nation in the world, but we have no colonies, no client states. Our military might is used in the defense of others, and in the defense of our people. If we have an "agenda," it is the desire that every human know the freedoms we enjoy as citizens of the United States. We believe, with President George W. Bush, that no country is beyond the hope of representative rule. In his 2004 State of the Union address, President Bush said,

> We also hear doubts that democracy is a realistic goal for the greater Middle East, where freedom is rare. Yet it is mistaken, and condescending, to assume that whole cultures and great religions are incompatible with liberty and self-government. I believe that God has planted in every human heart the desire to live in freedom. And even when that desire is crushed by tyranny for decades, it will rise again.

America is the only nation in history founded on an idea: the proposition that all men are created equal, and are endowed by their Creator with the inalienable right to life, liberty, and the pursuit of happiness. No other nation can make such a claim. This is what makes us unique. It is why, for more than two centuries, America has been a beacon of liberty for all who aspire to live in freedom. It is also why America has enemies. Those enemies hate the success with which the American idea has spread around the world. And they want to maneuver us into retreat or inaction. They want us to live in fear of defending freedom abroad. They want us to relinquish the freedom we have always enjoyed at home. They will not succeed.

We must strengthen our nation's moral and spiritual foundations so we can bear the weight of those who would lean on us in their own quests for liberty. We must instill in our young people an understanding that theirs is a nation founded by Providence to serve as a shining city on a hill—a light to the nations, spreading the good news of God's gift of human freedom.

For Americans, the apex of freedom is the freedom to worship as one chooses. The brave men and women who crowded into ships and sailed from

Europe to establish colonies an ocean away left everything they knew so they could follow their conscience and worship God without the restraint of government. This is not just an American right; this is a *human* right.

In the fall of 2000, Senator Paul Wellstone and I introduced an amendment to the bill that established permanent normal trade relations with China. We could put aside our well-known political differences because, as Americans, we wanted to encourage the Chinese government to extend this basic human right to the billions in China who are not free to worship as they choose. I was honored to support this amendment, and honored to cosponsor it with my friend from Minnesota. In this case, we both had the same conviction about what our government and our country ought to do before granting permanent normal trade relations to China.

Our amendment would have directed the President to certify that China had met a series of religious freedom conditions *before* granting them permanent normal trade relations.

The amendment was intended to tell China—and, just as importantly, the rest of the world—that we in America still stand for something other than profits, something other than whatever benefits were imagined by those willing to ignore injustice in order to forge a trading relationship.

What Senator Wellstone and I, and others who voted with us on this amendment, were saying was that we did not believe China should be welcomed into international organizations such as the World Trade Organization while China's government continues to repress, jail, murder, and torture their own citizens simply because those citizens have dared to exercise their faith.

Senator Wellstone and I were not exaggerating the problem. The State Department's own report on religious freedom that was delivered to the Congress of the United States just a week before we were asked to normalize trade relations said that in 1999, the Chinese government's respect for religious freedom had deteriorated markedly.

The questions we asked our fellow Senators were simple and stark. Were we going to ignore the facts—that China abuses, mistreats, and murders its own people? Were we going to ignore the crackdown on Christians that had begun that very month, during which three Americans—*Americans*, let me emphasize—were arrested by the Communist Chinese?

To this day, other crimes against religious believers in China abound. In the past few years, China has intensified its so-called patriotic reeducation campaign aimed at destroying Tibetan culture and religion. Similar horror stories are taking place in the Muslim northwest, where the Chinese government is persecuting and repressing anybody who attempts to display any kind of ethnic or true religious identity.

It was naive to believe these abuses would have been dealt with by the commission set up in the trade normalization legislation. The example of the newly created Commission on Religious Freedom had already been very instructive. After dramatically cataloging the barbaric crackdown on religious freedom in China, the commission recommended that permanent normal trade relations not be granted to China at that time. But nobody paid any attention to their findings. As far as the Senate was concerned, the commission had wasted its time.

So there we were, ready to toss all of those findings, all of the things we knew were going on, and say we ought to go ahead with our plans to normalize trade. They were going to do that without my vote. I believed then, and I believe now, that we should have insisted that progress on religious freedom precede China's entry into the WTO. Twenty-eight other Senators stood with Senator Wellstone and me to vote in favor of that amendment. Sixty of our colleagues opted to hope for the best. I do not know how they feel now, when they read of the ongoing persecution of the underground church in China or the relentless dismantling of the culture of Tibet. I do know that we lose more than we could possibly gain whenever America puts profit before principle.

And I know that while we are not a perfect country, we remain a blessed country, the beacon of hope to those who are oppressed. We have no more valuable export than personal freedom, no better gift to share than free enterprise, no higher priority than to help those who long to live free in their own homelands.

CHAPTER 32

The 1996 Campaign

W HEN THE 104TH CONGRESS convened in January 1995, Republicans controlled both houses of Congress, and I was now Chairman of the Foreign Relations Committee. Clearly, this was not the time for me to retire, and when asked the question on John McLaughlin's *One on One* program, I said that I would be running for reelection in 1996.

That probably wasn't the best way for Dot to learn that I had made up my mind—she was hoping that we might go home—but we both realized that I needed to keep on working.

As much as the Democrats wanted me out of office, they once again couldn't decide who might have the best chance of beating me. Once again I had to wait to see who my opponent would be. Charles Sanders (who had recently retired as CEO of Glaxo Pharmaceuticals) decided he would make a try for the nomination, and Harvey Gantt decided that he would run again. They were opposed by a third, lesser-known candidate, Ralph McKinney, whose campaign was overrun by the budgets and organization of the other two. For practical purposes, the Democratic primary was a two-man race.

As a political newcomer, Mr. Sanders had the handicaps of minimal organization and low name recognition, and while he had resources to improve his name recognition, his staff had a harder time engaging support. Mr. Gantt won the primary with 57 percent of the vote, in an election that had the lowest turnout in twenty years.

Once we knew our opponent would again be Mr. Gantt, we knew that we could expect the same sort of attacks and charges that had been flung at us in

1990. This invective hadn't worked in 1972, or in 1978, or in 1984, or in 1990, so we were hopeful that it wouldn't work this time either. I was happy to run on my twenty-four-year record and my same conservative principles.

My campaign staff and I also knew that Mr. Gantt and his advisors were well aware of the shift in the political mood of the country, and that they would want to reposition Candidate Gantt closer to the middle of the road.

My staff believed that the best way to keep the facts from getting lost in the fog was to keep them front and center. Early in the campaign, the staff prepared an ad with an anthology of Mr. Gantt's public speeches to groups all around the country. In those speeches he proclaimed that he was a liberal and proud of it!

We wanted to make sure the North Carolina electorate knew that their choice in 1996 was that old familiar decision from elections past. Did North Carolinians want to send a liberal to the Senate, who would vote in favor of the sorts of things liberals like (even though they lead to more taxes and more government intrusion in everyday life), or did they want to send *me* back to continue the fight for lower taxes, smaller government, and the traditional values liberals want to discard without a thought about the harm each loss causes our society?

In their drive to say anything to get rid of me, stories were dug up about the Jesse Helms Center and about Dot's real estate properties in Raleigh. The board of directors at Wingate University quickly and forcefully set the record straight about the purpose and operations of the Center, which has always been a nonpartisan 501(c)(3) organization whose prime mission is education.

Dot, for her part, was so angry about the twisted stories concerning her decades-old personal investments that she accepted an offer to appear on a Raleigh talk show and clear the air on this phony issue. I was fortunate enough to get into town in time to hear her that afternoon, and I was enormously proud of the way she handled herself in spite of her irritation at having her privacy invaded by people who prize innuendo over accuracy.

My last campaign finally ended after months of events that included visits on my behalf from former President Bush, Charlton Heston, Senators Fred Thompson and Kay Bailey Hutchison, and native daughter Elizabeth Dole, and rides in everything from boats and buses to planes and trains plus minivans and four-wheel-drives. I even did one fast lap in the official pace car around the track at the Charlotte Motor Speedway just before the flag dropped for a major Winston Cup race.

No wonder I was exhausted by November 5. Dot and I voted at 10:30 a.m. and headed home to rest.

The networks declared me a winner by 8:15 that night, but I waited to see the actual vote counts. The final results showed that when voters were asked to pick, their vote went our way by 53 percent to not quite 46 percent.

As hard as it still was for me to believe, I had been elected a fifth time to serve my state and my country.

I've seen some statistics recently on the vote percentages in each of my elections and some comparisons of the 1972 and 1996 campaigns that I found interesting. In 1996 the results were: Helms 53 percent, Harvey Gantt 46 percent. In 1990 they were: Helms 53 percent, Gantt 47 percent. The 1984 percentages were: Helms 52 percent, Governor Jim Hunt 48 percent. I had my biggest margin of victory in 1978—Helms 55 percent, John Ingram 45 percent—and in my first race the results were: Helms 54 percent, Nick Galifianakis 46 percent.

But the numbers behind the percentages are more revealing. In 1973, when I took office, the population of North Carolina was barely 5 million. By January 2001, when I retired, our state had grown to more than 8 million. The 54 percent of the vote I received in 1972 equaled 795,248. The 53 percent of the vote for me in 1996 came from 1,345,833 people, more than a half-million more supporters than I started with!

Our first campaign spent more than $650,000. The last one cost more than $14,500,000. I have heard all of the arguments explaining why a modern campaign is such an expensive undertaking, but I remain deeply concerned that today's high-dollar campaigns may be costing us some of our best new candidates simply because they do not have the personal resources to run competitively in states like North Carolina, where the urban TV markets cost millions to penetrate. I hope we will find a workable solution that is fair to candidates and fair to the electorate.

In 2001, as my thoughts turned to whether I should seek a sixth term in the Senate, Dot, my best friend and closest advisor for the last fifty-nine years, handed me a news clipping quoting a 1973 statement by a longtime friend and erstwhile patriot, the late Senator Sam J. Ervin Jr. Dot Helms suggested— "instructed" may be a better word—that I should give Senator Sam's words serious consideration. He said,

There's one inescapable reality that no man can ignore, and that is that time takes a terrific toll, which is of an increasing nature, with those who live many years. I would hate to be in the Senate and, in Kipling's words, have to "force my heart and nerves and sinew to serve their turn long after they are gone." . . . Intellectual honesty compels me to confront this inescapable reality.

Except for the fact that I was already a few years older than Senator Ervin was when he made his decision, on December 13, 1973, not to run for reelection in 1974, my family counseled me that my situation was not materially different from that of Senator Ervin.

Therefore, I made the decision not to run again in 2002. If I had run in 2002 and been elected and lived to finish a sixth term, I would have been 88 years old. Only the rarest of octogenarians could have the stamina to handle their responsibilities as a U.S. Senator at that advanced age.

I served the people of North Carolina for thirty years, longer than any other Senator elected by the people of North Carolina, and never in my wildest imagination did it occur to me that such a privilege would be mine.

It is a fact that in five different elections I was never endorsed by one of North Carolina's major daily newspapers. I had to take my message directly to the people and go over the heads of the liberal media.

There is no way I can adequately express my gratitude to the many thousands who made this possible by pitching in with their financial support and hard work in all five of my elections to the United States Senate. Without that help and without the prayers of so many, I would never have made it.

CHAPTER 33

George W. Bush

I T WAS MUCH EASIER to make my decision to retire in 2002 after Al Gore finally conceded the Presidential election in 2000. I was then comfortable that the direction of our country, and particularly its foreign policy, was in capable hands—with George W. Bush in the White House.

I believe there's something to be said for growing up over the family store as a way of gaining real understanding of the challenges and responsibilities expected of you. George W. Bush could not have had a better mentor than his father for the process of learning how to guide the United States in the foreign-affairs arena.

President George H. W. Bush is himself the son of a U.S. Senator, and his varied career in government included not only serving in Congress and as Ambassador to the United Nations, but also appointments as Chief of the U.S. Liaison Office to the People's Republic of China and Director of the Central Intelligence Agency.

He had twice been elected Vice President and had served the nation as President for four memorable years. His wealth of experience influenced his oldest son, George, and it influenced his second son, John Ellis Bush, the Governor of Florida (better known as Jeb), to also use his considerable skills in public service.

While it is true that the first President Bush goes out of his way to avoid "backseat driving," it is equally clear that he and Barbara raised sons who were watching their father carefully and learning more at home than they ever could have in a class on public policy.

As I write this, after watching the 2004 campaign—and knowing of the Bush family's commitment to doing what they can to leave the world in better shape than they found it—I have every reason to suspect that another generation of public servants by the name of Bush is growing up right now.

I first got to know George W. Bush when he was assisting in his father's first campaign for President. I immediately liked his direct manner and his businesslike approach to solving problems. There was a personable warmth about him that put everybody at ease from the minute he greeted them. (It was obvious to me early on that this plain-talker, who had sunk his roots in Texas, could be a future vote-getter himself.) I was therefore not at all surprised when he ran for Governor of Texas in 1994. Nor was I surprised when, with 53.5 percent of the vote, he defeated the incumbent, Ann Richards. When he ran for reelection in 1998, he won with a 68.6 percent margin!

Nor was I surprised when Governor Bush announced that he would run for the Republican nomination for President. There was, in 2000, a genuinely good field of candidates, but voters responded with approval to the Bush message—and to the man himself. (They sensed his honesty and his deep commitment to do everything he could to make America a nation whose President would be an example of principled behavior.)

My first opportunity to meet privately with Governor Bush was in October 1999, after he had announced his candidacy for the GOP Presidential nomination. The Governor had scheduled a fund-raiser in Raleigh, and while my staff knew that I was not endorsing anyone in the race or attending any of their events, they correctly assumed that I might want to meet and get to know Governor Bush a little better. So when I was asked if I would like to have a meeting with the Governor, my immediate response was that, based on my observation of the competition to that point, we indeed should meet this gentleman because he very well might be the next President of the United States.

It so happened that the day of that meeting coincided with a football game in Austin, Texas, between North Carolina State University and the University of Texas. Knowing of the Governor's strong interest in sports, I brought along an N.C. State football jersey as a small gift to our visitor. He enjoyed the joke and we immediately sat down to a wide-ranging conversation about current issues, including the need for immigration reform and ways to actively engage Hispanic voters, many of whom closely identified with conservative values, in the coming election.

Dot joined us for this meeting, and during our visit we were also joined by

Laura Bush. Dot liked Mrs. Bush at once, especially when she realized that they shared a love of books.

Just as we were about to leave, Governor Bush turned to me and said, "By the way, Dr. Condoleezza Rice of Stanford University is my foreign affairs advisor." I gave him the thumbs-up and told him that Dr. Rice was an excellent choice.

Our paths didn't cross again until 2000. The Governor had scheduled a large rally in Winston-Salem at Wake Forest University. Dot decided that she would like to attend the event, but as it happened, I could not join her because I was then taking care of "the people's business" in Washington.

Dot didn't seek any special accommodations and waited along the rope line with hundreds of others. Although they had met only once before, the Governor remembered her, and his greeting was very warm and personable, as if they had known each other for years.

I did not see the Governor thereafter for at least a couple of months. But when I did finally run into him, he went out of his way to stress how much he had enjoyed seeing Dot in Winston-Salem. (No wonder the American people genuinely like this President so much!)

Even though the liberal media tried to belittle his accomplishments, his record as Governor stood up to the scrutiny of critics. So did his vision of the United States as a country where we could do better. George Bush dared to expose the prejudice in schools, where it was assumed that the poor and minorities could not do well. He warned of the signs of a coming economic downturn and had solutions ready to prevent a major recession.

The national defense, another of his concerns, had been dealing with a significant increase in attacks on American interests and American citizens around the world—without any firm response from the United States. George Bush came to office with a plan to restore the international reputation of the United States for its steadfastness in the face of challenge.

In February 2001, the Conservative Political Action Conference invited me to speak. I was pleased to accept and to see so many of my conservative friends, such as Dick Cheney. Best of all, we had something pleasant to talk about as we looked forward to the Bush administration. I had always felt that George W. was a bit more conservative than his daddy, for whom I have great affection, and I was proud to be on his team.

When George Bush was in office just eight months, a plan that had been years in the making (unknowingly abetted by a series of failures, from carelessness about deporting illegal immigrants to treating terrorists as criminals with access to our criminal justice system) achieved its horrible goal with the attacks on the World Trade Center and on the Pentagon.

Courageous unarmed citizens aboard a fourth plane prevented a possible attack on either the White House or the U.S. Capitol itself, and on that day we saw the full caliber of the statesman we had elected President.

In spite of the criticisms by those who do not understand that their peace is made possible only because of the bravery of those who stand up to tyrants, President Bush has held to the course he knows is best for his country. This President is not distracted by any personal scandal or motivated by poll numbers. He takes the long view, and the results, even in this challenging time in our history, have been good.

As I write this, it has been more than three years since the dreadful attacks of 9/11—and no further attack has succeeded on our soil. To the contrary, potential threats have been exposed and dismantled, terrorist connections have been broken, and hideouts around the world have been raided. Afghanistan, the country whose government proudly gave sanctuary to the terrorists' leaders, has been returned to democratic rule.

In Iraq, terrorists mistook the depth of the United States' commitment to freedom. They believed we were soft and not willing to stand up to their cowardly attacks. They thought their barbarism would fill us with fear. What they now see is that we are all the more resolved to do what no one else has done and put an end to their brutal control of others.

We have the courage to say that men who hide in a religious shrine (while claiming they are fighting for their faith) are the worst infidels. We have the boldness to declare that those who waste the lives of their own people, even their families, in order to mount an attack on the very soldiers whose presence is intended to give them real freedom are contemptible no matter how they may characterize their behavior.

Those who are called brave martyrs by their misguided leadership are to be pitied—and their would-be successors should be put out of action. To his eternal credit, George W. Bush understands all of this, just as he understood that the Iraqis' desire to be free would be stronger than the desire to cower at home on their historic election day in January 2005.

He has rejected the arguments about a clash of cultures. He knows the issue is freedom—for us and for millions of others who risk living their lives under the heel of tyrants, whether in uniforms or the robes of religion.

The tenor of the times has limited President Bush's opportunities to exhibit his warm side, which his wife Laura has said she wishes we could all see more often. Because we have known each other for a good while now and had many meetings together—as well as shared trips to North Carolina for Presidential visits—I know what Laura means: George W. Bush is, as Dot now describes him, "as comfortable as an old shoe."

George Bush has returned structure to the White House by applying his management skills from the top down, and he has done this without imposing a stiffness that stifles the creativity and freedom of expression of his staff. In that kind of environment, he has been able to attract the best of people, including some of my former staffers and others whose work I admire.

Of course we have had our differences. I wished that the tax cuts put into place to stimulate the economy (which they have!) had been accompanied by cuts in government spending on nonessentials (which Congress ignored). I also would have been less patient with the Democrats who have held up outstanding nominees for judgeships and other posts over issues that have nothing to do with their fitness for their assignment.

People like Bob Conrad, who was honored by former Attorney General Janet Reno for his outstanding work as a U.S. Attorney, should not have been left dangling as a much-needed judicial nominee for the Fourth District simply because former Senator John Edwards claimed, for almost two years, that *he hadn't had time* to study this fine man's record. (It's interesting that the very people who expressed outrage when I demanded a thorough review of nominees now use orchestrated obstruction to keep anyone whose conservative philosophy they fear from reaching the bench.)

The President and I would have differed on bills that negatively impacted the deficit, and I certainly would have been leading the opposition against pork-barrel spending, even when it was attached to items as important as homeland security. It makes no sense to appropriate money to every little hamlet in the country when we must first protect our cities and our power and water resources. While I would absolutely vote in favor of providing any items the military needs in order to fulfill its mission, I would nonetheless urge fiscal responsibility to make sure that we're paying for what we need and not overpaying for things that don't meet the needs of the troops. Even in the face of a grave national challenge—no, let me say *especially* in the face of such a challenge—we must take care of the taxpayers' money, and of our sons and daughters who risk their lives for the cause of freedom. But our differences would be minor and our areas of agreement significant, especially when it comes to President Bush's second-term agenda on Social Security and tax reforms. These issues have been among my priorities for many, many years.

I sent my first tax overhaul bill to Congress in 1982. It was S.2200 and it was titled "The Flat Rate Tax Act of 1982." At the time I pointed out that higher taxes had never boosted production and that a simple flat rate tax would significantly broaden the tax base by eliminating all exemptions, with the exception of a $2,000 basic individual deduction. By closing loopholes and reducing the need for professional tax preparers and an "underground" cash economy, we would have the funds the government needs for its legitimate expenditures and our citizens would have more of the money they earned to use for their own priorities.

Of course, in Washington an idea as revolutionary as simplifying the tax system was greeted with fear and suspicion by bureaucrats and special interests alike, so I was not stampeded by fellow Senators hoping to add their names to my bill—or vote for it. But I was confident that good sense was on my side. (There was a flurry of interest during the Presidential primaries in 1996 when Steve Forbes and Phil Gramm both embraced flat-tax proposals, but the idea sank with their candidacies.)

Now, with his reelection secured, President Bush has promised to lead the charge in overhauling the most complicated and confusing set of rules and exemptions ever devised. I am watching with more than a little interest to see if real reform is possible. It will come down to a battle between what's good for all of our citizens, particularly those who are heavily burdened by taxes, versus the will of the people who are too selfish or shortsighted to give up the accommodations they enjoy from the current mess of deductions and exemptions that are, in fact, gifts from the people who *pay* the bills on behalf of those who do not.

If there is genuine tax reform in 2005, it will have been twenty-three years since I first proposed the idea. That's close to "fast-tracking" in Washington.

The President's plan for reforming Social Security has my support, too. Following a disappointing "status quo" report issued by a bipartisan, do-nothing commission that actually proposed a solution to Social Security problems by cutting benefits *and* raising taxes, I went on the record with a different solution.

My initial bill, the Social Security and Individual Retirement Security Act of 1983, was designed to convert the Social Security system to a tax-deductible private retirement account system. My bill would have guaranteed the payments of those already receiving benefits and a scaled system to assure that no one was harmed by a lack of time for investments to build. My goal was to see every working American benefiting from his or her own carefully managed investments.

What may have seemed radical in 1983 seems totally sensible now, a little more than two decades later, especially among young people who are tired of hearing that the current system may be bankrupt before they see any direct benefits. These young people are also aware of how our economy functions. They know that long-term investments gain value, often significant value, over time. They've seen the charts indicating the amount of return the typical Social Security tax amount would have yielded in a mutual fund or the bond market. They know the best way to save Social Security is to invest in American enterprise, not American bureaucracy.

The voices of fear will do all they can to thwart even the modest start President Bush is proposing with the investment of a small portion of Social Security taxes from those who volunteer for this option.

However, I believe their tired arguments will be drowned out by the growing demand for this option among those who have "done the math." (I also believe that in another twenty years or so, people will look back and wonder how we could have denied folks the freedom to invest for their retirement instead of relying on the government alone.)

In countries where this system has been tried, not only have the people received greater benefits from their investments, but the economy has been stimulated by the extra capital available for loans to build businesses, therefore creating more jobs. (I'm counting on George Bush to fulfill this particular campaign promise, no matter how much political capital he has to spend in the process.)

In George Bush, the country has found a man who has embraced the conservative philosophy and adapted to the needs of the times. He has exposed the personal side of conservatism with his emphasis on improving the quality of education and enabling citizens who want to help others to forge partnerships instead of adversarial relationships with government. Best of all, he has called us as citizens to stand together, to express our pride in America, and to unite in our determination to keep her safe and strong.

The 2004 Presidential campaign was of particular interest to me as a politician and a political observer. If I had listened only to the media, I would have despaired over the liberal direction our citizens seemed to want for our country.

Fortunately, my friends in Washington and in the field with the campaign kept me well informed about the real situation. They assured me that I would have been very much at home in a campaign like the one they were waging. I knew what it was like when the media simply would not or could not comprehend the desire of ordinary, decent people to vote for someone who respected and supported their values. I also knew those folks would work tirelessly for a candidate whom they could trust to work for them in Washington.

The American people understood and appreciated George Bush. They saw the man I know, the leader who insists on doing what is right without worrying about the way the press will cover the decision. They knew that the economy was recovering from the blow it was dealt on 9/11, and they knew the Bush tax cuts were the stimulus, not the problem. They knew—because they heard firsthand from the folks who had served in Iraq—that the Iraqi people wanted our help and knew we had rescued them from tyranny. They knew that the war on terrorism is real and that the United States must be able to do whatever it takes to defend our people. They understood that the opinions or advice of countries that had been doing business with the tyrants were of little consequence to us. They saw the formidable determination to take action and overcome evil. They saw the character of the President and the faith that guides him—and they knew George W. Bush had to stay on for four more years, no matter how unhappy that made his detractors.

There are those who want me to be a "Monday morning quarterback" regarding the war in Iraq. I am obliged to say to them that I no longer receive classified reports like the ones we used to guide us before the Congress gave its authorization to go to war. So I would not dare to critique the details of current policy decisions. But I do know this: A brutal and aggressive dictator who used his own troops to kill thousands of their countrymen is no longer in power.

Those who supported him and his kind of cruelty are desperate to prevent progress. They and the outsiders who have shown up to attempt to impose their extremist ideas on the Iraqi people may be making all the noise and thereby seeking the headlines, but the vast majority of the people of Iraq are embracing the light of freedom and all the blessings that the United States intends to bring to them and to their children.

I'll admit that I was more than a little nostalgic as I watched the results on election night and saw the faces of those network reporters as they realized that the President was doing well and the Congress was going to be solidly in the control of the Republicans. I never tire of watching those folks squirm as they realize their candidates are not going to be in power—and they had *plenty* to squirm about that night: Almost 63 million voters, the largest number in history, had voted for my friend George W. Bush. And my own granddaughter, Jennifer Knox, won *her* race to become a judge.

November 2, 2004, was a great day for America—and for our family!

CHAPTER 34

The Challenges We Face

THE 1990S WERE A DECADE of enormous democratic advances around the world. In the first years of that decade, we witnessed the collapse of Communism in Central and Eastern Europe; and in the final year of that decade, we saw the peaceful transfer of power from long-ruling parties to democratic oppositions in Taiwan and Mexico, as well as the fall of authoritarian leaders in places like Yugoslavia and Peru.

This progress notwithstanding, the global movement toward the rule of law, democracy, civil society, and free markets still meets resistance in many quarters. Our challenge, early in this new millennium, must be to consolidate the democratic advances of the recent past, while increasing the pressure on those who still refuse to accept the principle that sovereign legitimacy comes from the consent of the governed.

A good place to start was our own hemisphere—specifically, just across our own border. In Mexico, after seventy-one years of one-party rule, the corrupt Institutional Revolutionary Party (or PRI) was finally voted out of office. President Vicente Fox's victory in July 2000 opened avenues for genuine friendship and cooperation between the United States and Mexico.

We helped set in motion the move toward truly democratic government in Mexico several years ago by pointing out the realities of life under a socialist-leaning government—with no effective plans in place to improve the economy of their country other than taking over private businesses and amassing huge debts with international banks.

We were especially critical of our own government's permissiveness in failing to set conditions for assistance or establish safeguards to keep our country from being flooded with illegal aliens fleeing a 50 percent unemployment rate at home.

Now we can work for genuine partnership and a shared vision for dealing with the problems that challenge both countries. When we work together, we can secure our border, discourage illegal immigration, and strengthen our nation's second-largest trading partner by helping true reformers rejuvenate Mexico's economy.

Next, we can broaden and deepen law enforcement cooperation against the deadly drug trade if both countries attack corruption with impunity. Progress will not come easily, but it will come—if we do not abandon our mutual respect for each other.

Believing that we could strengthen our relationship through personal contacts, I was honored in 2001 to lead a visit of the U.S. Senate Foreign Relations Committee to Mexico for a joint meeting with the Mexican Senate Foreign Relations Commission. This was the first meeting of its kind on the part of the U.S. Senate, but our purpose was much more important than establishing a record. We were committed to doing what we could to solidify the emerging friendship between our two governments, and to make a contribution toward strengthening the long-standing friendship between our two peoples.

To that end, the Jesse Helms Center has taken an active role in working with educators in Mexico to institute Free Enterprise Leadership Conferences for young people, and to introduce the "Laws of Life" essay competition established by Sir John Templeton to promote sound character education in schools around the world.

In May of last year, Senator Fernando Margain, the Chairman of the Senate Foreign Relations Commission of Mexico, with whom I have remained in close contact since my visit, met with me at the Jesse Helms Center to discuss more ways we might work together in order to expose even more young people to the potential they now have before them as citizens living under a free and democratic government, where free enterprise is welcome and encouraged.

For eight years, I had the privilege of serving as Chairman of the Senate Foreign Relations Committee. During those years, the committee had a positive influence on foreign policy and led the way on some important accomplishments of which we could all be proud.

For example, we enacted into law the LIBERTAD (or "Helms-Burton")

Act, tightening the noose around the neck of the last dictator in the Western hemisphere—Fidel Castro.

Working with Joe Biden, our committee's distinguished ranking member, we took the first steps toward reforming our nation's foreign policy institutions for a post–Cold War world, passing historic, bipartisan legislation in the form of the Helms-Biden Act. And we passed the National Missile Defense Act, mandating the deployment of missile defenses as soon as the technology is ready.

For the most part, we did our work in a bipartisan manner wherever we could. That was possible because Senator Joe Biden of Delaware and I had an excellent working relationship that both of us worked to build and keep in good order.

I hope the spirit of bipartisan cooperation that Joe and I established will be the standard from here on in at the Senate Foreign Relations Committee, no matter who the ranking personalities might be. The work of the committee is too important to become a backdrop to power plays. And while the margin in the Senate has certainly narrowed, let's be honest: Unless either party has sixty votes (enough to invoke cloture and stop debate), very little can be accomplished in the U.S. Senate without some measure of bipartisan support—no matter who is in control or by how narrow a margin.

Our pleasure over the growth in democracy in Mexico gives us hope that change will come sooner rather than later in Cuba. The hemisphere's last totalitarian dictatorship still sputters on—like a cat with nine lives—just ninety miles from our shores.

Fidel Castro survived the Clinton years for one reason: The Clinton administration *never* made the dictator's removal from power a goal of its foreign policy. Embargo opponents correctly sensed that the Clinton people were never really committed to Castro's isolation and removal, and the administration did nothing to dissuade them of that notion. So they pushed on, dominating the debate.

As a result, instead of focusing on developing strategies to *undermine* Castro and hasten his demise, the last several years in Washington were spent wasting precious time and energy on a senseless debate over whether to lift the Cuban embargo unilaterally.

In his memoir, President Clinton claims that Castro sent him word in 1996 that he had never intended for the Brothers to the Rescue mercy flight to be shot out of the sky by his military aircraft, and President Clinton believed Castro. When I read that, I marveled at the gullibility. I suppose all the documented brutality against the people of Cuba and the theft of their freedom and prosperity were all accidental, too!

Things changed when the Bush administration came into office. There was an understanding of the nature of the tyrant and his crimes. It is my prayer that one day soon our President will be able to visit a new Cuba, one with an emerging civil society, with financial and other means of support supplied by its friends in the United States, who will welcome it as both a friend and a trading partner. I hope the President will be in Havana to attend the inauguration of the new democratically elected President of Cuba, and I hope that I may be able to join him.

When Cuba becomes free, there will be no Marxist powers in all of the Americas, unless Venezuela continues to slide. In each continent, on every island, the people of the Americas will have rid themselves of people who would take away their freedom and replace it with a system that devalues the worth of individuals while destroying their ability to pursue their dreams.

Are ideal governments now in power in all of these countries? No. Were some of the preceding governments repressive or corrupt? Yes. Does much remain to be done to remove the influence of drug interests or personal greed or old conflicts? *Absolutely*.

Have we always supported "good guys"? Maybe not. But this much is sure: It was *never* a mistake to give our support to the person or group who did not embrace Communism rather than the person or faction who did.

Communism has been tried and found wanting in countries around the world. In every case, the rule of Communism brought the death of dissidents, the banning of religion, the destruction of revered cultures, and the devaluation of human life.

In no case is the ancient rule that "the enemy of my enemy is my friend" truer than when that enemy is Communism. And Communism is not truly dead. How the issue of Taiwan is dealt with will continue to be one of our great challenges, and is of such importance that I felt compelled in this book to deal with it separately.

At the start of this century, we were awakened to the true scope of a different kind of enemy: terrorism. These new aggressors abide by no conventions and hide their hateful acts behind a screen of supposed religious devotion. Such zealotry is hard for most people to understand, but we must learn all we can so that not only can we put an end to the violence that we see now, but we can keep new groups from forming as we remove the old ones from their hideouts.

And we must once again learn the lessons of history and resist the lure of leisure. This great experiment in democracy, our beloved America, will always be the enemy of those who are afraid of freedom, jealous of the rewards of free enterprise, and in rebellion against the God who has blessed us.

We must train our children and grandchildren so that they will understand what it means to be American, both the manifold benefits and the important responsibilities.

Finally, we must not grow cold in our love for our country. We must vote. We must stay informed. We must make our opinions known, and we must be loyal to the principles that make this country the beacon of freedom and opportunity among all the nations on earth.

CHAPTER 35

Reflections and Retirement

REFLECTIONS

I'VE BEEN ASKED MANY TIMES what I would like to see in the future in the U.S. Senate. I am not so presumptuous, as a Senate retiree, as to try to direct such deliberations one by one, but I will say that I pray the Senate will never become a forum where the right of the majority snuffs out the voices of the minority.

Indeed, I hope—and I pray—that Senators and candidates for any and all public offices will turn aside those who seek to "package" them. America does not need "empty suits" with perfectly combed hair, preprogrammed sound bites, and rewritten biographies. America does not need people in public office who want mainly to make a name for themselves by running every option by a focus group before they themselves dare to take a stand on the issues. America does not need people in public office who are afraid that someone will get vehemently unhappy if they dare to point out what's right or what's wrong. America certainly does not need people who have no personal core of morality—and no love and understanding of the history of the United States of America.

What America *does* need are courageous leaders who are willing to take on "the establishment" in order to correct wrongs. America *does* need people with the courage of their convictions. America *does* need people who tell the truth and are willing to deal with the consequences. America *does* need people who wear ridicule as a badge of honor because it shows that their message is getting through. America *does* need people willing to take the time to learn to pursue excellence by becoming students of the jobs they hold—and making a commitment never to settle for anything less than their personal best.

And America needs leaders who possess a sense of history and recognition of the difference between the free-enterprise system and all the other systems in the world, past and present.

I have been asked if there's one person or a handful of people who are responsible for the changes in the Senate in the past thirty years. I've reflected on that question, and I can honestly say that there is no such entity. The changes have been more like the spread of kudzu, incremental and unnoticed until one day you realize that the vine has taken over the field and started up the side of the barn. Hire by hire the Senate staffing has exploded from the handful it was when I went to Washington as assistant to Senator Willis Smith. Perhaps it is because there are so few staff assistants with the kind of skills the late Clint Fuller brought to his job.

Clint was adept at listening to people's concerns and helping them get the help they needed. He did such a good job that most visitors to our office who thought they needed to see me were quite satisfied with the results of their meetings with Clint. There was nothing magical about what Clint did. He simply acted out of his nature as a kind gentleman whose most important assignment was to treat *all* people who asked for our help with courtesy and respect.

In today's Senate office environment, someone like Clint would get labeled and pigeonholed in the area of his "specialty," constituent relations. People outside of his department would never have the benefit of learning by observing a good example in action. Congress has deepening layers of directors of this or that specialty, all with deputies and staff members who report to them—and staffers who report to those staffers. Even the rookies in the mailrooms have even younger interns they supervise!

The sense of family that makes a workplace more than just somewhere to spend time is lost in a stratified and impersonal environment where no one really cares about anything outside of his or her direct area of control. The Senate's standing committees have built their own staffs, often duplicating the efforts of individual members' staffs, especially in the area of communications—now considered a necessary full-time job on just about every staff, whether there's any demand for news about their work or not.

Other staffs exist to serve the Majority and Minority Leaders, many subcommittees, study committees, joint commissions, and the committee on committees. Some of these people use their positions to further their own views or their own agendas, making sure that the information favorable to the action they prefer is what reaches the "boss."

The result is a fence of humanity that insulates Senators from their constituents and their constituents' concerns, often keeping the real facts at bay and allowing the staff to run the Senators. Senators who are too busy to read pending legislation for themselves find out too late that they were ill advised and have therefore cast votes they never would have cast if they had been given all the facts.

Running for office is no longer confined to a once-every-six-years exercise, with campaign events consigned to the days between Labor Day and Election Day. Almost from the first day in office, campaign consultants are taking the electorate's temperature and constantly warning their Senatorial candidates not to take controversial positions on bills or policy matters, lest they be voted out of office.

It has always been my contention that there is no sense in being in office if you don't have the courage to do what is right, even if it is the most unpopular position in the world. But too many of our Senators have given in to the concerns of their critics.

Even the defense of marriage was too hot a topic for most Senators to champion in 2004. Who could have imagined, even a decade ago, that Senators from both sides of the aisle would not have quickly united around sponsorship of a bill stating unequivocally that in the United States of America marriage is the union of a man and a woman who, if they are blessed with children, will do all in their power to raise them with the loving involvement of a mother and a father?

Fear of appearing "narrow-minded" or being labeled "hateful" overtook basic common sense. I can state with confidence that in every state in the union more people favor laws that protect traditional marriage than oppose them, but fear of a vocal minority silenced almost every Senator—or had them anxiously seeking a safe middle ground. (As if there *is* a middle ground between morality and immorality!)

I won't pretend to be pleased when I see the Senate waste the nation's taxpayers' time with intramural squabbles, or pander to the media's agenda, but I am encouraged by the many young people whom I have met who are committed to public service and to conservative principles. I believe they will be wiser than their elders about the need to stay true to their core beliefs and govern wisely—without an interest in building a fan base or getting "good press."

RETIREMENT

I don't have a lot to say about retirement—other than that I hope I will enjoy it if and when I find the time!

In the days since I left my Washington Senate office, I've gotten comfortable in my Raleigh office, where I have welcomed a steady stream of friends and guests. Some of my most enjoyable visitors have been friends who dropped by to just say hello and tell me they appreciated something the young folks in my Raleigh office had done to help their family or a stand I had taken on some issue. My favorites have included a young man in uniform who wanted me to know that my support of a strong military mattered to him. That made this old Navy man proud.

My office has regular calls about constituent concerns, and we help when we can or else direct the caller to Senator Elizabeth Dole's or Senator Richard Burr's office. Sometimes it's just as easy for me to personally cut through the red tape and get a matter settled, which makes both the constituent and me happy.

I enjoy watching the Senate in session on C-Span, although I will admit to occasionally wishing I could join in a debate—or raise an objection to an attempt to disguise a bad bill with tempting amendments.

I've realized once again that I've had a very good life. I have dined with kings and princes—and with mill hands and farmers. I've been on every continent and warmly welcomed in every county in my state. I have appeared on television around the world and had the privilege of writing for my hometown weekly. I've met the most powerful women on the world stage and been fortunate to have the best woman in the world by my side for more than sixty years.

And I can say that I think my father would be proud to know that I followed his advice and went to Washington to do what I said I was going to do.

CHAPTER 36

Our Responsibility to the Future

F AR TOO MANY AMERICANS are content to assume that the freedoms they have traditionally enjoyed and come to accept as the order of nature were initiated by the Declaration of Independence in 1776 and reaffirmed in the Bill of Rights in 1791. The truth is that the War for Independence was only one short skirmish in a struggle whose origins hark back into the mists of history.

Ultimately, the author of human liberty is almighty God, who endows every human being with free will.

Every human being since Adam has been free to obey the laws of God—or to disobey them; to enjoy, in the words of Scripture, the glorious liberty of the sons of God, or to submit to his own slavery in sin. God Himself does not constrain our wills; in His infinite majesty, He respects the choices made by men.

At various times over the past thousands of years, the human race has attempted in faltering ways to set up for itself governments that would respect the sense of freedom that, however dimly, each individual perceives in himself.

Very few nations in all recorded history ever achieved this goal. We see starts in this direction among the early Greeks and early Romans, but these were soon extinguished. It is a sobering fact that the freedom that has been the possession of Americans for over two centuries has been a unique achievement. Only a small fraction of one percent of humanity has ever enjoyed the benefits of American citizenship and the liberties that it confers.

By far, the overwhelming majority of human beings who have lived on this earth have done so as the captives or the subjects or the slaves of somebody else.

This is still true at this hour. Our indebtedness for the freedom Americans enjoy today spans many millennia. Remarkably enough, our debt is not to the great empires of ancient history, the Syrians or the Egyptians or the Romans who made civilization a reality, but to several tribes of wanderers who lived along the fringes of great empires and kept alive their identity and independence against the super states of their day.

I refer, first of all, to the Jews, who preserved the exalted concept of the one God and the moral code He laid down for the human race, and who prepared the way for the true Liberator of mankind, Jesus Christ. From them we received the ethical foundation of our liberty. Early in the Bible, in the Book of Leviticus, God instructs Moses to ". . . proclaim liberty throughout all the land unto all the inhabitants thereof. . . ."

For the genesis of our political institutions, we must look to a region on the remotest fringes of the gigantic Roman Empire, to a region now known as the German province of Schleswig-Holstein. Here, along the banks of the rivers that poured into the North Sea, lived a collection of primitive tribes—the Angles, Saxons, and Jutes—who practiced a form of self-government. Even though Roman law was among the greatest achievements of human society, it is from these rude barbarians, rather than from the Romans, that we gained the all-important concept of limited government and the germ of those institutions that made delegated power possible and workable.

About the time the Roman Empire was collapsing, before wave after wave of barbarian invaders, bands of Angles, Saxons, and Jutes were slowly emigrating from their homelands to the inviting meads of Britain that lay across the sea. With them went their ancient traditions of folk assemblies and local government.

Those who subjugated the native Britons were themselves laid low in succeeding centuries by the Vikings and then, most devastatingly, by the Normans, who imposed the strict hierarchy of the feudal system on the England of the eleventh century. This system supplanted the earlier free holdings almost without exception.

All across England, the tenants of the land quickly accepted the overlordship of the conquering nobles. The nobles held land from the king in return for military service. They subdued their fractious tenants and their rebellious neighbors and provided the security and stability that allowed the activities of daily life to continue unhindered.

Though many generations would go by under such conditions, the English never completely lost the impulse for self-government. Gradually, the unending taxes, tolls, and other exactions to which they were subject taught them what their progeny centuries hence would discover in colonial America: Security can sometimes be provided at too high a price, and what they needed most was relief from all this "protection."

And so the stage was set for the Magna Carta and the acceptance of the traditional practices that are the very substance of English common law. Through trial and error, through the accumulated experience of centuries of Christian teaching, the English expressed their native genius in the institutions that in the ensuing ages would make personal freedom a practical idea and would curb the power of the all-powerful state.

The great truth to be noted in this is the gradual evolution of personal rights and responsibilities in a nation whose instincts and experience led in this direction. Liberty in any form is not guaranteed by edicts or proclamations or slogans from the mob, but by order and discipline and a fundamental self-control. And this is what makes the American war for independence different in nature from the revolutions and wars of alleged liberation that followed it.

The Americans fought to *reclaim* their traditional rights as Englishmen. They did not resort to arms to fulfill the fantasies of some wild-eyed fanatic, but rather to preserve their own heritage and patrimony, which the political and commercial interests in Britain were intent on taking away. We can be sure that the colonists—the descendants and neighbors of those who risked their lives crossing the stormy Atlantic in fragile wooden vessels to secure, by their own efforts, a better life—knew well the value of liberty and property. In 1976, when America celebrated its bicentennial year, those points were rightly stressed by writers and speakers and television producers who understood the priceless heritage of freedom that had endured for two hundred years.

We have had our derelictions, it is true. Individuals and groups have in the past opted for other "arrangements." But until recently in this nation's history, ideology *never* prevailed for long over common sense. We need only examine the documents of the time to see that even the estimable Pilgrim fathers had some alien ideas tucked away in their own baggage. It might even be said, with some truth, that Communism came over on the *Mayflower*.

The full story of the first Thanksgiving in New England is an eloquent answer to those who pretend that mankind can be better served by more governmental controls, handouts, and restrictions. The Pilgrims actually tried the very thing that many politicians are advocating today. These Pilgrims nearly starved to death. Then they turned to God for an answer—and they got it.

It is not a well-known fact that the Pilgrims' experiment with Communism failed within three years' time. In order to survive, they had to turn to a system that rewarded individual initiative! Before landing in Massachusetts, the Pilgrims entered into what is known as the Mayflower Compact. Under this covenant, Plymouth Colony was established as a share-the-wealth community. No one owned anything. Whatever was produced belonged to the community as a whole—to "all the people," as some modern politicians occasionally put it.

The system was called, in the quaint writing of that day, "the comone course and condition." The Pilgrims lived under this system from the desperate, disease-ridden first winter of 1620–21 until the hungry spring of 1623. Then they changed to private enterprise.

Why? William Bradford, the second Governor of Plymouth Colony, tells why in his book titled *Of Plimoth Plantation*. Governor Bradford writes that the Pilgrims weren't long under this so-called "comone course and condition" before it "was found to breed much confusion & discontent."

Governor Bradford writes that "work was retarded that would have been to [our] benefit and comforts." The Governor then explains that the young men who were most efficient and able to work had no incentive to produce, because they knew they would not be rewarded any more than the lazy or inefficient men in the colony. So no one did any more work than he had to do. Instead of a Thanksgiving feast in the fall of 1622, there was literal starvation and hopelessly low morale. In his book, Governor Bradford relates what was done about this grim condition:

> So they begane to thinke how they might raise as much corne as they could . . . that they might not still thus languish in misere. At last, after much debate of things, the governor [Bradford himself] gave way that they should set corne every man for his own particular. . . . This had very good success, for it made all hands very industrious . . . much more corne was planted than other [wise] would have been.

The governor reflected on this incident. He condemned the theory that his people had tried and found wanting—the theory of socialism and Communism: "As if—" Governor Bradford noted sadly, "as if they were wiser than God."

Yes, the older I get, the more firmly persuaded I become that America was intended to be a manifestation of the intent of the Lord, who was experimenting with the frailties and the strengths of mankind by extending to those hardy Pilgrim souls who came here seeking a freedom of worship an opportunity to work and prosper unfettered by kings and kingdoms.

Ben Franklin was a part of the deliberations in Philadelphia when the Founding Fathers met to decide the final details of this new republic. But he sensed as well an attitude of self-interest festering, a forgetfulness of what freedom is all about.

Dr. Franklin's alarm at what he was hearing and seeing grew into an obligation to seek recognition from the presiding officer. Gaining that necessary recognition, Dr. Franklin began to speak in candor about what was going on. He was concerned, he said, that the group had somehow lost sight of the source of their blessings. So he urged that the doors and windows be shut and that all present should fall to their knees to ask the Source of their blessings to guide them in these final deliberations.

The doors and the windows were closed, and those men did pray, it is said, for a lot of things—including forgiveness for their selfish inclinations—but most of all they prayed for guidance. Those Founding Fathers, as we now reverently refer to them, lowered their voices. They prayed together with reverence and gratitude and for the ability to emphasize the great spiritual manifestation that would be America. And it was then that the miracle manifested itself—the birth of this great new land of freedom and opportunity. To their astonishment, the pathway to freedom was achieved, their work was finished, and they climbed aboard their carriages and their horses and headed for home.

As Ben Franklin emerged from that Philadelphia building, a lady is said to have rushed up and, with great anxiety, asked: "Tell me, Dr. Franklin, what do we have—a monarchy or a republic?"

To which Dr. Franklin replied in measured syllables: "We have a republic, my dear lady—if we can keep it."

Ours is a nation founded on the idea of virtue in action. The virtues that animated our Founding Fathers—faith, courage, and a selfless dedication to the truth of human freedom—are what have set us apart as a people and a nation.

The terrorists who struck the Pentagon and the World Trade towers were attacking us because of what America stands for: freedom, religious toleration, and individual liberty. They despise what we represent. And they want to terrorize us into retreat and inaction so that we will be afraid to defend freedom abroad and live as free people at home.

They will not succeed.

The terrorists we fight today are not the first aggressors of their kind to challenge the American people. Indeed, at this moment of trial, it is altogether fitting to honor the memory of that great man Sir Winston Churchill, whose courage, conviction, and steely resolve led the Allies to victory over Fascism. Mr. Churchill then warned us about the danger of the emerging Communist threat and the Iron Curtain descending across Europe.

As was the case in Churchill's time, our freedom and way of life have once again come under vicious attack. Today, we face a new and different enemy, one who hides in caves and who strikes in new and unexpected ways. Yet in many ways this new enemy is no different from the enemy Churchill faced six decades ago.

The terrorists of the twenty-first century are, in truth, the modern successors to the murderous ideologies of the twentieth century. And let there be no doubt: Like Fascism and Communism before it, terrorism will one day soon lie smoldering on the ash heap of history.

But as shocking as the September 11 events were, it should have come as no surprise that our nation was once again challenged by aggressors bent on her destruction.

Jefferson warned us that "the price of liberty is eternal vigilance." And since our founding, Jefferson has been proven right time and time again. New enemies have constantly emerged to threaten us, and the lesson of history is that to secure our liberty, America must be constantly on guard, preparing to defend our nation against tomorrow's adversaries even as we vanquish the enemies of today.

America is indeed the greatest nation on the face of the earth—a beacon of freedom for the entire world. We have met greater challenges to our freedom before September 11 and defeated them.

We will do so again. But in the long run, the greatest emerging threat to America may not come from without, but rather from within. I have said it often during my years in public life, and I will say it again: *We will not long survive as a nation unless and until we restore the moral and spiritual principles that made America great in the first place.*

Consider this: On September 11, three thousand Americans were killed by a foreign enemy. The American people responded with shock, sadness, and a deep and righteous anger—and rightly so. Yet let us not forget that every passing day in our country, more than three thousand innocent Americans are killed at the hands of so-called doctors, who rip those little ones from their mothers' wombs. They are the most innocent Americans of all—small, helpless, defenseless babies. For these unborn Americans, every day is September 11.

We must never forget that America was attacked by terrorists on September 11 because of what America stands for—our dedication to life, liberty, and justice under God. As we defend those principles abroad, let us also renew them here at home. As we go after the terrorists who committed those unspeakable acts against our people, let us at the same time get about the task of restoring the moral and spiritual foundations on which our country was founded in the first place.

No matter how successfully we prosecute the war against terrorism, no matter how brilliantly we prepare for the threats of the future, we will *never* be truly secure if we do not return to the principles on which America was founded and which made America great.

We must instill in our young people an understanding that theirs is a nation founded by Providence to serve as a shining city on a hill—a light to the nations, spreading the good news of God's gift of human freedom.

On that fateful evening in 1972 when I went before the Lord as North Carolina's newly elected Senator, I made several commitments to my Maker. The first, of course, was to be a man of my word and keep my promises as my father advised. But I also made a commitment that night that I would not fail to meet with any group of young people from North Carolina who wanted to see me.

I am pleased to say that, to the best of my ability, I kept this commitment, and the young folks on our staff documented that I had met with well over one hundred thousand of North Carolina's finest young people before leaving office on January 3, 2003. It is said that I even kept a few Ambassadors, CEOs, and heads of state waiting in order to fulfill this promise. In fact, one such meeting occurred shortly before I left the Senate that gave me much encouragement with regard to the future of our country and the world.

A group of North Carolina's young citizens was in Washington taking in the sights, and they stopped by my office to visit with "good old Jess." After I regaled them with a few stories on the history of the Senate, the Senate buzzer system alerted me that I was needed on the Senate floor for a vote. I then asked the young folks if they would like to go with me to the Senate chamber to observe the vote from the Senate gallery. As we rose to go, one young lady grabbed my arm and earnestly asked, "Senator, before we go, can we have a word of prayer?"

We prayed—just as Ben Franklin and the Founding Fathers had—for forgiveness and guidance. And we prayed not only for ourselves, but for our leaders and allies, as well as for our enemies. I was deeply touched by the faith and grace of these young people, and encouraged that from this type of young people, leaders will emerge as did the stouthearted souls who established our nation and government.

My experience with young people like these and my faith in God's Providence give me faith that this young generation of patriots has what it takes, and this gives me hope for the future. I believe that they will honor and protect the Miracle of America.

ACKNOWLEDGMENTS

Just as no life is an island, this book was certainly no one-man project. I must thank the people who worked closely with me on it; their efforts are surely reflected in this finished assignment.

To John Dodd, President of the Jesse Helms Center, and the rest of his fine staff; Jimmy Broughton and Pat Devine, who were on my Senate staff and were determined that this book should be published; Judy Edwards, my personal and dedicated assistant and faithful "retypist" as we moved from draft to draft; and Stella Snyder, who served as my researcher and editorial assistant, and encouraged me to write my story with candor—just the way I would tell it in person—I say, "We made it!"

And to so many of my good friends, like Hoover Adams, Tom Ellis, and Tom Joyner, and all the former staffers whose memories of events helped me recall important names and dates, I am grateful for your part in this collaborative effort.

And thanks, too, to my new friends, Jonathan Jao, my editor at Random House, and Joe Vallely, who serves as my agent.

APPENDIX 1

Dr. Norman Geisler's
"10 Reasons for Voluntary Prayer"

—

1. Our government was based on religious principles from the very beginning. The Declaration of Independence says: "We hold these truths to be self-evident, that all men are created equal, that they are endowed by their Creator with certain unalienable Rights . . ." Indeed, it speaks of God, creations, God-given moral rights, the Providence of God, and a final Day of Judgment—all of which are religious teachings. Indeed, the Supreme Court affirmed (*Zorach*, 1952) "We are a religious people whose institutions presuppose a Supreme Being." And school prayer has been an important part of our religious experience from the very beginning.

2. The First Amendment does not separate God and government but actually encourages religion. It reads: "Congress shall make no law respecting the establishment of religion, nor prohibiting the free exercise thereof." The first clause merely declares that the federal government cannot establish one religion for all the people. It says nothing about "separation of church and state." In fact, five of the 13 states that ratified it had their own state religions at the time. The second clause insists that the government should do nothing to discourage religion. But forbidding prayer in schools discourages religion.

3. Early congressional actions encouraged religion in public schools. For example, the Northwest Treaty (1787 and 1789) declared: "Religion, morality, and knowledge being necessary for good government and the happiness of mankind, schools and the means of learning shall forever be encouraged." Thus, religion, which includes prayer, was deemed to be necessary.

4. Early presidents, with congressional approval, made proclamations encouraging public prayer. President Washington on Oct. 3, 1789, declared: "Whereas it is the duty of all nations to acknowledge the providence of Almighty

God, to obey His will, to be grateful for His benefits, and humbly to implore His protection and favor; and Whereas both Houses of Congress have, by their joint committee, requested me 'to recommend to the people of the United States a day of public thanksgiving and prayer. . . .'"

5. Congress has prayed at the opening of every session since the very beginning. Indeed, in a moment of crisis at the very first Continental Congress Benjamin Franklin urged prayer and observed that "In the beginning of the Contest with G. Britain, when we were sensible to danger, we had daily prayer in this room for Divine protection.—Our prayers, Sir, were heard, & they were graciously answered. . . . And have we now forgotten that powerful Friend? or do we imagine we no longer need His assistance? . . . I therefore beg leave to move— that henceforth prayer imploring the assistance of Heaven, and its blessing on our deliberations, be held in this Assembly every morning before we proceed to business, and that one or more of the clergy of this city be requested to officiate in that service." Congress has begun with prayer ever since. If the government can pray in their session, why can't the governed pray in their (school) sessions?

6. Public schools had prayer for nearly two hundred years before the Supreme Court ruled that state-mandated class prayers were unconstitutional (*Engel*, 1962). The fact that prayer was practiced for nearly two hundred years establishes it by precedent as a valid and beneficial practice in our schools.

7. Since the court outlawed prayer, the nation has been in steady moral decline. Cultural indexes indicate that between 1960 and 1990 there was a steady moral decline. During this period divorce doubled, teenage pregnancy went up 200%, teen suicide increased 300%, child abuse reached an all-time high, violent crime went up 500% and abortion increased 1000%. There is a strong correlation between the expulsion of prayer from our schools and the decline in morality.

8. Morals must be taught, and they cannot properly be taught without religion. There cannot be a moral law without a moral Law Giver. And there is no motivation for keeping the moral law unless there is a moral Law Giver who can enforce it by rewards and punishments.

9. Forbidding prayer and other religious expressions in public schools establishes, in effect, the religion of secularism. The Supreme Court has affirmed that there are religions, such as "secular humanism," which do not believe in God (*Torcaso*, 1961). Justice Potter (*Abington*, 1963) rightly feared that purging the schools of all religious beliefs and practices would lead to the "establishment of a religion of secularism." In fact, the beliefs of secular humanism are just the opposite of the Declaration of Independence. By not allowing theistic religious expression, the courts have favored the religious beliefs of secular humanism, namely, no belief in God, God-given moral laws, prayer and a Day of Judgment.

10.   To forbid the majority the right to pray because the minority object is to impose the irreligion of the minority on the religious majority. Forbidding prayer in schools, which a three-quarters majority of Americans favors, is the tyranny of the minority. It is minority rule, not democracy. Why should an irreligious minority dictate what the majority can do? The majority wishes to preserve our moral and spiritual values and, thus, our good nation.

APPENDIX 2

Provisions of the
Unborn Children's Civil Rights Act

—

The Unborn Children's Civil Rights Act was proposed to challenge all Senators to give thought to the need to put an end to the legalized slaughter of innocent, helpless babies. The bill contained four provisions:

First, to put Congress clearly on record in declaring (1) that every abortion destroys, deliberately, the life of an unborn child, (2) that the U.S. Constitution sanctions no right to abortion, and (3) that *Roe v. Wade* was improperly decided.

Second, to prohibit federal funding to pay for or to promote abortion, and to defund abortion permanently, thereby relieving Congress of annual legislative battles about abortion restrictions in appropriations bills.

Third, to end indirect federal funding for abortions by (1) prohibiting discrimination at all federally funded institutions against citizens who as a matter of conscience object to abortion, and (2) curtailing attorneys' fees in abortion-related cases.

Fourth, that appeals to the Supreme Court are provided as a right if and when any lower federal court declares restrictions on abortion unconstitutional, thus effectively assuring Supreme Court reconsideration of the abortion issue.

APPENDIX 3

Excerpt from a Column by Jane Chastain

—

When I retired from the Senate in 2003, Jane Chastain, now a well-known national media personality, wrote a column about the first time she and I met in 1967, when she decided to move to Raleigh to marry her fiancé. She said:

I had managed to carve out a career as a television sportscaster at WAGA in Atlanta—which was a progressive city. I was quite sure my sportscasting days were numbered because I had heard they rolled up the sidewalks every night in Raleigh. Nevertheless, I decided to visit the (then) two television stations in the area before walking down the aisle to say, "I do."

The station in Durham offered me a job as a weather girl. WRAL [in Raleigh] was my last and best hope.

As I stood in the expansive office of the president of Capitol Broadcasting, which owned WRAL, Fred Fletcher took one look at me and said, "Sports? You just can't do sports for us." That's when his executive vice-president in charge of programming spoke up and said, "Oh, yes she can!" Jesse Helms hired me on the spot.

At that time, television, particularly in the South, was a white male bastion, but I found WRAL had employed a number of women and minorities. Everyone was treated with fairness and respect. Much to my surprise, opportunities there had no gender or color barrier.

APPENDIX 4

Remarks to Fellow Senators on the Clinton Impeachment

—

First, I believe a President cannot faithfully execute the laws if he himself is breaking them. Second, I know the foundations of this country were not laid by politicians running for something—but by statesmen standing for something.

But I must put it to you that we will, at our own peril, look to opinion polls to decide how we vote, when the real need is to look to our hearts, to our consciences, and to our souls. So many decisions are made in the Senate—be it on the fate of treaties, or legislation, or even Presidents—decisions having implications not merely for today, but for generations to come, reminding us that if we don't stand for something, the very foundations of our Republic will crumble.

Perjury and obstruction of justice are serious charges, as nobody knows better than you, Mr. Chief Justice, charges that have been proved during the course of this trial. Therefore, the outcome of this trial may determine whether America is becoming a fundamentally unprincipled nation, bereft of the mandates by the Creator who blessed America two hundred and ten years ago with more abundance, more freedom than any other nation in history has ever known.

There is certainly evidence fearfully suggesting that the Senate may this week fail to convict the President of charges of which he is obviously guilty. What else can be made of the behavior of many in the news media whose eyes are constantly on ratings instead of the survival of America?

This trial has been dramatized as if it were a Hollywood movie, trivializing what should be respected as our solemn duty.

The new media technology is creating an explosion of media outlets and twenty-four-hour news channels—and a brand-new set of challenges.

A friend back home called me after an impressive presentation by one of the House managers and said, "You know, Jesse, I found Asa Hutchinson persuasive.

But I had to tune in to CNN to see whether it was effective—because I knew without the media's immediate stamp of approval, it wouldn't make a damn bit of difference."

He had a valid point. Mr. Chief Justice, the awesome power of the media, with its instant analysis, is frightening. A political event occurs. The TV commentators immediately offer their lofty opinions; overnight surveys are taken, and many politicians are all too often cowed into submission by poll results.

In these proceedings, the House managers of course provided a forest of evidence clearly indicating that the President of the United States perjured himself before a federal grand jury and obstructed justice. The imaginative White House attorneys of course chopped down a few trees here and there—and then proclaimed that the whole forest had burned down. The press gallery bought that whole concept.

Some years ago, there was a Western movie starring Jimmy Stewart and John Wayne called *The Man Who Shot Liberty Valance.* Jimmy Stewart portrayed a tenderfooted young lawyer who ran afoul of the local outlaw, Liberty Valance.

Through a twist of fate, the character played by Jimmy Stewart received credit for ridding the county of the outlaw, even though it was John Wayne's gun that brought Liberty Valance down. Yet it was Stewart who rode public acclaim into a political career in the United States Senate, while Wayne's character faded into obscurity.

Late in life, Stewart's character, still a Senator, returned from Washington to attend John Wayne's funeral. Stewart felt guilty, of course, that the truth of Wayne's heroism remained untold. He related the entire story to the local newspaper, only to find the editor totally disinterested.

"When the legend becomes fact," the editor said, "print the legend."

With its vote on articles of impeachment, the United States Senate is preparing to add to the legend of this whole sordid episode, Mr. Chief Justice. We have the facts before us and we should heed those facts because *truth* must become the legend.

APPENDIX 5

Letter from Senator Jesse Helms
to President Bill Clinton

—

Dear Mr. President:

There is great apprehension, which I know many in the Senate share, regarding your upcoming meeting with President Jiang in New Zealand, a meeting that was obviously hastily arranged in the wake of Taiwan President Lee's recent remarks on Taiwan's status. It is clear that the meeting was arranged to assuage China's anger.

Given your administration's tilt toward China amidst this latest dispute, I feel obliged to register with you my conviction that no more should be said or done in New Zealand at the further expense of Taiwan.

In fact, I strongly recommend that you use the meeting as an opportunity to reverse the dangerous direction of United States policy during the past weeks and months. . . .

In addition, it would be a profound mistake for you to issue any kind of joint statement with President Jiang that even hints at Beijing's definition of the one-China policy or which in any way signifies U.S. pressure on President Lee to backtrack from his recent remarks on Taiwan's status.

Lastly, it goes without saying that nothing should be said about arms sales to Taiwan other than to restate clearly the legal obligations of the United States under the Taiwan Relations Act.

APPENDIX 6

Address by United States Senator Jesse Helms, R-N.C., Chairman of the Senate Committee on Foreign Relations, Before the United Nations Security Council, January 20, 2000

———

Mr. President, distinguished Ambassadors, ladies and gentlemen:

I genuinely appreciate your welcoming me here this morning. You are distinguished world leaders and it is my hope that there can begin, this day, a pattern of understanding and friendship between you who serve your respective countries in the United Nations and those of us who serve not only in the United States government but also the millions of Americans whom we represent and serve.

Our Ambassador Holbrooke is an earnest gentleman whom I respect, and I hope you will enjoy his friendship as I do. He has an enormous amount of foreign service in his background. He is an able diplomat and a genuine friend to whom I am most grateful for his role and that of the Honorable Irwin Belk, my longtime friend, in arranging my visit with you today.

All that said, it may very well be that some of the things I feel obliged to say will not meet with your immediate approval, if at all. It is not my intent to offend you and I hope I will not.

It is my intent to extend to you my hand of friendship and convey the hope that in the days to come, and in retrospect, we can join in a mutual respect that will enable all of us to work together in an atmosphere of friendship and hope — the hope to do everything we can to achieve peace in the world.

Having said all that, I am aware that you have interpreters who translate the proceedings of this body into a half-dozen different languages.

They have an interesting challenge today. As some of you may have detected,

I don't have a Yankee accent. (I hope you have a translator here who can speak Southern—someone who can translate words like "y'all" and "I do declare.")

It may be that one other language barrier will need to be overcome this morning. I am not a diplomat, and as such, I am not fully conversant with the elegant and rarefied language of the diplomatic trade. I am an elected official, with something of a reputation for saying what I mean and meaning what I say. So I trust you will forgive me if I come across as a bit more blunt than those you are accustomed to hearing in this chamber.

I am told that this is the first time that a United States Senator has addressed the UN Security Council. I sincerely hope it will not be the last. It is important that this body have greater contact with the elected representatives of the American people, and that we have greater contact with you.

In this spirit, tomorrow I will be joined here at the UN by several other members of the Senate Foreign Relations Committee. Together, we will meet with UN officials and representatives of some of your governments, and will hold a committee "field hearing" to discuss UN reform and the prospects for improved U.S.-UN relations.

This will mark another first. Never before has the Senate Foreign Relations Committee ventured as a group from Washington to visit an international institution. I hope it will be an enlightening experience for all of us, and that you will accept this visit as a sign of our desire for a new beginning in the U.S.-UN relationship.

I hope—I intend—that my presence here today will presage future annual visits by the Security Council, who will come to Washington as official guests of the United States Senate and the Senate's Foreign Relations Committee, which I chair.

I trust that your representatives will feel free to be as candid in Washington as I will try to be here today so that there will be hands of friendship extended in an atmosphere of understanding.

If we are to have such a new beginning, we must endeavor to understand each other better. And that is why I will share with you some of what I am hearing from the American people about the United Nations.

Now, I am confident you have seen the public opinion polls, commissioned by UN supporters, suggesting that the UN enjoys the support of the American public. I would caution that you not put too much confidence in those polls. Since I was first elected to the Senate in 1972, I have run for reelection four times. Each time the pollsters have confidently predicted my defeat. Each time, I am happy to confide, they have been wrong. I am pleased that, thus far, I have never won a poll or lost an election.

So, as those of you who represent democratic nations well know, public opinion polls can be constructed to tell you anything the poll takers want you to hear.

Let me share with you what the American people tell me. Since I became Chairman of the Foreign Relations Committee, I have received literally thousands of letters from Americans all across the country expressing their deep frustration with this institution.

They know instinctively that the UN lives and breathes on the hard-earned money of the American taxpayers. And yet they have heard comments here in New York constantly calling the United States a "deadbeat."

They have heard UN officials declaring absurdly that countries like Fiji and Bangladesh are carrying America's burden in peacekeeping. They see the majority of the UN members routinely voting against America in the General Assembly.

They have read the reports of the raucous cheering of the UN delegates in Rome when U.S. efforts to amend the International Criminal Court treaty to protect American soldiers were defeated.

They read in the newspapers that, despite all the human rights abuses taking place in dictatorships across the globe, a UN "special rapporteur" decided his most pressing task was to investigate human rights violations in the U.S.—and found our human rights record wanting.

The American people hear all this; they resent it, and they have grown increasingly frustrated with what they feel is a lack of gratitude.

Now, I won't delve into every point of frustration, but let's touch for just a moment on one: the "deadbeat" charge. Before coming here, I asked the United States General Accounting Office to assess just how much the American taxpayers contributed to the United Nations in 1999. Here is what the GAO reported to me:

Last year, the American people contributed a total of more than $1.4 billion to the UN system in assessments and voluntary contributions. That's pretty generous, but it's only the tip of the iceberg. The American taxpayers also spent an additional $8,779,000,000 from the United States' military budget to support various UN resolutions and peacekeeping operations around the world. Let me repeat that figure: $8,779,000,000.

That means that last year [1999] alone the American people furnished precisely $10,179,000,000 to support the work of the United Nations. No other nation on earth comes even close to matching that singular investment.

So you can see why many Americans reject the suggestion that theirs is a "deadbeat" nation.

Now, I grant you, the money we spend on the UN is not charity. To the contrary, it is an investment—an investment from which the American people rightly expect a return. They expect a reformed UN that works more efficiently, and which respects the sovereignty of the United States.

That is why, in the 1980s, Congress began withholding a fraction of our arrears as pressure for reform. And Congressional pressure resulted in some worthwhile reforms, such as the creation of an independent UN Inspector General and the adoption of consensus budgeting practices. But still, the arrears accumulated as the UN resisted more comprehensive reforms.

When the distinguished Secretary-General, Kofi Annan, was elected, some of us in the Senate decided to try to establish a working relationship. The result is the Helms-Biden law, which President Clinton finally signed into law this past November. The product of three years of arduous negotiations and hard-fought compromises, it was approved by the U.S. Senate by an overwhelming 98–1 margin. You should read that vote as a virtually unanimous mandate for a new relationship with a reformed United Nations.

Now, I am aware that this law does not sit well with some here at the UN. Some do not like to have reforms dictated by the U.S. Congress. Some have even suggested that the UN should reject these reforms.

But let me suggest a few things to consider: First, as the figures I have cited clearly demonstrate, the United States is the single largest investor in the United Nations. Under the U.S. Constitution, we in Congress are the sole guardians of the American taxpayers' money. (It is our solemn duty to see that it is wisely invested.)

So as the representatives of the UN's largest investors—the American people —we have not only a right but a responsibility to insist on specific reforms in exchange for their investment.

Second, I ask you to consider the alternative. The alternative would have been to continue to let the U.S.-UN relationship spiral out of control. You would have taken retaliatory measures, such as revoking America's vote in the General Assembly. Congress would likely have responded with retaliatory measures against the UN. And the end result, I believe, would have been a breach in U.S.-UN relations that would have served the interests of no one.

Now, some here may contend that the Clinton administration should have fought to pay the arrears without conditions. I assure you, had they done so, they would have lost.

Eighty years ago, Woodrow Wilson failed to secure Congressional support for U.S. entry into the League of Nations. This administration obviously learned from President Wilson's mistakes.

Wilson probably could have achieved ratification of the League of Nations if he had worked with Congress. One of my predecessors as Chairman of the Sen-

ate Foreign Relations Committee, Henry Cabot Lodge, asked for fourteen conditions to the treaty establishing the League of Nations, few of which would have
raised an eyebrow today. These included language to ensure that the United
States remain the sole judge of its own internal affairs; that the League not restrict
any individual rights of U.S. citizens; that the Congress retain sole authority for
the deployment of U.S. forces through the League, and so on.

But President Wilson indignantly refused to compromise with Senator Lodge.
He shouted, "Never, never!," adding, "I'll never consent to adopting any policy
with which that impossible man is so prominently identified!" What happened?
President Wilson lost. The final vote in the Senate was 38 to 53, and the League
of Nations withered on the vine. Ambassador Holbrooke and Secretary of State
Albright understood from the beginning that the United Nations could not long
survive without the support of the American people—and their elected representatives in Congress. Thanks to the efforts of leaders like Ambassador Holbrooke
and Secretary Albright, the present administration in Washington did not repeat
President Wilson's fatal mistakes.

In any event, Congress has written a check to the United Nations for
$926 million, payable upon the implementation of previously agreed-upon com-
monsense reforms. Now the choice is up to the UN. I suggest that if the UN were
to reject this compromise, it would mark the beginning of the end of U.S. support
for the United Nations.

I don't want that to happen. I want the American people to value a United
Nations that recognizes and respects their interests, and for the United Nations to
value the significant contributions of the American people. Let's be crystal clear
and totally honest with each other: All of us want a more effective United Nations. But if the United Nations is to be "effective," it must be an institution that
is needed by the great democratic powers of the world.

Most Americans do not regard the United Nations as an end in and of itself—
they see it as just one part of America's diplomatic arsenal. To the extent that the
UN is effective, the American people will support it. To the extent that it becomes ineffective—or, worse, a burden—the American people will cast it aside.

The American people want the UN to serve the purpose for which it was
designed: They want it to help sovereign states coordinate collective action by
"coalitions of the willing," where the political will for such action exists; they
want it to provide a forum where diplomats can meet and keep open channels of
communication in times of crisis; they want it to provide to the peoples of the
world important services, such as peacekeeping, weapons inspections, and humanitarian relief.

This is important work. It is the core of what the UN can offer to the United

States and the world. If, in the coming century, the UN focuses on doing these core tasks well, it can thrive and will earn and deserve the support of the American people. But if the UN seeks to move beyond these core tasks, if it seeks to impose the UN's power and authority over nation-states, I guarantee that the United Nations will meet stiff resistance from the American people.

As matters now stand, many Americans sense that the UN has greater ambitions than simply being an efficient deliverer of humanitarian aid, a more effective peacekeeper, a better weapons inspector, and a more effective tool of great-power diplomacy. They see the UN aspiring to establish itself as the central authority of a new international order of global laws and global governance. This is an international order the American people will not countenance.

The UN must respect national sovereignty. The UN serves nation-states, not the other way around. This principle is central to the legitimacy and ultimate survival of the United Nations, and it is a principle that must be protected.

The Secretary-General recently delivered an address on sovereignty to the General Assembly in which he declared that "the last right of states cannot and must not be the right to enslave, persecute, or torture their own citizens." The peoples of the world, he said, have "rights beyond borders."

I wholeheartedly agree.

What the Secretary-General calls "rights beyond borders," we in America call "inalienable rights." We are endowed with those "inalienable rights," as Thomas Jefferson proclaimed in our Declaration of Independence, not by kings or despots, but by our Creator.

The sovereignty of nations must be respected. But nations derive their sovereignty—their legitimacy—from the consent of the governed. Thus it follows that nations can lose their legitimacy when they rule without the consent of the governed; they deservedly discard their sovereignty by brutally oppressing their people.

Slobodan Milosevic cannot claim sovereignty over Kosovo when he has murdered Kosovars and piled their bodies into mass graves. Neither can Fidel Castro claim that it is his sovereign right to oppress his people. Nor can Saddam Hussein defend his oppression of the Iraqi people by hiding behind phony claims of sovereignty. And when the oppressed peoples of the world cry out for help, the free peoples of the world have a fundamental right to respond.

As we watch the UN struggle with this question at the turn of the millennium, many Americans are left exceedingly puzzled. Intervening in cases of widespread oppression and massive human rights abuses is not a new concept for the United States. The American people have a long history of coming to the aid of those struggling for freedom. In the United States, during the 1980s, we called this policy "the Reagan Doctrine."

In some cases, America has assisted freedom fighters around the world who were seeking to overthrow corrupt regimes. We have provided weaponry, training, and intelligence. In other cases, the United States has intervened directly. In still other cases, such as in Central and Eastern Europe, we supported peaceful opposition movements with moral, financial, and covert forms of support. In each case, however, it was America's clear intention to help bring down Communist regimes that were oppressing their peoples, and thereby replace dictators with democratic governments.

The dramatic expansion of freedom in the last decade of the twentieth century is a direct result of these policies.

In none of these cases, however, did the United States ask for or receive the approval of the United Nations to "legitimize" its actions.

It is a fanciful notion that free peoples need to seek the approval of an international body (some of whose members are totalitarian dictatorships) to lend support to nations struggling to break the chains of tyranny and claim their inalienable, God-given rights. The United Nations has no power to grant or decline legitimacy to such actions. They are inherently legitimate.

What the United Nations can do is help. The Security Council can, where appropriate, be an instrument to facilitate action by "coalitions of the willing," implement sanctions regimes, and provide logistical support to states undertaking collective action.

But complete candor is imperative: The Security Council has an exceedingly mixed record in being such a facilitator. In the case of Iraq's aggression against Kuwait in the early 1990s, it performed admirably; in the more recent case of Kosovo, it was paralyzed. The UN peacekeeping mission in Bosnia was a disaster, and its failure to protect the Bosnian people from Serb genocide is well documented in a recent UN report.

And, despite its initial success in repelling Iraqi aggression, in the years since the Gulf War the Security Council has utterly failed to stop Saddam Hussein's drive to build instruments of mass murder. It has allowed him to play a repeated game of expelling UNSCOM inspection teams which included Americans, and has left Saddam completely free for the past year to fashion nuclear and chemical weapons of mass destruction.

I am here to plead that from now on we all must work together, to learn from past mistakes, and to make the Security Council a more efficient and effective tool for international peace and security. But candor compels that I reiterate this warning: The American people will never accept the claims of the United Nations to be the "sole source of legitimacy on the use of force" in the world.

But, some may respond, the U.S. Senate ratified the UN charter fifty years ago. Yes, but in doing so we did not cede one syllable of American sovereignty to the United Nations. Under our system, when international treaties are ratified they simply become domestic U.S. law. As such, they carry no greater or lesser weight than any other domestic U.S. law. Treaty obligations can be superseded by a simple act of Congress. This was the intentional design of our Founding Fathers, who cautioned against entering into "entangling alliances."

Thus, when the United States joins a treaty organization, it holds no legal authority over us. We abide by our treaty obligations because they are the domestic law of our land, and because our elected leaders have judged that the agreement serves our national interest. But no treaty or law can ever supersede the one document that all Americans hold sacred: the U.S. Constitution.

The American people do not want the United Nations to become an "entangling alliance." That is why Americans look with alarm at UN claims to a monopoly on international moral legitimacy. They see this as a threat to the God-given freedoms of the American people, a claim of political authority over America and its elected leaders without their consent.

The effort to establish a United Nations International Criminal Court is a case in point. Consider: The Rome Treaty purports to hold American citizens under its jurisdiction—even when the United States has neither signed nor ratified the treaty. In other words, it claims sovereign authority over American citizens without their consent. How can the nations of the world imagine for one instant that Americans will stand by and allow such a power grab to take place?

The court's supporters argue that Americans should be willing to sacrifice some of their sovereignty for the noble cause of international justice. International law did not defeat Hitler, nor did it win the Cold War. What stopped the Nazi march across Europe, and the Communist march across the world, was the principled projection of power by the world's great democracies. And that principled projection of force is the only thing that will ensure the peace and security of the world in the future.

More often than not, "international law" has been used as a make-believe justification for hindering the march of freedom. When Ronald Reagan sent American servicemen into harm's way to liberate Grenada from the hands of a Communist dictatorship, the UN General Assembly responded by voting to condemn the action of the elected President of the United States as a violation of international law—and, I am obliged to add, they did so by a larger majority than when the Soviet invasion of Afghanistan was condemned by the same General

Assembly! Similarly, the U.S. effort to overthrow Nicaragua's Communist dicta-torship (by supporting Nicaragua's freedom fighters and mining Nicaragua's har-bors) was declared by the World Court as a violation of international law.

Most recently, we learn that the chief prosecutor of the Yugoslav War Crimes Tribunal has compiled a report on possible NATO war crimes during the Kosovo campaign. At first, the prosecutor declared that it is fully within the scope of her authority to indict NATO pilots and commanders. When news of her report leaked, she backpedaled.

She realized, I am sure, that any attempt to indict NATO commanders would be the death knell for the International Criminal Court. But the very fact that she explored this possibility at all brings to light all that is wrong with this brave new world of global justice, which proposes a system in which independent prosecu-tors and judges, answerable to no state or institution, have unfettered power to sit in judgment of the foreign policy decisions of Western democracies.

No UN institution — not the Security Council, not the Yugoslav tribunal, not a future ICC — is competent to judge the foreign policy and national security de-cisions of the United States. American courts routinely refuse cases where they are asked to sit in judgment of our government's national security decisions, stat-ing that they are not competent to judge such decisions. If we do not submit our national security decisions to the judgment of a court of the United States, why would Americans submit them to the judgment of an International Criminal Court, a continent away, comprised of mostly foreign judges elected by an inter-national body made up of the membership of the UN General Assembly?

Americans distrust concepts like the International Criminal Court, and claims by the UN to be the "sole source of legitimacy" for the use of force, be-cause Americans have a profound distrust of accumulated power. Our Founding Fathers created a government founded on a system of checks and balances and dispersal of power.

In his 1962 classic, *Capitalism and Freedom*, the Nobel Prize–winning econ-omist Milton Friedman rightly declared: "Government power must be dispersed. If government is to exercise power, better in the county than in the state, better in the state than in Washington. [Because] if I do not like what my local community does, I can move to another local community, . . . [and] if I do not like what my state does, I can move to another. [But] if I do not like what Washington imposes, I have few alternatives in this world of jealous nations."

Forty years later, as the UN seeks to impose its utopian vision of "international law" on Americans, we can add this question: Where do we go when we don't like the "laws" of the world?

Today, while our friends in Europe concede more and more power upwards to supranational institutions like the European Union, Americans are heading in precisely the opposite direction.

America is in a process of reducing centralized power by taking more and more authority that had been amassed by the federal government in Washington and referring it to the individual states, where it rightly belongs.

This is why Americans reject the idea of a sovereign United Nations that presumes to be the source of legitimacy for the United States government's policies, foreign or domestic. There is only one source of legitimacy of the American government's policies—and that is the consent of the American people.

If the United Nations is to survive into the twenty-first century, it must recognize its limitations. The demands of the United States have not changed much since Henry Cabot Lodge laid out his conditions for joining the League of Nations eighty years ago: Americans want to ensure that the United States of America remains the sole judge of its own internal affairs, that the United Nations is not allowed to restrict the individual rights of U.S. citizens, and that the United States retains sole authority over the deployment of United States forces around the world.

This is what Americans ask of the United Nations; it is what Americans expect of the United Nations. A United Nations that focuses on helping sovereign states work together is worth keeping; a United Nations that insists on trying to impose a utopian vision on America and the world will collapse under its own weight.

If the United Nations respects the sovereign rights of the American people and serves them as an effective tool of diplomacy, it will earn and deserve their respect and support. But a United Nations that seeks to impose its presumed authority on the American people without their consent begs for confrontation and, I want to be candid, eventual U.S. withdrawal.

Thank you very much.

APPENDIX 7

Dedication of the Jesse Helms School of Government, Liberty University, October 6, 2004

—

It is both an honor and a great pleasure to be with you this morning as we mark the dedication of the Jesse Helms School of Government here at Liberty University. I can think of no institution of learning with which I would rather have my name associated. I am truly humbled.

For almost twenty-five years, I have been honored to have Jerry Falwell as my friend. I admire the way he has always fought the good fight without compromising.

When I went to Washington as a United States Senator, I did not set out to win a popularity contest nor to be the "darling of the news media." I'm told that I succeeded fairly well!

I went with the sole purpose of defending the values that made America great. They are timeless values and they are the same values that our Founding Fathers defended and which you are learning to defend today!

When I retired from the Senate last year, many friends inquired as to what I intended to do. Well, I can tell you that the Jesse Helms School of Government is the realization of part of my hope and dream—my vision to train young men and women to carry the message of freedom and hope throughout this great nation of ours.

I have seen time and again that when good men and women sit on the sidelines, evil triumphs!

As I finish the mission entrusted to me, I often think of that day when I will face my Maker. And when I do, my greatest desire is to hear Him say:

"Well done, thou good and faithful servant."

Young men and women, don't ever miss an opportunity to stand up for what is right in the sight of God.

At this school, you will learn how to be godly citizens so that you can impact your communities and, ultimately, our nation in a profound way.

In some circles today, there's an effort to silence those who practice their Christian faith in the public arena. But, contrary to many modern voices, biblical truths have never threatened America. They have, instead, helped to make this nation great!

My longtime and dear friend and our great President Ronald Reagan said, "Without God, there is no virtue because there is no prompting of the conscience. . . . Without God, there is a coarsening of the society. Without God, democracy will not and cannot long endure. If we ever forget that we are one nation under God, then we will be a nation gone under."

Every one of you can make a remarkable difference in our society.

I agree with Theodore Roosevelt, who said that the success or failure of our nation will depend upon the way in which the average citizen does his duty. In 1910, President Roosevelt further noted that "it is not the critic who counts. . . . The credit belongs to the man who is actually in the arena, whose face is marred by dust and sweat and blood, . . . who spends himself in a worthy cause."

One of the most important lessons that I learned in my years serving in the United States Senate is that with God's help we really can make a difference. We did not make the world a perfect place. But with the help of many like-minded citizens, I believe we have been able to stem the tide of evil for a season!

We were able to save "precious, little lives" with legislation which helped protect the unborn. Along with many others, we were able to bring down the walls of Communist tyranny—both in this hemisphere and across the ocean.

We fought every day to defend our inviolable Constitution and the principles of our Founding Fathers.

We have fought to protect the American taxpayer, to keep America's defense strong, and to protect America's interests all around the world!

We have fought to protect our flag; to protect our inalienable right to worship God as we choose!

My prayer is that those of you who are graduating from the Jesse Helms School of Government will pick up the baton where my generation is leaving off.

It is up to each generation to step into this arena. The victories of yesterday will not last long. Evil is always on the march. But as we know, God is greater than the evil forces of this world.

There is a possibility that you will be bloodied and that you will probably be ridiculed, but take this as a sign that you are on the right side! You will always make a difference by doing what is right!

I am so grateful to Dr. Falwell for creating this school of government, which will prepare future generations to be good soldiers in this war for truth and freedom!

It is my prayer that God will guide those responsible for shaping the hearts and minds of the fine young people who study here.

It is also my hope that God will grant all of you the courage and the strength to run the race that He has set before you. Always remember that as believers in Jesus Christ, we are pilgrims passing through this land, and that our true citizenship is in heaven!

Thank you, and God bless you!

INDEX

ABOUT THE AUTHOR

SENATOR JESSE HELMS served for thirty years in the
United States Senate until his retirement in January 2003.
He is considered one of the most influential individuals
in American government and has received scores of
awards for his distinguished service to his state, his
country, and freedom-loving peoples around the world.
He lives in Raleigh, North Carolina, with his wife,
Dorothy, and can be reached at
www.jessehelmscenter.org.
All of the author's proceeds from this book go
to supporting the work of the Jesse Helms
Center Foundation.